The Old Brown Dog

CORAL LANSBURY

The Old Brown Dog

Women, Workers, and Vivisection
in Edwardian England

The University of Wisconsin Press

Published 1985

The University of Wisconsin Press
114 North Murray Street
Madison, Wisconsin 53715

The University of Wisconsin Press, Ltd.
1 Gower Street
London WC1E 6HA, England

First printing

Printed in the United States of America

For LC CIP information see the colophon

ISBN 0-299-10250-5

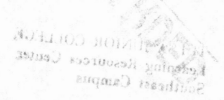

For Malcolm and Lucy

Contents

Preface

Some travellers feel uneasy without a detailed guidebook in their hands and a clear notion of their destination. They enjoy the security of knowing where they are going and what they are likely to see along the way. But for others this is a wretched way to set out on a journey, rather like turning to the end of a detective story when barely half the book is read. All those who are of this mind are requested to stop immediately at this point and proceed forthwith to chapter 1, where certain events will be found taking place in the London borough of Battersea. But others who prefer roadmaps and as few surprises as possible when travelling may find this brief introduction useful.

In 1907 an extraordinary series of antivivisection riots took place in Battersea over the statue of a brown dog in the Latchmere Recreation Ground. Medical students came across the river from London University and tried to destroy it, and a crowd of trades unionists and feminists, momentarily united by their opposition to vivisection, battled to defend the brown dog. What made the riot so remarkable at a time when suffragettes and the unemployed were regularly competing for the attention of the public and government was this conjunction of trades unionists from the most radical borough in London and a group of middle-class women who had shown they were ready to endure prison and force-feeding to secure the vote. The trades unions were not only accustomed to ignoring the demands for women's suffrage; they bitterly opposed those middle-class women who had arrogantly appropriated a traditional working-class mode of protest: it was only as a last desperate resort that a trades unionist broke windows and destroyed property. Here then is a brief outline of a riot with a number of contradictions and ambiguities already emerging, and clear indication that a great many people were acting from impulses which had very little to do with the fate of a dog that had been vivisected twice in a London University laboratory.

Our journey begins with a narrative of events in Battersea, making use of a form of historical structuralism to interpret the paradoxes and passions of the riot. Just as a text may be said to conceal a multitude of subtexts, an urban landscape presents a vista of ranked roofs, streets, and power wires, but underneath that landscape there is a hidden world of fields and manor houses with rivers that still run below the traffic of people and cars. None of this is visible as we stand and look at Battersea today, but the buildings in front of us may well have had their architecture determined by a river far below the street. When Lloyds Bank bought land at the junction of Battersea Rise and St. John's Road, they found it impossible to excavate for vaults: the Falcon River ran below the site. There are still few tall buildings at the Junction in Battersea, but I doubt if there are many along those busy streets who pause to contemplate the lost world beneath their feet.

We then look at the various groups that joined to defend the dog and particularly the ways in which those people saw each other. First, there are the workers, and some surprising facts are discovered when we examine working-class attitudes to animals and women. Then we pause to see how the doctors regarded working-class opinions of animal experimentation and the vivisection of the brown dog, and why both workers and women were so distrustful of the medical profession. Women were the most fervent supporters of antivivisection, not simply for reasons of humanity but because the vivisected animal stood for vivisected woman: the woman strapped to the gynaecologist's table, the woman strapped and bound in the pornographic fiction of the period. We turn next to the group who tried to tear down the statue of the brown dog—the doctors and students who were becoming known as the "New Priesthood." And we end where we began, with a small brown dog, and conclude that it was the dog and animals generally who lost in this passionate collision where so often the words spoken concealed quite contrary emotions.

Of course, many people will be puzzled and disturbed by this book, for they will open it expecting to find what I clearly have not provided. The literary critic may well be irritated by accounts of borough politics, the urban historian will probably feel shortchanged by long discussions of fiction and pornography, and the intellectual historian will find nothing at all to interest him. There is little concern here with quantification, statistics, and tables, for this is essentially a history of emotions and prejudices, attitudes, and opinions, of "mentalities," to use the currently fashionable term. What concerns me is not how many women preferred pekes to people, but why so many were prepared to devote their lives to the antivivisection movement.

It should also be made clear that this is not a history of the animal rights' movement—although some reasons for the failure of the early antivivisection movement may be discerned from this study. The modern animal liberation movement, characterized by the works of Stephen Clark, Peter Singer, Tom Regan, and Mary Midgley, is less than twenty years old and bears only occasional reference to the antivivisection movement of the nineteenth century. Quite simply, the way we look at animals today is very different as a result of a changed consciousness towards the whole natural world. The debate between Singer and Regan over the moral status of animals would have bemused the Victorians, with the exception, perhaps, of Henry Salt. The whole issue of animal rights and the moral implications for our treatment of animals is a major concern of modern philosophy, and that fact alone would have astounded our forebears.

If asked to give a defining theme of this book in a few words, I would say that it is a study of the ways in which experience, and the intimations of experience, are translated into fictions, adding that those fictions then have the power to shape belief. I know of only one law in history, and that is that people will always believe what they want to believe, despite all evidence to the contrary. And sometimes those attitudes and beliefs will be directed by unconscious imperatives that speak for the human ability to act from wildly contradictory impulses. Surely, no human activity is more imbued with prejudice and paradox than our attitude towards animals and, in this context, the way men have regarded women. When emotions are the subject, quantification and statistics have proved notably deficient, and the historian is wise to defer to the poet and the novelist. There is much in this book that readers will find objectionable: I only hope they will appreciate my honesty in presenting such material. I have no desire to shock or titillate, but I cannot ignore the buried river beneath my feet. *Virtutem doctrina paret, naturane donet?*

Acknowledgments

I owe much to a great many people. A Guggenheim Fellowship gave me that most precious of all commodities, time, to complete this study. The librarians of my own university worked to bring documents and books to me from sources all over the world—the miracle of computers! Certain other libraries provided me with information that I could not have gained anywhere else. In particular, Richard Allen of the Battersea Municipal Library demonstrated what a model local historian can do to help a scholar. Richard Pankhurst of the Fawcett Library was similarly helpful, and I was ably assisted at the Wellcome Institute, the Physicians' Library in Philadelphia, and at several antivivisection society offices, the Research Defence Society, and the RSPCA. At Sydney University, I was permitted to use items in the W. A. and Elizabeth M. Deane Collection of Fisher Library.

Above all else, I must thank my fellow Victorian scholars, so many of whom have read parts, or the whole of this manuscript, and who have never failed to give me information and advice even though they may not have agreed with my conclusions. Richard Altick, Samuel Hynes, Frank Turner, Harriet Ritvo, Martha Vicinus, and Barbara Gates have all helped me in these ways. Perhaps my greatest debt is to the members of the Northeast Victorian Studies Association, which at times seemed to constitute a research group for the benefit of this study.

Coral Lansbury
Rutgers University

The Old Brown Dog

1

The Brown Dog Riots of 1907

In 1980 there was only one old resident of Battersea who could recall the Brown Dog Riots of 1907, when police, feminists, medical students, and trades unionists fought over the statue of a brown dog in the Latchmere Recreation Ground.[1] It was a time when the most unlikely allies found common cause, and for a few turbulent weeks some of the most passionate issues of the day were debated violently in the streets. Cecil Hart, ninety years old, a retired solicitor and vestryman of St. Luke's Church remembered the riots vividly but thought they were concerned with the antivivisection hospital in Battersea Road. The dog was—and clearly he was at a loss to account for the dog's role at the time—the dog was just an "advertizing story."

For Cecil Hart, memory had established its own logic and hierarchy of events, and what had been for many the very heart and cause of the riots had dwindled into a commercial fiction. We will have reason to discuss memory and the tricks it plays in the course of our investigation: the ways in which memory edits and interprets the past, and the tendency of fictions to live longer than the experiences which inspired them. The brown dog of Battersea had once been a living creature; later it came to be a symbol of feminist outrage and working-class resentment. Those in authority in society sought to destroy it, denouncing it as the embodiment of traditions and attitudes that had been shaped by a past beyond conscious recall. For these people it stood as a denial of progress, relic of a time when sorcery and sentimentality dragged at the skirts of science. Again and again the opponents of the brown dog declared that they were rational and reflective

3

men of science, whereas the women and workers defending the dog were emotional and irresponsible acolytes of a brutal and unsanitary past. On both sides statements were made that were not the logical consequence of circumstance but the result of accumulated experiences going back to forgotten social rites and customs. What people said and did at that time was shaped as much by literature as by history, and the fears and phantoms invoked by the brown dog were often more real than the actual events. William Hogarth was present at the riots; so too were Black Beauty and the body snatchers, Burke and Hare. Fiction collided continually with facts, and in a sense Cecil Hart was wiser than he knew when he described the brown dog as a "story." What we will try to do now is explore the subterranean motives and ideas that erupted in Battersea and spread across the river to Trafalgar Square, where two cavalry charges of police were required to disperse the "brown-doggers" and their opponents.

Let us begin then with appearances, the superficial structure of the story, remembering that the most discreet and uniform streets may well conceal the landscape of another world, another time. Gillian Tindall has described how Kentish Town erected bricks and cement across sleeping fields and walled over the streams that once carried a freight of ships down to the Thames.[2] Stroll along St. Pancras Way and you are passing over the buried Fleet; in Battersea it is the Falcon Brook which runs under the corner of Battersea Rise and St. John's Road, only making its presence felt in the occasional flooded basement along Falcon Road. It is an image that speaks to the heart of this study, for what happened in 1907 was, like most riots, a congeries of apparently inexplicable actions performed by an eccentric and disparate cast of players having nothing in common except a brown dog. And yet for each of those people the dog was a potent symbol capable of determining action and belief.

First, we can walk around Battersea and see for ourselves where the riots began, then set up a narrative, remembering always that dates and even events are no more than signposts which may often point to a lost age as well as to a present place. The Lavender Hill of 1900, with its respectable small shops and ranked cottages, was once a garden where lavender was grown and its fragrance then dried or preserved in oil for medicines and perfumes. Battersea lavender was as well known in the eighteenth century as Battersea enamel with its primly pastel arcadian patterns. John Burns, president of the Local Government Board and member of the House of Commons, had moved up to Lavender Hill, to "Athelstane," a square, shuttered house, in 1906. We will meet him soon as one of the main opponents of the brown dog.

Nine Elms, colored black and blue as a place of "most degraded poverty" in Charles Booth's maps, was where in the 1800s the Battersea artichoke was cultivated and asparagus blanched for West End dinner tables.[3] That was the time when there were farms and market gardens from the river's edge to Clapham Common, and a century before that, sheep grazed on Battersea Rise. A report issued in 1813 mentions that "the garden-grounds at Battersea occupying a dry and kindly soil, are much famed for the seeds of vegetables grown on them, and the gardeners at Clapham and some other places in the neighbourhood . . . procure their seed from the former parish. In consequence of this demand for seed, much of the garden ground in the Parish of Battersea is employed in raising vegetables for seed."[4]

It was not always easy to find that agricultural past under the streets of Battersea in 1907; nonetheless, the countryside was not so remote from the factories and tenements as it is today. Sally Plornish of Bleeding Heart Yard in *Little Dorrit* had a rustic cottage painted on her living room wall to remind her father of his childhood home, but the people of Battersea did not need pictures to recall the country. Most of them had heads well furnished with rural memories, and those who may have forgotten the open fields and farm animals had only to walk down Latchmere Road, "Pig Hill," when the cattle and pigs were being driven to Chesney Street and Semple's slaughterhouse. Indeed, one small farm could still be seen on the corner of Battersea Rise and Limburg Road until the First World War.[5] Rabbits and chickens were kept behind the cottages along Battersea Road and children sent there for fresh eggs. But all this was changing at the turn of the century: tenants were not permitted to keep livestock in council houses, and blocks of flats had begun to displace cottages.

Gipsies used to camp in the fields by Usk Road; by the turn of the century the fields were gone, but the gipsies still returned in winter to put up their caravans in stable yards and bring the sounds and smells of the country with them. Horses were flogged up the Battersea Rise in icy weather, and many people would stop to pity the straining animals and remember the sufferings of Black Beauty on Ludgate Hill. Anna Sewell's book was not only a perennial favorite in the Battersea Municipal Library; it was also prescribed as a school text and a regular Sunday school prize. Down by the river, the two hundred acres of Battersea Park were set out with lawns and trees and flowering shrubs, and here family groups from Battersea came to picnic in the summer, and children could feel grass under their feet and look up through leaves to the sky. A number of artists and writers lived by the park, among them, G. K. Chesterton, John Burns's friend and ally in his campaign against the brown dog.

From Battersea Rise to Clapham Common the houses were larger, and professional people and tradesfolk made their homes there. This was South Battersea, which worked in the West End like Cecil Hart and insisted that its address was Wandsworth. Rents, land, and servants were cheaper here than across the river; Cecil Hart had a live-in maid and "morning's only" cleaner for seven and sixpence a week. It was a part of Battersea that tried to hold itself aloof, politically and socially, from the factories and slums by the river.

Battersea in 1907, belching smoke across the river, was the creation of the nineteenth century and the railroads.[6] The population had grown from 6,617 in 1841 to 168,907 in 1901, and a good proportion of the men had come to find work in the railway yards and shunting stations. It was the railway which dominated Battersea: the large flat lands where artichokes and asparagus once flourished were now found to be ideal for depots and sidings. Battersea was on the approach to two major terminals, Waterloo and Victoria, and here in Nine Elms the air was always heavy with coal dust and greasy with oil fumes. Today it is the site of Covent Garden Markets, and boxes and barrows of fruit and flowers recall its buried agricultural past: underneath the cement floors of the produce sheds is still that "dry and kindly soil" where vegetables were once grown for seed.

In 1907 Nine Elms was "an area shaped like a narrow triangle lying on its side, bounded on the north by the Thames and on the other two sides by railway lines. . . . In the centre of the triangle, dominating Nine Elms, were the gasometers, retorts and purifiers of the London Gas Light Company. Nearby there were limeworks, flour mills, breweries and an iron foundry."[7] With only two exits from the area, both to the south, Nine Elms was, to use Booth's phrase, "a poverty trap," but it was here in the most squalid part of a degraded neighbourhood that one of the main supporters of the brown dog chose to make her home. We will meet Charlotte Despard—feminist, novelist, and social reformer—when she leaves Currie Street to defend the statue of the brown dog against her arch-enemy, John Burns.

Across the river, people said you could smell Battersea long before you saw it. Ernest Morris, who worked at Morgan's Crucibles for over forty years, remembered Battersea as a place of dirt and foul odors where the stench from paint manufacturers contended with the sulphur fumes of the gasworks: "But the Daddy of them all was the Morgan Crucible Co. then known as the plum which blackened the borough with its lamp black, carbon and plumbago and the dust carried over the Thames into Chelsea."[8] But it's an ill wind, and Battersea women took in washing by the basket and the cart load. As Booth observed, "Central London washes its dirty linen at home. Battersea undertakes this duty for a large part of the West End."[9]

Over in the city, Battersea was famous for more than its reeking smokestacks; it was notorious as a hotbed of radical politics and militant trades unionism. People had not forgotten August 19, 1889, when John Burns marched with the striking dockworkers around the City of London, the same year that the Battersea gas workers went on strike and secured an eight-hour working day. In 1902 the Battersea Borough Council, controlled by the local Trades and Labour Council, belligerently refused to sign the loyal address to the King, and in December would not even consider a donation from Andrew Carnegie for the municipal library because Carnegie's cash was "tainted with the blood of the Pittsburg strikers."[10]

It was also true that if Battersea was mentioned in a music hall, there would be an immediate chorus of barks and howls because of the Battersea Dogs' Home, the largest of its kind in England. Despite the jokes from neighboring boroughs, Battersea residents regarded the Home with a good deal of affection. Part of the folklore of Battersea which found its way into the *South-Western Star* and the *Battersea Mercury* turned upon tales of distraught owners reunited with lost dogs at the kennels. When it was suggested in 1907 that Battersea Dogs' Home should supply animals for vivisection, the chairman of the board, the Duke of Portland, rejected the suggestion as "not only horrible, but absurd . . . and entirely unacceptable to the Home."[11] The Battersea Dogs' Home, the Battersea Polytechnic, and the Antivivisection Hospital were landmarks like Arding and Hobbs' store at Battersea Rise. In the Town Hall with its sweeping staircase and fluted columns, the Borough Council had gained the reputation of being "the most democratic council in the metropolis ever since the London Government Act was passed."[12] Certainly the Council could point with considerable pride to its housing estates: the Town Hall and Shaftesbury Estates set a standard for the many private and co-operative building societies in the area.

The Latchmere Housing Estate was formally opened in 1902, and John Burns stood with Mayor Howarth in the centre of the Recreation Ground, where four years later the statue of the brown dog was to be erected. Burns was at his magniloquent best, and after lauding the virtues of hearth and home, he pronounced a general blessing on all those who were going to rent the small detached houses at seven and sixpence a week: "May this little colony never know the curse of drink or the blight of betting; may it be free from the minor nuisances of life; may its children be bright and cheerful, and may all its members be as mindful of their proper neighbours as the Borough Council has been public-spirited in looking after them."[13] It was a fair sample of Burns's bombast and the patronage that was beginning to make him sound more like Mr. Honeythunder than a radical labor leader. The *South-Western Star* observed that a number of unionists present had jeered at his rhetoric, and noted with approval that the three thousand inhabitants of the Latchmere Estate had failed to go cap in hand to Burns to thank him for his generosity. Battersea workers were never known for their deference.

These were the workers who became the champions and defenders of the brown dog when it was placed in the very centre of the Recreation Ground: a bronze statue of a terrier dog, muzzle lifted, staring pensively towards the houses, the fountain at its base inviting people and animals to drink. Now, drinking fountains had always been a touchy subject among the working class, for they were frequently erected by temperance societies as well as by those who sincerely wanted to slake the thirst of horses and dogs. A workingman resented being told to forgo his pint of bitter and drink alongside his horse, so these monuments to middle class concern for working-class sobriety were regarded as being particularly offensive. In 1903, when the Battersea Council was run by Progressives, it flatly turned down an offer from the Metropolitan Drinking Fountain and Cattle Trough Association to donate a drinking fountain and dog trough with the terse response that "the Council regret that they have no available site."[14] As many people suspected, when the brown dog and its fountain were placed in Latchmere with the authority of the Council, it was there for other reasons than those of alleviating thirst.

Here then in Battersea we have the scene for our story, and now we must cross the river and meet some of the men and women who made the brown dog the expression of their most fervent beliefs. The immediate cause of the riot was in the physiology laboratory of University

College, where Louise Lind-af-Hageby and her friend Liese Schartau witnessed the vivisection of a brown dog and noticed that the dog had an unhealed wound in its side which indicated that it had recently been used for another experiment. They both made a record of the incident in their diaries.

Louise Lind-af-Hageby was twenty-four when she enrolled with her friend at the London School of Medicine for Women, with the deliberate intention of becoming medical students in order to master the science of physiology and then use that knowledge to expose the practice of vivisection. Both of them were scornful of those sentimental women who drowned themselves and their listeners in floods of tears when they spoke about the suffering of animals under the vivisector's knife: they were determined to arm themselves with the language and arguments of the enemy and speak as doctors. The resolution to dedicate their lives to the antivivisection movement had been born during a visit to the Pasteur Institute in Paris, when they had seen hundreds of animals dying in agony. Fortunately, Louise Lind-af-Hageby came from a wealthy Swedish family and possessed a woman's passport to independence in those days, "private means." She knew that in England the antivivisection movement was strong and well organized if divided in the means required to protect animals from experimental use.

English antivivisectionists were grouped in two main societies, with a number of smaller associations that often seemed more at odds with each other than opposed to vivisection. Despite its fragmentation, however, the movement had won a number of victories with the 1876 Act to Amend the Law Relating to Cruelty to Animals standing as the only legal restriction in the world against the experimental use of animals.[15] But vivisection was still being practiced, and it was known that men who held licenses to vivisect were on the council of the Royal Society for the Prevention of Cruelty to Animals, and were even appointing the inspectors whose charge it was to regulate the Act.[16]

The British Union for the Abolition of Vivisection, under Dr. Robert Walter Hadwen, had been founded in 1898 when Frances Cobbe demanded that the National Antivivisection Society seek the total abolition of vivisection through a single legislative act. The Hon. Stephen Coleridge, a barrister and son of Sir John Coleridge, lord chief justice of England, argued that abolition could be accomplished only by means of successive legislative amendments. It was on this issue of gradualism versus instant and revolutionary change that the movement had split into two distinct societies, with Coleridge assuming the presidency of the National Antivivisection Society, and Frances Cobbe founding the British Union. Far from being unique to the antivivisection movement, these two attitudes reflected theories of change that were being propounded daily by feminists and leaders of the working class. Millicent Fawcett was calling for women's suffrage to be accomplished by successive electoral reforms; the Pankhursts of Manchester were demanding votes for women by means of one legislative act. H. M. Hyndman predicted violent social revolution, whereas John Burns had pledged himself to a piecemeal progress so slow that his critics claimed he was walking backwards into the arms of the Liberals.

Louise Lind-af-Hageby and Liese Schartau, like most educated young women, had been taught to keep diaries, and in vivid and dramatic prose they recorded what they had seen at University College in the Department of Physiology. Later we will spend some time with the language and metaphors that these young women chose to use in their diary; unconsciously they were evoking images that went beyond, and often contradicted, the immediate meaning. Over a period of months they compiled a series of vignettes which they felt could become a book. They took what they had written to Stephen Coleridge at the Antivivisection Society offices in Victoria Street, and he immediately saw that if what they had recorded was correct, then there had been a serious infringement of the 1876 Act. Under the Act a vivisected animal could not be revived after one experiment and used for another: it had to be destroyed. But the young women, in a section called "Fun," had described a brown terrier dog with a recent abdominal wound which had been carried into the laboratory strapped to a board. The dog was then subjected to an operation in the throat by Professor William Bayliss. The dog had struggled throughout the course of the demonstration and was still alive when it was taken from the lecture room.

Coleridge questioned the two women and, when convinced of the accuracy of their observations, helped them find a publisher for the diary.[17] As soon as *The Shambles of Science* was in print, Coleridge publicly charged the physiologist, Bayliss, with having broken the law. Bayliss in turn had no recourse but to sue Coleridge for libel in order to protect his reputation, and the case was heard in November 1903. Coleridge did not expect to win the case: what he wanted was publicity and an opportunity to ventilate the deficiencies and anomalies of the 1876 Act.

The case was widely reported, but already, clear social divisions could be seen in the press. The *Times* referred to the diary as a mischievous work, and Coleridge's actions were impugned in the *Telegraph*; but the Liberal and working-class press—the *Star*, the *Daily News*, the *Sun*, the *Standard*, and the *Tribune*—came out strongly in support of Coleridge. The *Daily News* published the court proceedings in full and concluded:

> Let us grant for the moment that man has the right to make use of animals for experimentation in the means of alleviating human suffering and saving life. But surely there must be some limit to this right. Has it not been reached in such a case as this? Here is an animal which worships and trusts mankind with an unreasoning fidelity. The dog may almost be said to have surrendered himself into our safe keeping. Does not this overwhelming trust—this absolute confidence that glistens in the dog's eye—lay upon us some obligation?
>
> Is it not worth considering whether the human race may not pay too heavy a penalty for knowledge acquired in this manner? Are we to leave out of count altogether the hardening of heart and searing of sensitive feeling that must be produced by the constant spectacle of such unmerited suffering? Let us suppose that the Swedish ladies were wrong, and that this dog was anaesthetized. But a correspondent points out that the certificate possessed by Dr Bayliss is not the only certificate allowed by law. There are other physiologists who are permitted to perform such operations as these on conscious animals, and no one who alleged that the animals were conscious would be saying anything libellous.[18]

Implicit in this statement is not merely a concern for animals, but a challenge to a form of social authority sanctioned by law. For reasons that we will examine in some detail the antivivisectionist movement had become associated with radical politics and the interests of the working class and women. Coleridge had anticipated the outcome of the trial. The chief justice ordered that the section "Fun" be removed from *The Shambles of Science*, and Louise Lind-af-Hageby and Liese Schartau complied in all subsequent editions, replacing the offending vignette with a lengthy account of the trial. Since the burden of proof lay on the defendant, the jury found for Bayliss: Coleridge was fined two thousand pounds to the delighted cheers of the medical students who packed the court throughout the trial—their behavior had been described by the *Times* as "medical hooliganism." The *Daily News* immediately opened a subscription fund to pay Coleridge's damages, and the money was oversubscribed within the month.[19] If Coleridge and Lind-af-Hageby had lost in court, they were not vanquished in public opinion. The case had brought them the publicity they desired, and the sales of *The Shambles of Science* increased. Yet the verdict rankled, for William Bayliss had been found innocent of any charge of cruelty or failure to abide by the provisions of the 1876 Act. Moreover, the medical students were jubilant, and at every antivivisection meeting they added three cheers for Professor Bayliss to their usual catcalls and groans. If there is a mob in this story, it is not the Battersea workers, but these medical students who now had a long tradition of noisy opposition to antivivisectionists.

As early as 1830 medical students in London had rioted and forced the professor of anatomy, G. S. Pattison, from his chair because of his "*total ignorance of* and *disgusting indifference* to new anatomical views and researches."[20] All Pattison's attempts to lecture were shouted down by the students, and eventually the college council was forced to compromise between the students' protests and Pattison's obdurate refusal to learn new methods by appointing him to the chair of surgery. There was always considerable tolerance of medical students' boisterous behavior because it was felt that the nature of their work made such outbursts necessary. What would never have been countenanced in a law student was accepted in a medical student because he had frequently to do the work of a butcher on living flesh. For this reason many early physiologists like Koch believed that the cries of vivisected animals helped to habituate the student to the pain of a human patient—an argument which continued after the introduction of anaesthesia.

For William H. Lister, a medical student at University College, the Bayliss case was less an instance of "old women of both sexes" holding back the cause of science than an opportunity to set gown against town and in the process make London University students behave and feel like Oxford and Cambridge undergraduates. Lister's ambition was to create a political estate from the students of London University and, if possible, to represent those students himself.[21] He was to seize that opportunity three years later at the Latchmere Recreation Ground.

Antivivisection vied for public attention with a great many other issues, foremost among them unemployment and women's suffrage. The old spontaneous market and election riots bore little relation to the planned and occasionally rehearsed demonstrations of public anger in Trafalgar Square and through the streets of the City of London. The liveliest cause of the day was women's suffrage, and Charlotte Despard, as secretary of the Women's Social and Political Union, was one of the leaders of the radical wing, always ready to march and harangue politicians. For her, as for many feminists, one of the greatest obstacles was John Burns, member of Parliament for Battersea.

In 1906 Burns was prepared to renounce his radical past and run for election as a Liberal with the cabinet post of President of the Local Government Board as his reward. Over the years Charlotte Despard had grown to dislike and despise John Burns. She had led deputations of the unemployed to his door, she had begged him to give his support to women's suffrage like her friend George Lansbury in Poplar, and Burns had always dismissed her with a mouthful of platitudes. A shrewd politician, Burns knew that workingmen had never shown the slightest interest in giving women the vote. For Charlotte Despard, Burns was the great apostate, Mr. Bumble incarnate, and she was not alone in this opinion. The Socialists and many of the Progressives in Battersea abhorred the man. Unfortunately for the radicals of the electorate, Burns proved he had a political base that did not require the support of the Trades and Labour Council or even his own union, the Amalgamated Society of Engineers. In 1906 the TLC presented its own slate of candidates for the borough elections and was successful in capturing forty of the fifty-four Council seats, but they could not break Burns's majority in the parliamentary election. Battersea laughed at Burns's bombast, but it continued to vote for him.

Burns was at his ebullient best in January of 1906. His friend and admirer G. K. Chesterton had spoken on his behalf at the Battersea Town Hall, and Chesterton's dazzling paradoxes met with enthusiastic applause. George Bernard Shaw had just attacked Burns's policies, or the lack of them, in a speech at the Latchmere Baths, and Charlotte Despard followed Shaw with a bitter denunciation of Burns's failure to help women and the unemployed. However, with a majority of over two thousand votes in the election, Burns could afford to disregard his enemies. What the socialists and the suffragettes feared was that as President of the Local Government Board Burns would now be controlling one of the greatest sources of patronage in London.

At this point we can see a number of angry and frustrated individuals: Louise Lind-af-Hageby was still outraged by the Bayliss verdict; Stephen Coleridge was appalled when a commission was appointed to review the working of the 1876 Act and it was proposed to include known vivisectors among the commissioners, closing all its inquiries to the press and the public; Charlotte Despard together with a great many disappointed electors in Battersea deplored the election of John Burns. Into this group now came Miss Louisa Woodward, secretary of the Church Antivivisection League, a wealthy woman from an old Wiltshire family and a close friend of the vicar of St. Luke's Church, where Cecil Hart worshipped. The vicar, Erskine Clarke, was not only an antivivisectionist, but was also a supporter of Charlotte Despard and her work among the poor of Nine Elms. Louisa Woodward met Louise Lind-af-Hageby, and the two decided to present the Battersea Council with a most unusual drinking fountain. Stephen Coleridge discussed the plan with the mayor and council, which approved the design and the inscription on the base of the statue. It was agreed that it should be placed in the Latchmere Recreation Ground.[22]

The fountain was designed to be provocative. The inscription rang out like a challenge: "In Memory of the Brown Terrier Dog Done to Death in the Laboratories of University College in February, 1903, after having endured Vivisection extending over more than Two Months and having been handed over from one Vivisector to Another Till Death came to his Release. Also in Memory of the 232 dogs Vivisected at the same place during the year 1902. Men and women of England, how long shall these Things be?" That there was strong antivivisection sentiment in the Council is obvious. Only the conservatives and a few of the radicals were opposed to accepting the fountain, warning that there might be legal action from London University. Indeed, when University College did threaten to take proceedings against the Battersea Borough Council unless the memorial was removed from the statue, the Council bluntly told the university to mind its own business.[23]

There was a large crowd on September 15, 1906, when the fountain was unveiled, and for once, John Burns was not invited. However, Charlotte Despard was there with Louisa Woodward, George Bernard Shaw, and the Reverend Charles Noel, who spoke on behalf of the Anti-Vivisection Council. It was a public snub for Burns, who had always looked on the Latchmere Estate as a testimony to his beneficent care of the borough. The Mayor of Battersea, J. H. Brown, welcomed the statue and all that it stood for. Brown was a thirty-eight-year-old trades unionist, honorary secretary of the General Labourers' Union and secretary of the Battersea Trades and Labour Council.[24] As well as being a vocal critic of Burns for having taken office under a Liberal government,

Brown was an antivivisectionist and remained one of the strongest supporters of the brown dog. When the ex-mayor of Chelsea praised Battersea for its bravery in accepting such a gift, Brown said that Battersea would always lead the way in improving conditions for the working class. Clearly, for Brown vivisection was a means used to oppress the working class, and his words were met with cheers. Sufficient to record now that it was a stirring occasion brought to a conclusion by the Reverend Noel, who led the crowd in singing "Ring the Bells of Mercy," the antivivisectionist hymn.[25]

The fountain was in place, the brown dog stared across to the neat ranks of council houses, and if ever a riot had been deliberately instigated, this was it. The wonder is that it took so long for the medical students to respond to the challenge. The *South-Western Star* wrote enticingly: "It is rumoured that the students of the hospital intend to pull it down and that electric bells have been placed on the statue to give notice of any such attempt."[26] However, it was just over a year before the students crossed the river into Battersea. Of course, those who have had some experience of student demonstrations will appreciate that they occur most frequently on campus; there is a marked disinclination to walk any distance for the purpose of rioting. In this case, it is doubtful if the London University students would have done more than complain had they not been organized and led by that politically astute young medical student William Lister.

In Battersea the Socialists were still complaining about John Burns and threatening to run their own candidate against him in the next elections. They were joined by the antivaccinationists, who were outraged when Burns voted in favor of the Vaccination Act, which made inoculation a condition of employment in government service.[27] Half a century later Cecil Hart may have forgotten the brown dog, but he did not forget the Battersea General Hospital and what it stood for in the borough. "The Old Anti" had always served the working folk of Battersea, but now abruptly it was refused funds from the Metropolitan Hospital Sunday Fund.[28] The Battersea Council saw John Burns's influence at work here and organized carnivals to raise money for the hospital and what it stood for—an institution where every doctor was pledged not to engage in any form of vivisection.

It was a time of furious activity for Charlotte Despard; she led deputations of Battersea's unemployed to the Town Hall, and smaller groups of women to see John Burns, who was no longer able to conceal his contempt for this angry old woman. The Pankhursts, however, were delighted to have Charlotte Despard as secretary of the Women's Social and Political Union, and they made it known that the reason she had not been arrested was because the government feared a riot in Battersea and because there was alarm that her brother might resign from the army—Sir John French being regarded as the most promising general and Haldane's choice for Inspector-General of the Forces.[29] Neither statement was true, but the violence and incoherence of the threats was typical of many of Emmeline Pankhurst's utterances.

In November William Lister decided the time had come to attack the brown dog in Battersea. He had campaigned vigorously throughout the university and felt he had sufficient support to conduct something more elaborate than the customary heckling at antivivisection rallies. On November 20, 1907, an exceptionally foggy day, Lister summoned a group of thirty students from University College and Middlesex Hospital. They purchased a massive hammer and crowbar and set out a little after three to their meeting place at the top of the Tottenham Court Road, where other medical students had assembled. They all caught a Royal Blue Omnibus to Battersea and then quietly, concealed by the fog, made their way along Battersea Park Road to the Latchmere Recreation Ground. But the police had been warned, and when the students rushed to the fountain and one man "took a mighty blow at the creature with the sledge hammer," he was seized by two plainclothes policemen.[30] Battersea men rushed out of the council houses and helped the police arrest ten of the students, who were formally charged and fined five pounds each the following day at the South-West London Police Court. The magistrate, Paul Taylor, not only rebuked the students: he sent them off with a warning of two months' prison with hard labor and no option of a fine if they created any further disturbances.[31]

Lister now had a cause which would rouse his fellow students to action, and they responded with bonfires in front of University College and demonstrations against Paul Taylor. What infuriated these young men was that they had been treated in the same manner as the suffragettes, who were now being routinely arrested after their disturbances and given prison sentences. Charlotte Despard, for example, had served twenty-one days in Holloway after her part in the February 12 riot in front of the Commons. Despite the fact that some suffragettes were known to approve of vivisection, the students began to attack every women's suffrage meeting with howls, barks, and cries of "Down with the Brown Dog!" Millicent Fawcett, a close friend of several noted vivisectionists and the sister of the medical pioneer Elizabeth Garrett Anderson, had her suffrage meeting at the Paddington Baths broken up in disorder on December 5.[32] Even Edward K. Ford, who wrote a contemporary account of the riots, was puzzled at this association of antivivisection with the women's cause when men like Coleridge and Hadwen had not shown any particular sympathy for women's suffrage.[33] Yet, for the students and increasingly for the public, antivivisection and women's rights were now part of the same movement. Inevitably, as we shall see, each was to lose by this association.

The medical students were now an organized body, and Lister drew up a campaign to destroy the statue. On November 25 students made another attempt to enter the Latchmere Recreation Ground and were driven back in considerable disarray, so Lister planned a demonstration in Trafalgar Square. He knew that on December 10 the Oxford and Cambridge undergraduates would be in town for the 'Varsity Rugby football match: if only he could enlist their support, then London men would be seen standing shoulder to shoulder with their Oxbridge companions. The demonstration was advertised, and the police made ready.

Lister was chagrined when the Oxford and Cambridge men down for the match refused to join his cause, but decided to sally forth without them. Shouting and singing, the medical students marched in procession down Kensington High Street, holding aloft effigies of the brown dog and the magistrate Paul Taylor. In Trafalgar Square fights broke out between students and groups of workingmen. Immediately the mounted police moved in, scattering the crowd and arresting several students. Lister led the main band across the river to Battersea, where there were more police and a hostile crowd.

Driven out of the Latchmere Ground the students fought their way down Battersea Park Road, where they tried to attack the Antivivisection Hospital. Again the crowd forced the students back, and when one fell from the top of a tram and was slightly injured, the *Daily Chronicle* reported that the crowd had shouted jubilantly, "That's the brown dog's revenge!"[34] His friends tried to carry him across to the Antivivisection Hospital, but a group of workers barred the door and refused to let him enter.

Battersea's new mayor at this time was Fred Worthey, a master printer, Congregational temperance worker, and fervent antivivisectionist. When the Police Commissioner asked the Battersea Council to pay for the cost of the two policemen who were now required to guard the brown dog twenty-four hours a day, Worthey told the Commissioner to stop badgering the Council and start doing the job for which he was paid.[35] It was a chance for the borough to assert itself against the city and, indirectly, show the London County Council that it could not bully Battersea. A Conservative member of the Battersea Council, A. E. Runeckles, then suggested that the inscription be removed, but the Council had the following statement recorded in the minutes: "That the inscription on the memorial being founded on ascertained facts, the Council declines to sanction the proposal to remove it, and that the Chief Commissioner of Police be informed in reply to his letter that the care and protection of public monuments is a matter for the police and any expense occasioned thereby should be defrayed out of the public rate to which this Borough contributes so largely; also that the Council considers more strenuous efforts should be made to suppress any renewal of the organised ruffianism which has recently taken place in the Metropolis in connection with the Memorial."[36] Letters supporting the Council's stand were received from ratepayers and from an incongruous group of supporters. The Battersea Labour League wanted to see the students removed from Battersea before anyone thought of moving the brown dog, the National Canine Defence League formally applauded the Council for its actions, and the Battersea branch of the Operative Bricklayers' Society pledged its members to defend the statue. Working-class support for antivivisection was now a matter of public record. If medical students had identified the movement with women, people were now beginning to see it as a working-class issue.

When Louise Lind-af-Hageby held a ticketed antivivisection meeting at the Acton Central Hall on December 16, 1907, she had a guard of Battersea workers, yet over a hundred students managed to smuggle their way in, and soon the meeting was pandemonium, with broken chairs, fistfights, and smoke bombs. Again, police were required to restore order and arrest the rioters.[37] The students appealed to Sir Philip Magnus, M.P. for London University, to have the inscription removed from the fountain, and he in turn asked the Home Secretary at question time in the Commons what it was costing the government to protect the Brown Dog Memorial, assuring the House that "a large body of students in the London University were quite prepared to remove this offensive monument free of charge."[38] A petition signed by over a thousand London University students was presented to the Battersea Council demanding that the libellous inscription be erased.[39]

At a public meeting in the Battersea Town Hall on January 15, 1908, Stephen Paget, speaking as president of the newly formed Research Defence Society, moved that another inscription be placed on the statue. Stephen Paget was the son of Sir James Paget, who had once remonstrated with Queen Victoria over her opposition to vivisection. The younger Paget was by no means as eminent a doctor as his father, but for several years he had been secretary of the Association for the Advancement of Medicine by Research. On this occasion the students rioted in their customary fashion, and more than three hundred stewards were required to drag the demonstrators from the hall.[40]

The following month in London the Municipal Reformers defeated the Progressives for control of the London County Council. Sir Herbert Jessel had waged a brilliant campaign for the Municipal Reformers, appropriating Socialist slogans and images and using them against the Progressives. Campaign songs were promoted, and one poster showed a Progressive with "a bloated ugly face, chewing a cigar and wearing a top hat, hand outstretched, with the caption *It's Your money we want!*"[41] Battersea was caught up in the same struggle, but here the issues were increasingly debated in terms of the brown dog and the Antivivisection Hospital.

The Battersea General Hosital had always been controlled by a board of local residents: three of the four vice-presidents were women, and these women were antivivisectionists.[42] With its painted sign announcing its principles and practice to passersby the hospital was felt to be an insult to a modern medical profession dedicated to research by means of animal experimentation. Sir William Church of the Metropolitan Hospital Fund declared that "no self-respecting medical man would for one moment consent to the governing body of a hospital which consisted mainly of laymen." Thomas Bryant stated in the same report that the "Antivivisection Hospital casts a great slur upon the profession generally, and that they ought not to support a hospital which was based upon such principles."[43]

Cutting off funds to the hospital was one means of closing it, but here the Hospital Fund had not reckoned with the loyalties of men like Cecil Hart and the local trades unions, which helped run carnivals and collect money for the "Old Anti."[44] Finding it impossible to close the hospital by starving it financially, the Hospital Fund charged it with neglecting its patients. This charge was upheld in the Battersea Coroner's Court in December 1909, when the coroner, John Troutbeck, investigated the deaths of two patients who had initially received treatment at the hospital. He observed that there had been "great neglect at the Anti-Vivisection Hospital."[45] In consequence the hospital was closed and patients transferred to the Wandsworth Infirmary, where doctors sat on the governing board and there were no restrictions against vivisectors being allowed to practice.

Throughout 1908 the Moderates campaigned to take control of the Battersea Council, and when an additional threepence on the pound was imposed on ratepayers to assist the unemployed, the Moderates knew they could count on an increased vote. After all, not every man could vote under the restricted franchise of this period. In 1907 only 22,914 in a population of more than 180,000 could go to the polls, and these were ratepayers and heads of household most affected by the increase in rates. There were complaints of a Socialist Council pouring money into the pockets of "the wastrels and loafers of that Borough."[46] And the symbol of Socialist authority in Battersea was now the brown dog.

Meetings were held, each more riotous than the last, but it was clear now that so long as the Socialists and Progressives held a majority in the Council the brown dog would remain in Battersea. Nevertheless, at the 1908 elections the Moderates were able to gain control, and among the first acts of the new Council was an order to remove the statue. The mayor, Peter Haythornthwaite, a Moderate, tried at first to persuade the Council to alter the inscription to one suggested by Stephen Paget:

> The dog was submitted under profound anaesthesia to a very slight operation in the interests of science. In two or three days it was healed, and remained perfectly well and free of all pain. Two months later it was again placed under profound anaesthesia for further experiment, and was killed under the anaesthetic. It knew nothing of what was being done to it on either occasion. None of us can count on so easy death. We doubtless shall suffer pain or distress, both mental and physical. This dog was free alike from fear and suffering. It died neither of starvation nor of overfeeding, nor of burdens from old age. It just died in its sleep.[47]

The fatuous stupidity of Paget's declaration did not go unremarked, and even the *Daily Mail* wondered if the dog had felt in the best of health between the two operations.[48] Louise Lind-af-Hageby was outraged that known facts should be falsified by a new inscription from an acknowledged vivisector. This was not what she had seen in the laboratory of University College, and she demanded the right to speak again at the Battersea Town Hall. Even though she was met with wild applause, the same fights and brawls broke out between medical students and the stewards.

William Lister was now convinced that in the brown dog he had at last found a cause to unify the London University students, and he led them from one antivivisection and women's suffrage meeting to another. The Police Commissioner was still insisting that the Battersea Council pay for the protection of the statue, and on February 10, 1910, the Council moved that the fountain should be returned to its donor, Louisa Woodward of the Church Antivivisection Society. She promptly sought a restraining injunction from Chancery, and Charlotte Despard and Louise Lind-af-Hageby addressed a mass meeting at the Latchmere Recreation Ground. The ex-mayor Fred Worthey said the Council was making "a concession to organised violence," and handed out pamphlets which he had composed and printed at his own cost.[49]

Before Miss Woodward could secure the restraining injunction, the Council had acted, and about two o'clock on the morning of March 10, four Council workmen guarded by 120 police carried the statue away and hid it in a bicycle shed.[50] Battersea exploded in rage, but now there were mounted police ringing the Recreation Ground. Speakers who tried to place a box there and address the crowd were led away, and the demonstration was effectively quashed.

Ten days later over three thousand people assembled in Trafalgar Square to hear the leaders of the antivivisection movement demand the return of the brown dog. Scuffles broke out between medical students and police, but this time the speakers—Sir George Kekewich, Louise Lind-af-Hageby, and Stephen Coleridge—made themselves heard.[51] Despite their fiery pronouncements and the enthusiasm of the crowd it was clear that the brown dog had gone from Battersea and would never return. Indeed, three weeks later it was broken up in the Council yard.

Most of the participants declared themselves well satisfied with the results of the riots. Stephen Paget regarded it as a victory for progress and science; William Lister felt that a corporate spirit had been created in the "*disjecta membra* of the University"; G. K. Chesterton playfully suggested that the Battersea banner should have a brown dog rampant although he would have preferred a chrysanthemum himself, and Stephen Coleridge stated that the brown dog had been "a splendid advertisement for our cause."[52] Louisa Woodward continued trying to secure legal redress against the Council, but even when she failed, she declared that the cause had become better known. Louise Lind-af-Hageby maintained the struggle by means of her own society and rented shops where antivivisection literature was displayed and sold. George Bernard Shaw continued to write and lecture against vivisection, but there was a *fin de siècle* feeling about the movement by this time, and for many the issues had become so influenced by other social movements that it was difficult to distinguish antivivisection from feminism or working-class socialism.

A chronological narrative like this is always as enigmatic and intrinsically superficial as the passing traveller's perception of a crowded street. You may be able to see London from the top of a bus, but you cannot hope to know and understand it. Just as the slums and suburbs of Battersea defined an obscure geography wherein architecture concealed the life and purpose of the inhabitants, the ranked tenements and paved streets concealed fields and streams which made their presence felt by covert means and unsuspected signs, like those half-forgotten memories which yet have the power to determine present action. Why people behaved and thought as they did at this particular time cannot be explained by reference to changes in local government or the rivalry between town and gown; there are too many incongruities and contradictions in this particular riot.

An immediate problem in such a brief narrative is the conjunction of workers and suffragettes, for if there was one issue which had no support among the trades unions and with working-class men generally, it was the demand that women be given the vote. Labour men routinely pledged their support for the cause, but when it was put to the test in a mass union vote it failed. Working-class men who were threatened with unemployment had no desire to enfranchise the cheap labor of women, and every strong union sought to exclude women, not give them added authority at the polling booth. George Lansbury discovered this in 1912 when he ran for his old seat in Poplar as a suffrage candidate: a majority of 863 became a minority of 731, and his biographer, Raymond Postgate, saw it as the most serious blunder of his career.[53] Yet in Battersea the suffragettes and trades unionists had worked for a common cause—a brown dog.

This straightway gives rise to another difficulty: R. D. French assures us that antivivisection was a dead letter for the working class. Indeed, all efforts to organize the workers ended in failure, and "the ultimate stumbling block emerged in the profound indifference of laborers towards the issue."[54] Who then were those cloth-capped stewards at Louise Lind-af-Hageby's lectures, and what were the local ironworkers doing when they voted to defend a memorial to a vivisected dog? In Battersea we find unionists protecting that dog, and men and women prepared to use their fists and meagre funds to support an antivivisection hospital. The RSPCA always maintained that the working class was callous in its treatment of animals, but perhaps this particular society was less concerned with protecting animals than with policing the workers. Statements of this order cannot be explicated in terms of events but only by exploring those attitudes which translate emotion into action, and we may well find that the workers of Battersea are typical of their class and that their concern with antivivisection is more deeply felt than that of any other social group.

French also notes the involvement of women with antivivisection, "among the very highest for movements without overtly feminist objectives."[55] Women like Frances Cobbe, Anna Kingsford, and Louise Lind-af-Hageby were willing to give their lives to this cause. Anna Kingsford even volunteered to give her own body for vivisection in order to save an animal.[56] Is this passionate involvement really the "displacement of guilt" that the prosperous middle class transferred from their employees to animals, as James Turner argues?[57] Surely the emotions are too extreme to make such an ingenious thesis possible, even if the middle class carried such a burden of guilt over the suffering of the working class. Certainly, many of the middle class women did not show the same concern for children or the poor, and it is doubtful whether guilt was as pervasive in Victorian society as it is with us today. It may well be that here we shall find a very dark river running beneath the architecture of social forms, a river bounded on one side by pornography and on the other by conventional medical practice.

The doctors of the future, the medical students of our narrative, behaved like a hooligan mob, but not only E. K. Ford was perplexed by their belligerent insistence that women's suffrage and antivivisection were parts of the same objectionable cause. A number of prominent antivivisectionists like Anna Kingsford, the novelist "Ouida," and Robert Hadwen were opposed to any extension of the suffrage, while among the suffragists there were many like Millicent Fawcett who saw antivivisection as an obstruction to scientific progress. It also may be that the young men denouncing the brown dog and its supporters were unconsciously responding to the same force that had drawn women into this cause, although there were few who recognized the nature of that force, and fewer still who would have been prepared to acknowledge it if they had.

Eventually, the whole incident became a question of opposed symbols in shop windows, and Cecil Hart's recollection of an "advertizing story" now has considerable point. The Anti-Vivisection Council set out a display in a shop front in Oxford Street.[58] Behind the glass were displayed saws, scalpels, and straps; boards designed to hold animals for vivisection; and a centrepiece which Patrick White describes in his novel *The Vivisector*:

> It was one of the greyest days, pierced by black monuments. Hurtle lost the others for a moment: they had all floated apart in the drizzle, the sound of wheels revolving in wet, the tramping of galoshes; when he found himself staring into a display window of horrible purpose. There was a little, brown, stuffed dog clamped to a kind of operating table. The dog's exposed teeth were gnashing in a permanent and most realistic agony. Its guts, exposed too, and varnished pink to grey-green, were more realistic still.[59]

Next to this shop was one managed by the Research Defence Society with photographs of Pasteur and the picture of a smiling young woman with a baby on her knee, and underneath it the inscription: "Which will you save—your child or a guinea pig?"[60] The images were contradictory, but the conclusion was plain in terms of symbol if not of fact. It was a case where fiction had supplanted reality; the icon of mother and child and the sacrifice of a dog concealed another grotesque image of a woman strapped to a surgical bed struggling to escape. Women's suffrage had very little in common with antivivisection, but the two had become confusedly entwined through the accident of circumstance: the image of the vivisected dog blurred and became one with the militant suffragette being force-fed in Brixton Prison.

There are many reasons why the antivivisection movement dwindled and almost disappeared between these years and the present surge of interest and concern, but one predominating cause is that people no longer saw it in actual terms but through coded messages of scientific progress, sacrificial redemption, and sexual victimization. It was at the time of the Brown Dog Riots that these messages first came to signify reality, but the origin of the messages goes back to the early years of the nineteenth century.

2

What about the Workers!

When Battersea was still a village in the last years of the eighteenth century and market gardens extended from the river's edge to Clapham Common, you could shoot pigeons at the Red House, attend cock-fights in the yard of the Plough, or bet on a rat-killing at the Falcon. Thames rates were regarded as being particularly plucky and courageous, and the spectators knew that they would fight to the death against any terrier. Of course, these sporting occasions were only a pale imitation of what might be found at places like Hockley-in-the-Hole, where sharp at three on Monday there was always a full card of bloodsports with "a *green bull* to be baited, which was never baited before, and a bull to be turned loose, with fireworks all over him; also a mad ass to be baited. With a variety of bull-baiting and bear-baiting, and a dog to be drawn up with fireworks."[1] Nothing as elaborate and diverse as this could be found at any of the Battersea inns, and certainly there were no special stands set aside for gentlemen, no "pleasant cool gallery" where gentlefolk could stand apart from the common people. In Battersea, as at most places, the men stood together around the pit, betting, swearing, and drinking prodigious quantities of beer.

Within walking distance of these sporting taverns was Broomfield House in Clapham, where William Wilberforce planned his campaign against slavery and helped Dr. John Bowdler found the Society for the Suppression of Vice and Encouragement of Religion.[2] The Clapham Saints were determined to establish Christ's Kingdom in England, and one step in that direction was to abolish all public occasions where

26

carnal passions were aroused. It was not so much compassion for animals that led Wilberforce to oppose bloodsports as his belief that men became worse than brutes when they witnessed the suffering of animals. In the House of Commons William Windham challenged Wilberforce's motives, declaring that "cruel sports do not make cruel people," and moreover, "if the cruelty of Bull-baiting was thus to be held up to the attention of the house in such glaring colours, why was not hunting, shooting, fishing, and all other amusements of a similar description to be judged by similar principles?"[3] Moreover, in the name of Methodism, Wilberforce and his friends were oppressing the poor so pitilessly that the result could only be riot and rebellion: "If to poverty were to be added a privation of amusements, he [Windham] knew nothing that could operate more strongly to goad the mind into desperation, and to prepare the poor for that dangerous enthusiasm which is analogous to Jacobinism."[4]

These two men had visions of an England as far removed from each other as earth from heaven: Wilberforce wanted a community of saints; Windham, the restoration of a rural age where the gentry mingled with their workfolk as though members of the same family. Threaded through Windham's speeches there is the image of the genial squire presiding over a dinner table that includes children and servants, or cheering on a jovial throng at the bullbaiting with men of all classes standing together on the same bloody ground. Although he was not a sportsman, and neither hunted nor fished himself, Windham regarded bloodsports as splendid examples of English fraternity, fostering harmony and good spirits in the community. Morals should be inculcated from the pulpit, he argued, or taught from the press, by precept, by exhortation, and above all else, by example. What could possibly be said in favor of legislation which deprived the poor of their pleasures while preserving the sports of the rich? "I defy a person," Windham wrote, "to attack bull-baiting and to defend hunting."[5]

At issue were two distinct psychologies of social response. Windham insisted that if the working class was permitted to watch bulls gored and dogs flayed, then it would be so sated with violence that it would accept the hardships of life without recourse to protest and riot. Wilberforce argued that the spectacle of suffering encouraged men to rebellion, making the transition a single step from cruelty to animals to cruelty to people. The fear of revolution lay behind most social theorizing at this time, and the likelihood of a market riot or a rick burning exploding into a reign of terror and a guillotine haunted the English. How to make the working class content with its lot, or, if not content, then disinclined to seek recourse in revolution was the question for which Wilberforce found the answer in faith and law, and Windham in a return to the traditions of the past.

E. P. Thompson has advised those who want to emphasize the sober constitutional ancestry of the working-class movement to look again at some of its rowdier aspects.[6] It also helps to see the working class in the context of a society where violence was a commonplace and everybody could expect more than one beating in his life. To be born a gentleman did not save one from the floggings and thrashings that were thought to be as necessary a part of education as a knowledge of Scripture. Physical violence as the manifestation of authority remained part of a child's experience when its worst excesses had been removed from public life. Long after the police had imposed a degree of order in the streets of London, with hangings conducted behind the high walls of the prison and many bloodsports abolished; thoughout the time when it was no longer fashionable for masters to kick and cuff their servants, the children of both the rich and the working poor continued to share the pain of the rod, the birch, or somebody's fist. Some, like Thackeray and Swinburne, developed a perverse taste for the birch, but for most it was a savage indignity they remembered with considerable anguish. Trollope recalled that at school he was not only beaten by his teachers but by his brother: "As a part of his daily exercize he thrashed me with a big stick. That such thrashings should have been possible at a school as a continual part of one's daily life, seems to me to argue a very ill condition of school discipline."[7] This was Harrow, yet it was much the same at that dismal church institution, the Clergy Daughters' School at Cowan Bridge, where Charlotte Brontë suffered as a child and which she described in *Jane Eyre* (1846) as Lowood. The refinement of punishment here was to make the offending student curtsey, then hand the birch to the teacher as a token of guilt and grateful acceptance of correction: "Burns immediately left the class, and, going into the small inner room where the books were kept, returned in half a minute, carrying in her hand a bundle of twigs tied together at one end. This ominous tool she presented to Miss Scatcherd with a respectful curtsey: then she quietly left without being told, unloosed her pinafore, and the teacher instantly and sharply inflicted on her neck a dozen strokes with a bunch of twigs" (chap. 6).

Elizabeth Gaskell, fortunate to be born a Unitarian and educated by the enlightened methods of that faith, was one of the very few children to escape flogging. When Flora Thompson recalled the kindly Miss Holmes of her village school, she noted that although this excellent teacher carried a cane from room to room, she never caned the very small children and only occasionally girls.[8] Poor Traddles in *David Copperfield* (1869), caned every day at Salem House and drawing skeletons on his tear-stained slate (chap. 7), could be found in most English classrooms.[9] We should not forget that animals were protected long before children in England and in the United States.

In 1884, John Colam, Secretary of the RSPCA since 1860, used the same arguments as the Clapham Saints to defend children from cruelty: those who tortured and abused animals would be sure to injure human beings. So a concern for the welfare of children grew naturally from the compassion felt for animals. Indeed, in that same year the executive committee of the Society for the Prevention of Cruelty to Children met regularly in the boardroom of the RSPCA's headquarters in Jermyn Street until they could afford quarters of their own. Twenty percent of the members of the new society were already members of the RSPCA, including John Colam. The words spoken by Henry Bergh, founder of the American SPCC, had become a rallying cry for the protectors of children. In 1874 Bergh had stated: "The child is an animal. If there is no justice for it as a human being, it shall at least have the rights of a cur in the street. It shall not be abused."[10]

Flora Thompson learned to accept the cane and was grateful when it was used with moderation to discipline the unruly. She knew that among themselves working-class children learned early that it was necessary to use their fists in order to survive:

It has been said that every child is born a little savage and has to be civilized. The process of civilization had not gone very far with some of the hamlet children; although one civilization had them in hand at home and another at school, they were able to throw off both on the road between the two places and revert to a state of Nature. A favourite amusement with these was to fall in a body upon some unoffending companion, usually a small girl in a clean frock, and to 'run her', as they called it. This meant chasing her until they caught her, then dragging her down and sitting upon her, tearing her clothes, smudging her face, and tousling her hair in the process. She might scream and cry and say she would 'tell on' them; they took no notice until, tiring of the sport, they would run whooping off, leaving her sobbing and exhausted.[11]

Boys' games tended to be considerably rougher, with stray dogs stoned and drowned, or cats caught and skinned alive.

The fate of most girls was domestic service or apprenticeship, and then there would certainly be bullying and, occasionally, blows from workmates and other servants. Oliver Twist was not beaten by his master, Mr. Sowerberry, but the other apprentice, Noah Claypole, took a positive delight in tormenting the boy. In due course Noah makes a profession of this taste for petty tyranny in a career suggested to him by Fagin after the lad has rejected bag-snatching from old ladies as being too dangerous: "The kinchins, my dear," said Fagin, "is the young children that's sent on errands by their mothers, with sixpences and shillings; and the lay is just to take their money away—they've always got it ready in their hands—then knock 'em into the kennel and walk off very slow, as if there was nothing else the matter but a child fallen down and hurt itself. Ha! ha! ha!" (*Oliver Twist* [1841], chap. 13).

In this area of abused children, fiction was a pallid imitation of the truth. Throughout the eighteenth century the death of apprentices and servants as a result of beatings was not uncommon: "The Middlesex Sessions papers, for example, record that in 1736 James Durant, a ribbon weaver, beat his thirteen-year-old apprentice to death with a 'mop-stick', and that in 1748 Elizabeth Dickens murdered her child apprentice by beating and ill-using her."[12] If the actual murder of servants became a rare occurrence in the nineteenth century, there was still a full measure of hurt and humiliation to be endured.

The large Victorian house was designed so that servants lived and ate in separate quarters from the family, and this physical division between workers and employers became the model for much poorer homes. It was the very antithesis of Windham's ideal community of "beneficence, humanity and hospitality," functioning like a family with the workers at the bottom of the table and the gentry at the top—but all eating from the same board. Windham was not alone in holding to this vision; it colored the minds and aspirations of the working class. Bitterly Mrs. Golding of Battersea recalled getting a job as "daily maid" at a small house on the Rise when she had just turned fourteen: "I might also add that although there was plenty of room to sit at the table with the Lady of the House and her two daughters 3 or 4 years younger than myself, I had to eat my dinner off the mangle, next to the scullery but in the same room."[13] The injustice of this remained with her, but at least she was not beaten by the "Lady of the House."

By contrast, Mrs. Scholefield of Illminster Gardens remembered her mother speaking of an employer's kindness in a way that set aside all questions of low wages and long hours: "My mother worked at 'Astors' the drapers in St. John's Road when she was a little girl. She remembered her boss was very kind and all the Staff had their meals with him at the head of the table carving the joint, always saying grace before they ate. In those days they had to be up to clean, fill and light oil stoves before breakfast to warm the shop for the customers."[14] It would seem that it was not an excess of paternalism that workers resented but its absence.

Windham deplored this growing division between classes, divisions that were forgotten when men stood cheering on the dogs at a bullbaiting. Not only were bloodsports democratic; they could give even the poorest member of society some release for his frustration and pain. And since children were the most helpless and persecuted, what was more natural than that they should want to torture and kill creatures even weaker than themselves? But if Windham saw this as natural and benefic in the community, Wilberforce and his Evangelical friends denounced it as cultivating the inherent savage in a child. Soon the working-class child was learning two contradictory lessons: he was to be coerced into goodness by means of the birch, and he must not inflict a similar pain upon animals.

Nobody has satisfactorily resolved the problem of cruelty in human nature, and I have no elaborate theory to propound now. Instead, at this point, I would like to use Philip Hallie's definition of cruelty as the paradoxical relationship between oppressor and victim whereby the latter is deprived of liberty and freedom and the persecutor is made a slave to his own brutality.[15] This was essentially William Hogarth's belief and the argument of Wilberforce. By extension, the torturing of a person or an animal is the overt assertion of the power and authority of an individual or a group. If you can kick me and get away with it, you have clearly demonstrated your physical and social authority over me, if not your moral ascendancy. So, it can be argued that cruelty, particularly towards animals, had a definite social and psychological function at a time when life was a progress of painful subservience to most people. As Ernest Morris said, looking back to the days of his youth in Battersea: "Those days one existed by cap in hand and fear of unemployment and the dole. Class distinction reigned and the dole. Class distinction reigned predominant."[16]

Rather than being seen as an aberration of human nature, the torture and killing of animals permitted those who had no rights, no possibility of ever imposing their will upon others, to demonstrate, often publicly, their strength and dominance. When men who were accustomed to being thrashed and abused could watch the chained bull harried by a pack of dogs, it was like seeing the authority of the master torn apart by the mob. Wilberforce and others of like mind saw the symbolic and social import of these sports and were deeply troubled: was the satisfaction derived from such a spectacle as a bullbait any different from that of the Paris mob at the foot of the guillotine? Windham responded in turn that it was the democratic nature of a bloodsport in England which precluded any danger of revolution. Masters and workmen, gentry and townsfolk, would all turn out to watch a bullbaiting. Gaskell wrote of Rochdale, where

> The bull was fastened by a chain or rope to a post in the river. To increase the amount of water, as well as to give their workpeople the opportunity of savage delight, the masters were accustomed to stop their mills on the day when the sport took place. The bull would sometimes wheel suddenly round, so that the rope by which he was fastened swept those who had been careless enough to come within its range down into the water, and the good people of Rochdale had the excitement of seeing one or two of their neighbours drowned as well as of witnessing the bull baited, and the dogs torn and tossed.[17]

Windham pleaded for this old England in the face of the abhorred "Methodists and Jacobins" who were resolved to coerce the people into morality, but his cause was lost.[18] Not only were the classes now segregated at sporting occasions; there was also a distinct policy that crowds of workers, invariably described as mobs, should be denied any opportunity to assemble. Above all else, it was necessary for workers to be educated from earliest childhood in deference; they must learn not to harm animals and, by extension, people. A docile, tractable, and energetic work force was the dream of every employer, who, on his part, was prepared to encourage Bible schools and wholesome team sports like cricket and football. Gaskell described an "industrial school" in Hollingford founded and maintained by the local gentry which trained girls, and ensured a supply of maids for their service: "Girls are taught to sew beautifully, to be capital housemaids, and pretty fair cooks, and, above all, to dress neatly in a kind of charity uniform devised by the ladies of Cumnor Towers; —white caps, white tippets, check aprons, blue gowns, and ready curtseys, and 'please, ma'ams', being *de rigueur*." In the Black Country, an enlightened manager recommended that "all manly games, such as cricket, all humanising and refined tastes, should be encouraged as soon as possible."[19] This in an area where cockfights had been the traditional sport of miners and their employers!

If the Evangelicals could abolish sports like bullbaiting and cockfighting with the assistance of those of humane instincts, it was not so easy, as Windham had sardonically observed, to deny the gentry their traditional pleasures. Therefore, throughout the nineteenth century we find the working class being deprived of the bloodsports they had always enjoyed in the company of the gentry and the middle class, while the latter appropriated those bloodsports which excluded the workers. Gentlemen could race horses, but it was frowned on when they attended ratfights. And unquestionably the reason was that at a race you stood apart from the lower orders, whereas around a ratpit you stood alongside them.

Foxhunting was an expensive sport and it became the pursuit of the rich and the rural gentry in all save a few isolated parts of Wales, where the miners turned out on ponies. So, too, stag hunting and shooting were reserved for those who could afford the time and money to kill animals preserved for the sport. Nothing is more misleading than to speak of the elimination of bloodsports from social life in this period. Instead what we find is the retention of all those bloodsports that could be enjoyed by the upper classes in the exclusive company of their own kind. However, if a gentleman were to indulge in a working-class sport like cockfighting or ratfights, he could expect neither the approval of his peers nor the mercy of the law. The point was made in Trollope's *Orley Farm* (1862), when Sir Peregrine Orme ruefully considered his grandson's predilection for Carroty Bob's establishment in Cowcross Street, where rats were killed in a barrel: "Rats have this advantage, that they usually come cheaper than race-horses; but then, as Sir Peregrine felt sorely, they do not sound so well" (chap. 4).

Cockfights had always been one of those democratic sports praised by Windham where rich and poor could mingle together. Gaskell re-

lated how as late as the 1850s the gentry of Yorkshire patronized cockfighting in defiance of clerical denunciations against those who preferred to spend Sunday gambling instead of praying:

> Another squire, of more distinguished family and larger prop-
> erty—one is thence led to imagine of better education, but that
> does not always follow—died at his house, not many miles from
> Haworth, only a few years ago. His great amusement and occupa-
> tion had been cockfighting. When he was confined to his chamber
> with what he knew would be his last illness, he had his cocks
> brought up there, and watched the bloody battle from his bed. As
> his mortal disease increased, and it became impossible for him to
> turn so as to follow the combat, he had looking-glasses arranged
> in such a manner, around and above him, as he lay, that he could
> still see the cocks fighting. And in this manner he died.[20]

Not only did men of all classes attend cockfights; it was within the
means of a working man to own and train a cock, or a terrier dog for
ratfighting. He could never hope to purchase a horse or join a hunt
club, and it was most unlikely that he would ever be invited to shoot at
a country house. It was not merely the composition of the crowd at a
bloodsport which had changed by the end of the century but its loca-
tion as well. All bloodsports were now confined to rural areas under
the patronage of the gentry. The scenes of the foxhunt were as brutal
as the flayed and torn birds at the conclusion of a cockfight: it was as
"natural" for cocks to fight as it was to set hounds in pursuit of a fox,
but those enjoying the carnage were now restricted to the upper
classes. Laborers and the like were told to play "manly games" like
cricket and football, but the old traditions did not die easily among
men who had been passionately devoted to cockfighting. Frances
Power Cobbe told the story of the lady taking a Ragged School class on
the subject of "Gratitude" and inquiring "what pleasure in the course
of the year they most thoroughly enjoyed. After a thoughtful pause, the
last boy in the class looked up and said, with simple candour—'Cockfighting, ma'am.'"[21]

By the middle of the century the RSPCA was actively prosecuting
the men who promoted cockfights no matter what their station in life.
The rank of Captain Augustus Berkeley did not save him from arrest
when he was caught by the society's officials while presiding over a
cockfight as referee.[22] It was easier to prosecute an illegal cockfight in

the city than in the country; nonetheless, in 1863 the marquess of Hastings was fined for setting up cockfights at Dorington Hall.[23] By the end of the century it had become an illicit sport that workingmen patronized in defiance of the law and gentlemen attended at the risk of name and reputation. Miners still held an occasional and secret cockfight in the north of England, but in other parts it became a specialty of the gypsies, particularly in Wales, where the "travelling people" would arrive with their gamecocks and be off on the road before the local magistrate could be informed.[24]

Those who had grown up in the early years of the century now tended to look back in dismay and astonishment at what they had been and done. Thackeray felt as though he had lived in two different worlds, and what troubled him was that the old world still had the power to lay claim on his spirit. He remembered with considerable shame how he had enjoyed bloodsports as a child and delighted in sporting writers like Pierce Egan, St. John, and Badcock with their boisterous account of gutted dogs and torn bulls. And he recalled how the ultimate bloodsport, a public hanging, was a very jolly occasion indeed, even if it was no longer possible to witness the spectacle of men having their ears and nose sliced off by the hangman.[25] Yet even though Thackeray could never quite forget the exploits of Egan's Tom and Jerry, he declared that he found it impossible to find a copy of the work after 1860. Taste had altered, and although the appetite for bloodsports had not vanished, it was now being driven underground or forced to take different forms.

If the middle class felt it had been irrevocably changed, putting aside forever all the barbarous ways of the past, general opinion held that the working class was becoming ever more dangerous, depraved, and numerous. Wordsworth lauded solitary reapers and the meek, lowly, patient children of toil, but there were few commendations for the virtues of rural workers as the age progressed. At least in the city the brutal cabman flogging his overworked horse was under the supervision of a watchful populace, but in the country the old barbarities persisted. In *North and South* (1855) Gaskell contrasted the shrewd and kindly common sense of the industrial worker with what could be found in a pleasant little village like Helstone where Margaret Hale is questioning one of her father's old parishioners:

"How old is Betty Barnes?"
"I don't know," said the woman rather shortly.

"We's not friends."

"Why not?" asked Margaret, who had formerly been the peace-maker of the village.

"She stole my cat."

"Did she know it was yours?"

"I don't know. I reckon not."

"Well! could not you get it back again when you told her it was yours?"

"No! for she'd burnt it!"

"Burnt it!" exclaimed both Margaret and Mr Bell.

"Roasted it!" explained the woman.

It was no explanation. By dint of questioning, Margaret extracted from her the horrible fact that Betty Barnes, having been induced by a gypsy fortune-teller to lend the latter her husband's Sunday clothes, on promise of having them faithfully returned on the Saturday night before Goodman Barnes should have missed them, became alarmed by their non-appearance, and her consequent dread of her husband's anger, and as, according to one of the savage country superstitions, the cries of a cat, in the agonies of being boiled or roasted alive, compelled (as it were) the powers of darkness to fulfill the wishes of the executioner, resort had been had to the charm. The poor woman evidently believed in its efficacy; her only feeling was indignation that her cat had been chosen out from all others for a sacrifice. (Chap. 46)

Here is a dialogue that must have taken place on countless occasions when middle-class reformers encountered "the savage country superstitions" of an agricultural past. G. Kitson Clark has written that the changed attitudes to bloodsports constituted a turning point in Victorian society: "This conflict was very often between what was to make for a more humane, more civilized and more equitable society in place of indefensible survivals or the product of mere primitive savagery."[26] This is undeniable; however, for a rural worker accustomed to killing animals as his daily work, these intrusions into time-honored customs were both unwarranted and resented. It was a tradition for wrens to be hunted and plucked alive on the Isle of Man on St. Stephen's Day and for cocks to be run in Huntingdonshire on Shrove Tuesday; and as late as 1835 there were riots in Wokingham on St. Thomas's Day when the corporation refused to let a bull be baited before it was killed and its meat divided among the poor, especially when it was believed that the flesh of an unbaited bull was unwholesome if not poisonous. Indignantly, the lower orders of Wokingham "vented their rage for successive years in occasional breaches of the peace. They found out, often informed by the sympathising farmer or butcher, where the devoted animal was domiciled; proceeded at night to liberate him from stall or meadow, and to chase him across the country with all the noisy accompaniments imaginable." On another occasion, "The mob broke into the place where one of the two animals to be divided was abiding and baited him, in defiance of the authorities, in the market-place; one enthusiastic individual, tradition relates, actually lying on the ground and seizing the miserable brute by the nostril with his own teeth. This was not to be endured, and a sentence of imprisonment in Reading Gaol cooled the ardour of the ringleaders, and gave the *coup de grâce* to the sport."[27]

By the end of the century the Dean of Rochester was writing that an addiction to bullfighting was proof of Spanish perversity and arguing that just as Protestants hunted and played cricket, Roman Catholics would always be drawn to the savagery of the bullfight.[28] Although the English countryside had become a much quieter place, general opinion held that the rural worker was a brutish fellow who needed an army of Margaret Hales to prevent him from reverting to his natural state. Wordsworth saw the lowly and patient children of toil standing very close to God. In "A Journey in Search of Nothing" (1863) Wilkie Collins revealed a typical Victorian view which conveys all the contemporary prejudices about rural workers:

It is getting on toward evening, and the sons of labor are assembling on the benches outside the inn to drink. What a delightful scene they would make of this homely every-day event on the stage! How the simple creatures would clink their tin mugs, and drink each other's health and laugh joyously in chorus! How the peasant maidens would come tripping on the scene and lure the men tenderly to the dance! Where are the pipe and tabor that I have seen in so many pictures; where the simple songs that I have read about in so many poems? What do I hear as I listen, prone on the sofa, to the evening gathering of the rustic throng? Oaths—nothing, on my word of honor, but oaths! I look out, and see gangs of cadaverous savages, drinking gloomily from brown mugs, and swearing at each other every time they open their lips. Never in any large town, at home or abroad, have I been exposed to such an incessant fire of unprintable words as now assail my ears in this primitive village. . . . This is an age of civilization; this is a Christian country; opposite me I see a building with a spire, which is called, I believe, a church; past my window, not an hour since, there rattled a neat pony-chaise with a gentleman inside, clad in glossy-black broadcloth, and popularly known by the style and title of clergy-man. And yet, under all these good influences, here sit twenty or thirty men whose ordinary table-talk is so outrageously beastly and blasphemous that not one single sentence of it, though it lasted the whole evening, could be printed, as a specimen, for public inspection in these pages. When the intelligent foreigner comes to England, and when I tell him (as I am sure to do) that we are the most moral people in the universe, I will take good care that he does not set foot in a secluded British village when the rural population is reposing over its mug of small beer after the labors of the day.[29]

In the popular mind, Collins's primitive savages carousing among the haystacks were rapidly overtaking Wordsworth's innocent children of toil. When the image of both was invoked, the difference was defined in terms of animals. Jude, who is trying to free himself from the brute existence of country life, cannot bring himself to bleed the pig to death in Hardy's *Jude the Obscure*, so Arabella (who first made her presence known by flinging a pig's testicles at Jude) finishes off the job herself. Throughout Hardy's novels the humane and sensitive cannot injure or ill-treat animals, and in consequence they are made to suffer for their sensibility in a brute society. The social implications are bleak, for Arabella succeeds in a community that reflects her own values, whereas Jude is doomed to failure because his aspirations go beyond the fleshly mundane. Arabella would be perfectly at home pulling beer for Wilkie Collins's savages. As for the city worker, he was seen as the village lout translated to an urban setting. And George Gissing depicted his rapacious cunning and drunken bestiality in the inhabitants of *The Nether World* (1889) and *Demos* (1886). In Galsworthy's novels lower-class men invariably beat their wives and kick dogs, and as Samuel Hynes observed, they are themselves described as a form of human animal.[30] The dog as a dog was the most admirable of creatures, but when it slouched the streets on two legs in the shape of Galsworthy's workingman, it ceased to be an animal and became the kind of beast that

H. G. Wells was to portray in *The Island of Dr. Moreau* (1896). Only by means of constant vigilance, as the RSPCA warned, could the working class be prevented from flogging horses to the ground and drowning dogs for sport.

At this time popular opinion held that the workers were inherently deficient in all feelings of compassion towards animals because they were so like animals themselves. Therefore it was the duty of all enlightened people to train and discipline them as though they were dogs that had never known a collar or a command. Brian Harrison has given us an account of an RSPCA that was determined to do more than just defend animals: it was going to civilize the lower orders.[31] Year after year the Society declared that workingmen were growing more callous and unfeeling and called for more education of working-class children. Certainly, at first sight it would seem that the RSPCA was correct, for almost every issue of the *Times* contains a small paragraph relating the arrest and sentence imposed on a carter or costermonger who had ill-treated his horse. These items were then reprinted in journals and publications concerned with the welfare of animals. The cumulative effect is to give the impression of workingmen who would torment and abuse any animal that fell into their hands. What is also remarkable is that these arrests were frequently brought to the attention of the police by private citizens, and the penalties and fines were often very severe. For example, at the Thames Police Court on August 16, 1894, Harry Leaman, aged twenty-four, was charged with having flogged his pony. He was found guilty and sentenced to a month's hard labor without the option of a fine.[32]

Admittedly, coercion of this kind was the last resort of those concerned with the welfare of animals. As Brian Harrison has observed, there was a continuing debate within the RSPCA over using force to restrain working-class brutality and about the need for the more conciliatory methods of persuasion and education, particularly among working-class children.[33] Bands of Hope preached a gospel of temperance and kindness to animals, Sunday schools taught the gospel of a gentle Jesus guarding his lambs, and by the end of the century, Catherine Smithies' Bands of Mercy were flourishing throughout the country with their own hymns and cautionary tales: the boy who delighted in pulling wings off flies was on a certain road to hell.[34]

One book was used by all these groups; it was the subject of sermons and was always on the list of books to be given as prizes by the

Education Council of the London County Council. *Black Beauty* presented a model of behavior for working-class children: they were to become "Christ's Police," to use the Band of Hope's term. It was not enough for the young Christian to be kind to animals; he had to keep his eyes open for any act of cruelty on the part of an adult, and then, like little Joe Green, he must actively help to apprehend the malefactor. Here indeed was a means whereby the child, that individual without rights or authority, could assert itself over the adult world. If children had once tormented animals in order to express a fragile sense of power, they were now presented with the means to assert their moral authority over adults. When Joe Green confronts the carter in the brickyard, he first warns the offender and offers to help him, then acts as one of "Christ's police":

> "Hold hard!" said Joe. "Don't go on flogging the horses like that; the wheels are so stuck that they cannot move the cart."
>
> The man took no heed, but went on lashing.
>
> "Stop! pray stop!" said Joe. "I'll help you to lighten the cart; they can't move it now."
>
> "Mind your own business, you impudent young rascal, and I'll mind mine!" The man was in a towering passion and the worse for drink, and laid on the whip again. Joe turned my head, and the next moment we were going at a round gallop toward the house of the master brickmaker. I cannot say if John would have approved of our pace, but Joe and I were both of one mind, and so angry that we could not have gone slower.
>
> The house stood close by the roadside. Joe knocked at the door, and shouted, "Halloo! Is Mr. Clay at home?" The door was opened, and Mr. Clay himself came out.
>
> "Halloo, young man! You seem in a hurry; any orders from the Squire this morning?"
>
> "No, Mr. Clay, but there's a fellow in your brickyard flogging two horses to death. I told him to stop, and he wouldn't; I said I'd help him to lighten the cart, and he wouldn't; so I have come to tell you. Pray, sir, go." Joe's voice shook with excitement.
>
> "Thank ye, my lad," said the man, running in for his hat; then pausing for a moment, "Will you give evidence of what you saw if I should bring the fellow up before a magistrate?"
>
> "That I will," said Joe, "and glad to." The man was gone, and we were on our way home at a smart trot.

"Why, what's the matter with you, Joe? You look angry all over," said John, as the boy flung himself from the saddle.

"I am angry all over, I can tell you," said the boy, and then in hurried, excited words he told all that had happened. Joe was usually such a quiet, gentle little fellow that it was wonderful to see him so roused.

"Right, Joe! you did right, my boy, whether the fellow gets a summons or not. Many folks would have ridden by and said 'twas not their business to interfere. Now I say that with cruelty and oppression it is everybody's business to interfere when they see it; you did right, my boy." (Chap. 20)

"Everybody's business" was the particular charge of the socially responsible child, and the theme was hammered home in tracts and pamphlets and Sunday school lessons. And if we look at the way working-class people in Battersea remembered their childhoods, it would seem that the RSPCA and groups of allied interest were far more successful than they ever chose to admit. There was the occasional young savage who relished the spectacle of suffering, but most found it almost unendurable. Looking back, Mrs. Scholefield remembered Battersea Rise in winter when "it would be a common sight to see men lashing their horses to get them up the hills on icy roads and it would distress me very much to see these horses flinch with pain and their veins standing out. I would breathe a sigh of relief when they finally made it." Her words recall Black Beauty struggling under the whip to reach the crest of Ludgate Hill and then collapsing at the side of the road. She continued: "Another unhappy memory was looking in a pet shop window and seeing all kinds of small wild birds in tiny cages where they could hardly turn round, let alone fly. I would also watch with horror a man with a stick, drive sheep, pigs, etc. into the slaughter house next to North's our Butchers. A few would escape and run down Usk Road screaming all the way for they seemed to know they were going to their death."[35]

A great many Battersea residents remembered with similar disgust how the cattle were driven down Latchmere Road. Mr. Morris, who as a child often gave his pennies to the "Old Anti," remarked drily that "it was a grand sight for some." Harry Kirkham was among the latter; he remembered only the excitement of chasing the fleeing cattle and that if "we helped to catch them we were allowed to watch in the Slaughterhouse."[36] The small boy who told his teacher that he enjoyed a cockfight more than anything else had not disappeared—he could still be found—but he was disapproved of as much by his own mates as he was by a reforming middle class.

If we read accounts of the working class, there is always a general condemnation of the way they ill-treat animals that serves to illustrate the reports of the RSPCA. However, when we find the occasional text by a worker, there is a very different picture given. It would almost seem as though little Joe Green had grown to be a man in the pages of B. L. Coombes, the miner, who was appalled at the way the pit ponies were treated by the owners and by many of his fellow miners.[37] Of course, the most remarkable text by a workingman is *The Ragged Trousered Philanthropists*, in which the painters and decorators are treated like animals by the jobbing contractors, and yet they can still pity those who are weaker and more defenseless than themselves.

The Ragged Trousered Philanthropists was probably written in 1907 at the same time as the Battersea workers were turning out to defend the statue of the brown dog: the author, Robert Tressell was dead by 1911.[38] The details of his life are scanty, like those of most workingmen, and the known facts of his biography would not fill more than a paragraph, but his novel with its long Socialist tracts does give us his dream of a better world. Tressell's laborers are not the grimed brutes of Arthur Morrison's stories of slum life; they are slaves who have come to accept their chains and servitude as a bitter birthright. By their unending toil they sustain the monied classes, for they are the true philanthropists giving their very lives to maintain a society where philanthropy was doled out by the rich in minute portions. Living hand-to-mouth, their tragedy is that they accept their condition as unalterable and fatalistically drink or gamble to ease the realities of pain, monotony, and hunger.

Yet in some there is a spark of hope, and in Frank Owen it is like a consuming fire; he is the socialist, the reformer who tirelessly preaches the gospel of social change to his fellow workers, receiving only apathy or derision in return. He is introduced by means of an incident that immediately denotes his compassion and decency. Owen is wet through and hurrying home when he decides to turn back and tell old Jack Linden, who has been "stood off," that there is a chance of work with Makehaste and Sloggit:

As he hurried along he presently noticed a small dark object on the doorstep of an untenanted house. He stopped to examine it more closely and perceived that it was a small black kitten. The tiny creature came towards him and began walking about his feet, looking into his face and crying piteously. He stooped down and stroked it, shuddering as his hands came in contact with its emaciated body. Its fur was saturated with rain and every joint of its backbone was distinctly perceptible to the touch. As he caressed it, the starving creature mewed pathetically.

Owen decided to take it home to the boy, and as he picked it up and put it inside his coat the little outcast began to purr. (Chap. 4)

It is a scene which accepts the rhetoric and emotional responses of a Band of Mercy tract, but the story is used to preach another lesson than the one customarily taught by Evangelicals. Tressell acknowledges that compassion for animals is a necessary condition of the humane individual, but caring for the defenseless does not lead in his case to Christ, but to the rejection of Christian faith and all those who preached its doctrines to the poor. Tressell's rogues, like Slyme and Misery, are fervent members of the Shining Light Chapel; his workingmen heroes cannot afford religion and its shallow hypocrisies. As Frank Owen tucks the kitten into his jacket, it provides him with the text for a sermon of doubt and disbelief. And we should not forget that when the working class was castigated for its savagery, what was frequently deplored, as in Wilkie Collins's criticism, was its refusal to attend church. As an Essex farmworker's son observed: "One thing as a boy I didn't like and it sticks in my mind today. I came to the conclusion that church-goers were something like the railway carriages were at one time—first, second and third class."[39] Ernest Morris of Battersea was not alone when he resented class distinction more than anything else in the society of his childhood. So if Tressell's sermon is derived from an Evangelical source, it takes a form that was to horrify a middle class which believed religion to be divine confirmation of deference and class:

This incident served to turn his thoughts into another channel. If, as so many people pretended to believe, there was an infinitely loving God, how was it that this helpless creature that He had made was condemned to suffer? It had never done any harm, and was in no sense responsible for the fact that it existed. Was God unaware of the miseries of His creatures? If so, then He was not all-knowing. . . . It was not necessary to call in the evidence of science, or to refer to the supposed inconsistencies, impossibilities, contradictions and absurdities contained in the Bible, in order to prove that there was no truth in the Christian religion. All that was necessary was to look at the conduct of the individuals who were its votaries. (Chap. 4)

Throughout Tressell rages at a church which condones exploitation and approves a congregation segregated by class. In this community it is poor Philpot who is the martyr, the one among all the men who works hardest and complains least. To the best of his limited understanding he tries to follow Owen's lessons, and when his mates are not looking, he feeds the birds:

> After dinner, when the others had all gone back to their work, Philpot unobtrusively returned to the kitchen and gathered up the discarded paper wrappers in which some of the men had brought their food. Spreading one of these open, he shook the crumbs from the others upon it. In this way and by picking up particles of bread from the floor, he collected a little pile of crumbs and crusts. To these he added some fragments that he had left from his own dinner. He then took the parcel upstairs and opening one of the windows threw the crumbs on to the roof of the portico. He had scarcely closed the window when two starlings fluttered down and began to eat. (Chap. 18)

No one cares for Philpot as he cares for the birds: he is killed when he is forced to climb the swaying sixty-five-rung ladder that is held to the roof of a crumbling building by a rotted rope. Tressell's anger is directed at the Grinders and Grabits who sent men into early graves and, in equal measure, at his fellow workers for their apathy and indifference. Owen cannot even persuade his mates to join the union: they accept their fates and go to their deaths like dumb animals.

Owen is first introduced to the reader, as we have seen, with an incident that replicates similar anecdotes in Band of Mercy and Sunday school tracts, but Tressell uses it to subvert the Christian message. In the tracts the stray kitten always belongs to a rich lady who befriends the boy, or else a wealthy stranger notices the act of kindness and rewards the boy handsomely. The bitter irony of *The Ragged Trousered Philanthropists* is that the story is resolved by means of the same device. George Barrington is a wealthy young man who has disguised himself in order to work with the painters and learn about their conditions at first hand. At the end, when Owen is sick and destitute, a letter arrives from Barrington, who is now living the life of a gentleman, and accompanying the customary good wishes is a ten pound note to help Owen and his family over Christmas. Despite all Tressell's argued socialism and his demands for economic reform, there is a yearning for paternalism, for the genial benevolence of employers who worked and ate with their workers—the world evoked by Windham in so many of his speeches.

Few social observers appreciated the conservatism of the working class, and fewer still were prepared to acknowledge that its feeling towards animals had changed radically from the days when there were dog fights and cockpits behind every large inn. The gentry still hunted and shot and went abroad to kill the more exotic animals of the jungle and veldt for sport. Gentlemen could be found relaxing at their ease in trophy rooms that were like charnel houses of stuffed heads, but workingmen had been taught to acquire different tastes and appreciate other values. They had taken to football and cricket and spent more time and money betting on horse races than people thought they should. When the two classes met these days on the occasion of a bloodsport, there was no longer the old fraternity praised by Windham, but anger and a sense of outrage. So the *Tribune* reported a clash between gentry and workers over a wounded stag:

> An exciting scene, in which a dreadfully-mutilated stag, chased by members of the Berks and Bucks Stag Hunt from the vicinity of Hawthorn Hill, took a prominent part occurred at the little village of Windlesham, Surrey, yesterday afternoon.
>
> The terrified beast, bleeding freely from the neck, suddenly made its appearance in the main street, and in a frantic endeavour to evade its pursuers dashed up a side lane bordering a grocer's shop and sank to the ground in an exhausted condition. A party of men who witnessed the scene hurried to its side, and having fastened a rope round its neck, were in the act of leading it to a neighbouring stable, when the animal detected sounds of the approaching hunt and in a terrible struggle to regain freedom strangled itself.
>
> A large number of villagers assembled on the spot, and on the arrival of members of the hunt the demeanour of the crowd be-

came hostile, some very uncomplimentary remarks being expressed concerning the nature of the sport.[40]

It would almost seem from an account like this—and increasingly there were incidents of a similar kind—that the working class was identifying with the wounded animal, not with the hunters and sportsmen. If we ask for evidence of a more civilized and humane society, then surely this will answer, but it was seldom reflected in literature or popular opinion. Societies concerned with animal welfare continued to deplore the cruelties of the working class, while writers like George Gissing and Arthur Morrison depicted it as brutish and dangerous. Even an experienced political reporter like Randal Charlton, who wrote some very perceptive pieces indeed about the suffragettes, described a meeting of Battersea unionists with guarded caution: "You see rows upon rows of cloth caps shadowing stolid faces, faces that look at you with a sort of sleepy strength as they pull lazily at their tobacco pipes. It is a work-roughened audience scornfully content in its grime and corduroys, its greasy mufflers, its cardigan jackets, and clay-caked boots. It is an audience that would certainly be impatient of cant or prattle."[41]

These were the men who fought to defend the brown dog, who escorted Louise Lind-af-Hageby to her meetings and pledged the support of their unions for antivivisection. On two issues workingmen seldom found any reason to argue: they were opposed to animal experimentation and they stood solidly against women's suffrage and women's rights. Yet, at the time of the riots, the two issues were blurred and the cause of women became the cause of animals. We must now see what our Battersea workingmen thought about women and vivisectors, and you may choose to attribute their opinions to ignorant prejudice or enlightened self interest according to your own particular prejudice.

3

Ignorant Prejudices

When Charlotte Despard took a Women's Freedom League caravan into South-east England in 1908 to lecture on the suffrage, she was met with "a hostility and a violence quite terrifying to the uninitiated; yelling, shouting and musical instruments drowned our arguments; rotten eggs, fruit and vegetables ruined our frocks—obscenity unspeakable offended our ears."[1] In the market square of Maidstone, as she stood on a chair to address the crowd, the sixty-three-year old woman was pelted with stones and her chair snatched from under her, smashed, and burned. Bleeding and shaken she was forced to leave the town to jeering abuse and volleys of granite chips.

It required just as much courage for a suffragette to speak to a group of workingmen in the East End of London, where she risked the chance of being catcalled and told to go home and look after her family—if she were lucky enough to have one. Working-class women had even less sympathy for the suffragettes, resenting the leisure of these middle-class ladies who were not burdened down with housework and children. Not one of the working-class women in Battersea who reminisced to the local historical association even bothered to mention the suffrage demonstrations, or showed the slightest interest in women's rights. They remembered the "Old Anti" and the dogs' home, but not the struggle to give women the vote. "I reckon they suffragettes wants half-a-dozen kids like this yer squad of mine. That'd steady 'em," was the attitude of most working-class wives.[2]

Charlotte Despard was accepted in Battersea because she lived and worked in Nine Elms, where the locals regarded her as eccentric but one of their own. She was always given a hearing when she spoke about unemployment, child-care, or vivisection, but when Emmeline Pankhurst lectured with her on the subject of women's suffrage at the Battersea Town Hall, the crowd kept calling for the brown dog. Like Mrs. Fawcett, Emmeline Pankhurst was bewildered by this association of women's suffrage and the fate of a brown terrier dog. John Burns knew the mind of his electorate when he refused to support the suffragettes and their cause until every adult male in England was given the vote. Keir Hardie remained their friend, and some said it was more for personal reasons than anything else; his secretary was one of Mrs. Pankhurst's followers.[3] As for George Lansbury, he was forced to admit in his autobiography that his support for women's suffrage had led him "into a head-on collision with the rest of the Labour Party. All the party were theoretically in favour of votes for women. But the rest did not appear as passionate as I was. . . . It was not a wise political decision."[4]

If the working class in general derided the suffragettes, trades unionists regarded them as a particular and most insidious enemy. From the beginning of the trades union movement, men like George Howell and Henry Broadhurst insisted that woman's place was in the home, not in a trades union, and certainly not at the annual congress. Broadhurst was speaking for his fellow stonemasons when he doubted the wisdom of sending women to these congresses, because "under the influence of emotion they might vote for things they would regret in cooler moments."[5] Wherever women were unionized it was to the benefit of the male unionist, and this applies so generally that it can almost be taken as a law in the history of labor.

The problem union men confronted with women was that they were always prepared to do the same work for less money. In the colonies it was possible to keep out blacks and Chinese by exploiting race prejudice and denouncing the competing work force as lazy, shiftless, and depraved. The White Australia Policy was as much the creation of the trades union movement as it was an expression of national sentiment. However, it was not so easy to exclude working women by the same means; after all, they were often sisters and mothers. So the language of exclusion took two forms: it could be pejorative, which was effective when dealing with those of a different race, or laudatory, as when disposing of women. Women were innately refined and virtuous, it was said, too pure to be defiled by contact with brute men in the factory or the mine.

It was extraordinarily effective, even though it ran counter to every social and economic interest of women. The aspiration was to be a lady, and it was not only Liza Doolittle who cherished that dream. Ramsay MacDonald said: "I have met with cutting reproofs from fore-women and others in the bookbinding houses when I tried, in my innocence, to find out why they did not turn their hands to simple and easy processes which were being done by men. 'Why, that is man's work, and we shouldn't think of doing it!' is the usual answer given with a toss of the head and a tone insinuating that there is a certain indelicacy in the question."[6]

The test of a strong union was always its ability to maintain wages and hours and exclude cheap labor. The miners had accomplished the latter by making it illegal for women to work in the pit; when the printers found it impossible to get rid of women in the same way, they set about unionizing them on terms to suit themselves. It was an issue appreciated from the first by Australian unionists, and in 1889 the Queensland Provincial Council of the Australian Labor Federation resolved: "It shall be one of the chief duties of District Organisers to organise women workers in unions of the Federation, and every member shall assist in this work, without which any attempt to permanently benefit Labor must be futile."[7] In the textile industry in the North of England women were relegated to the lowest-paid jobs, but they were still called upon to pay the largest share of the levy used for the parliamentary salary of David Shackleton, a man who had never given any support to women.[8]

In the past Robert Owen had sought the equality of the sexes, but this idealistic socialism had no influence upon the day-to-day work of the trades unions.[9] There, one rule applied: if women could not be removed from the workplace, they must be organized in such a way that they presented no competition to men. Charles Drysdale expressed this fear when he wrote: "Men were frequently told to go home and to send their wives in their stead. Every man who is engaged as an employee realises bitterly to-day how women are coming in and underselling him, and how difficult it is for him to raise his salary and feel secure of his position."[10] Drysdale argued that a major cause of unemployment amongst men was "the exceedingly rapid incursion of unorganised and unrepresented women into the labour market," and therefore, "even supposing that women did not want the vote, it is just as necessary for men to induce them to do so, as it is for members of a trade-union to get all the men in their industry enrolled in their society."[11]

Generally the English worker would have agreed with the first part and ignored the conclusion. The Battersea Council and several of the unions voted solidly for antivivisection but never for women's suffrage. Even in the visionary society which Robert Tressell sets against the world of his novel, there is no suggestion that women should be given equal opportunity to work. They cook and wash for their children, just as they do in William Morris's *News from Nowhere* (1891). Robert Owen's radical feminism was forgotten by trades unionists: what they kept in mind was Engels' warning that in a capitalist society men's labor would eventually be replaced by the cheaper work of women, and they in turn could expect to be displaced by children.

Single women and widows were expected to work, and generally they found themselves earning less than a living wage from employers like Tressell's Mr. Adam Sweater, who "employed a great number of girls and young women who were supposed to be learning dress-making, mantel-making or millinery. These were all indentured apprentices, some of whom had paid premiums of from five to ten pounds. They were 'bound' for three years. For the first two years they received no wages: the third year they got a shilling or eightpence a week. At the end of the third year they usually got the sack, unless they were willing to stay on as improvers at from three shillings to four and sixpence per week" (chap. 20). The aspiration of girls like these was not to acquire a better job, but to marry like Gaskell's Mary Barton, or Gissing's Monica Madden in *The Odd Women* (1893).

The home was a married woman's sphere, and what Tressell and workingmen admired most was a good manager.[12] It is Ruth Easton's tragedy in *The Ragged Trousered Philanthropists* that she can never make ends meet, and her housekeeping skills are so limited that she tries to feed a nursing baby with mashed potato and bacon. When Battersea folk looked back to their childhood, many of them recalled with considerable pride a mother who knew how to put a good meal on the table in the hardest times:

My brother used to have to go to Harrods early in the morning before school and buy 3d giblets and a bag full of turkey necks. Rich people didn't want them and sometimes he would get a 3d big bag full of fish. It was all good food but sometimes the kippers would be broken so the rich people wouldn't like them but my Mum used to feed us on the fat of the land. For 3d we could get pieces of cheese: the ends and the broken bits and all colours, and my Mum used to put it in a saucepan and melt it and it was lovely.[13]

Nothing irritated working-class women more than to hear a well-dressed lady, obviously with time on her hands, lecturing them on the need to campaign for the vote. When you were balancing pennies against sixpence to buy the Sunday dinner, the "New Woman" and her problems of boredom and lack of political power seemed as trivial as they were offensive. Vera Brittain wrote of the stresses of Edwardian society and the need for the Lady to become a Woman, but she did not have much idea of a Battersea housewife's dreams and goals.[14] The problems of Ann Veronica, stifled by convention in H. G. Wells' novel (1909), would have seemed hysterical to those Battersea women who cherished middle-class aspirations for themselves and their children.

When the suffragettes took to the streets in rioting mobs, breaking shop windows and shouting abuse, they were appropriating a traditional working-class mode of protest, and their actions were savagely resented by trades unionists. You broke windows and rioted as a last resort over issues of wages and hours, not for the feminine whim of idle women. With men like Harry Champion and Ben Tillett in charge, the spontaneous riot of the market or workplace had become a calculated expression of violence. Kenneth Brown notes the effectiveness of this kind of action in a society where the fear of poverty erupting into revolution was never far from middle-class minds: "In 1886 the Lord Mayor's Mansion House Fund, established to relieve the unemployed, shot up from £19,000 to £72,000 in the two days immediately following demonstrations in the heart of London's clubland. The rioters, most of them unemployed workers from the East End, were led by members of the Social Democratic Federation who had been drilling them for some time under the direction of H. H. Champion, a former soldier."[15]

Battersea had its own history of successful strikes: John Burns had been one of the leaders in the Fight for the Dockers' Tanner in 1889; Mark Hutchins led the gasworkers to victory in the same year. The issues then were those of a living wage for hungry families and the right to combine in a union: to set the cause of votes for women alongside these concerns was absurd. In consequence, when Labour politicians considered the questions of unemployment and women's suffrage, they worked to alleviate the former and paid lip service to the latter.

What roused Battersea in 1907 was not the plight of women but a fear that had its origins at Tyburn in the eighteenth century. Public hangings were undoubtedly the most popular of all bloodsports, and the "jingling antithesis between life and death," to use Thackeray's phrase, always roused the spectators to a frenzy. Brawls often broke out at the foot of the gallows between the friends of the dead and the servants of the Royal College of Physicians or Company of Barber-Surgeons, who had the right to claim ten corpses a year for dissection. Private surgeons too were ready to pay high prices for a fresh corpse, and in 1736 the grave-digger of St. Dunstan's, Stepney, felt the full fury of the law and the populace when he was convicted for having sold bodies to a private surgeon:

> Sentence was executed upon him very severely by John Hooper, the then common Executioner; and on the Day appointed for him to be whipped; there was, perhaps, the greatest Concourse of People that was ever known. A Mob of Sailors and Chimney Sweepers rendevouz'd in Stepney Church-yard, and when [the] poor Culprit was ty'd to the Cart, they led the Horses so slow, that he received some Hundreds of Lashes, the Hangman being encouraged by the Mob (who gave him a good deal of Money) not to favour the Delinquent, but to do his Duty.[16]

It was not only the corpses of convicted felons which provided subjects for anatomical research; the poor lived in constant fear that their dead would be taken and dissected on the surgeon's table. There were stories told of dead men suddenly reviving under the knife and meeting a death more painful than any received from the hangman's noose. Certainly, it is doubtful if the English working class went in dread of the pains of hell; what did concern many of them was the likelihood of some surgeon's hack stealing their bodies before they were cold and then cutting them up like carcasses of meat.

The progress from cruelty to animals to the dissection table in Surgeons' Hall had been horrifyingly depicted by William Hogarth in his *Four Stages of Cruelty* (1751). The prints were "intentionally explicit . . . to grip the attention of the ignorant and brutal."[17] Here the most dreaded working-class fears were cast into the form of a cautionary tract—four pictures that expressed the terrors of vivisection in a sequence from Tom Nero's skewering of a dog, to his flogging of a horse, the murder of his mistress, and his eventual death by hanging, with his body given over to the dissectors. In Hogarth's plates the persecutor of animals was the murderer of women—and this became more than a narrative concept: it was to be an article of faith in popular opinion. It was Hogarth's genius to borrow his images from life, cast them into the form of narrative art and then impose them upon the world as reality.[18]

James Mill stated that "nothing is remembered but through its IDEA. The memory, however, of a thing, and the idea of it, are not the same. The idea may be without the memory; but the memory cannot be without the idea."[19] And for the nineteenth century it was Hogarth's idea that framed arguments and shaped the form of working-class belief even when his pictures were not held in the mind's eye. In the first plate Tom Nero is driving a stake into a dog; he is surrounded by emblems of cruelty as boys blind a sparrow, set cats fighting from a lamp post, or tie a bone to the tail of a dog. In the next plate Tom has graduated to hackney coachman, and he flogs a horse that has collapsed with fatigue while another man beats a lamb with a club. The third plate shows Tom arrested for having murdered his pregnant mistress; and in the fourth and final plate, the reward of cruelty, his corpse is laid out before the surgeons who scoop out the eyes, drag forth the entrails, and cut the tendons of the foot. All around the spectators gossip and gloat, and as the intestines and heart are cast to the floor, a famished dog seizes on Tom Nero's cruel heart and devours it. In drawing these pictures for "the lower orders of society," Hogarth had done more than provide a tract: he had taken the fears of Tyburn and the surgeons and made them a direct consequence of the wanton cruelty of children torturing animals for sport. The horror in Hogarth's last plate is concentrated in the face of the corpse, for Tom Nero does not seem dead; it is as if he is silently screaming for help and for mercy. The idea of cruelty to animals leading to a murdered wife or mistress and ending under the surgeon's knife was to remain a recurring figure and traditional belief, for as Mill also stated, "Belief is a matter of habit and accident, and not of reason."[20]

The last two etchings of *The Four Stages of Cruelty* were sold for sixpence in the form of John Bell's woodcuts, but all of Hogarth's prints were widely disseminated. Just as the temperance societies used *Gin Lane* in their publicity, the antivivisection societies made Tom Nero familiar in their publications and flyers. However, it was the popularity

of Hogarth among the working class which made the progress from
cruelty to animals to murder and dissection seem part of the natural
order. Charles Mitchell has written of the way that "the prints were
cast adrift on an open sea and might fetch up anywhere. They were
pasted up in inns and taverns . . . country yokels pored over stray
'*pickters* come from Lunnon;' and any sort of person might stop to
join the crowds round the print-shop windows."[21] The colored print
shaped the mind and imagination of the working class at this time just
as television does today, and the recurring theme in many of these
prints was body snatching and the disposition of the poor dead.

If the rich and genteel seemed more concerned with the fate of
their souls in the next world, it was because their earthly remains were
laid to rest in stout coffins in closed crypts or deep graves. A poor man
like Silas Wegg in Dickens' *Our Mutual Friend* (1865) often came to feel
that his body was being disposed of, bought and sold, while he was
still alive. Wegg lost his leg as the result of a hospital amputation and
suspects that Mr. Venus, the "articulator," has the bone among a mis-
cellaneous collection from which he constructs skeletons. Plaintively
Wegg appeals to his friend's social conscience: "'I have a prospect of
getting on in life and elevating myself by my own independent exer-
tions,' says Wegg, feelingly, 'and I shouldn't like—I tell you openly I
should *not* like—under such circumstances, to be what I may call dis-
persed, a part of me here, and a part of me there, but should wish to
collect myself like a genteel person'" (chap. 7). No other writer at this
time had such insight into the almost mythic fears of his readers, and
it is not simply Jerry Cruncher sucking the rust from his fingers in *A
Tale of Two Cities* (1859) who speaks to the dread of the body snatcher,
but also Squeers' venomous intentions towards Peg Sliderskew in
Nicholas Nickleby (1839): "'Why, I suppose they can't do much to me
if I explain how it was that I got into the good company of that there
ca-daverous old Slider,' replied Squeers viciously, 'who I wish was dead
and buried, and resurrected and dissected, and hung upon wires
in a anatomical museum, before ever I'd anything to do with her'"
(chap. 60).

Working-class people paid into burial clubs and funeral funds to
ensure that death should be as sumptuous as life had been mean and
constricted. There was considerable comfort to be derived from a funeral with nodding sable plumes and velvet-shrouded hearse, the
mourners decked out in brand-new clothes for the occasion. Edwin
Chadwick recognized the impulses that led to the opulent displays of

a working-class funeral and deplored them as ridiculous and sinful, while the *Quarterly Review* lamented that if only "the poor were wise, their funerals would be as simple as possible; a plain coffin, borne by near male relations, and followed by the family and friends of the deceased in decent mourning, but without any of the undertaker's trappings on their persons, would be sufficient. The poor like funeral pomp because the rich like it; forgetting that during life the condition of the dead was entirely different, and that there ought to be a consistency in every thing belonging to the different ranks of society."[22] Here indeed was one reason why burial clubs flourished and people went into debt to keep up the payments. A solemn funeral attended by a throng of mourners was one of the most vehement expressions of social equality: if you could not live like the rich, then at least you could die like them. To be buried handsomely as a "genteel person" was a small compensation for the injustices of life. If some insisted that class distinctions should be maintained in death as in life, the sumptuary rites of the poor repudiated this belief.

The horror working-class people felt for the workhouse was equalled only by their resolve to avoid a pauper's funeral with its cardboard coffin bulging with the body of the corpse. The disgrace of poverty was made all too evident when paupers were buried like dogs, a phrase not uncommon with workhouse guardians. The poor were always being rebuked by middle-class critics for their lavish funerals. Arthur Morrison gives a typical impression in "On the Stairs" (1895):

"When I lost my pore 'usband," said the gaunt woman, with a certain brightening. "I give 'im a 'ansome funeral. 'E was a Oddfellow, an' I got twelve pound. I 'ad a oak caufin an' a open 'earse. There was a kerridge for the fam'ly an' one for 'is mates—two 'orses each, an' feathers, an' mutes; an' it went the furthest way round to the cimitry." 'Wotever 'appens, Mrs. Manders,' says the undertaker, 'you'll feel as you've treated 'im proper; no-body can't reproach you over that.' An' they couldn't. "E was a good 'usband to me, an' I buried 'im respectable."[23]

Undertakers competed for every corpse: for ten pounds H. J. Larner's of Battersea would provide a glass-sided carriage with velvets on the horses, drapes all round, and two coaches for the mourners to make the fourteen-mile round trip from Battersea to the burial ground at Morden. Competition was always keen, and undertakers hovered like vultures around the doors of the dying. Robert Tressell described them as ghouls, prepared to snatch a body from one coffin and put it in another of their own. This is, of course, poor Philpot's fate in *The Ragged Trousered Philanthropists*; his old landlady complains about the undertakers who have clamored for the job of burying him:

> "I shall be very glad when it's all over," she said, as she led the way up the narrow stairs, closely followed by Hunter, who carried the tressels, Crass and Sawkins, bringing up the rear with the coffin. "I shall be very glad when it's all over, for I'm sick and tired of answerin' the door to undertakers. If there's been one 'ere since Friday there's been a dozen, all after the job, not to mention all the cards what's been put under the door, besides the one's what I've had give to me by different people. I had a pair of boots bein' mended and the man took the trouble to bring 'em 'ome when they was finished—a thing 'e's never done before—just for an excuse to give me an undertaker's card." (Chap. 47)

It seemed that no amount of criticism or advice could persuade the poor to exercise economy or common sense when it came to funerals, because nothing could assuage the fear of a pauper's funeral and the dreadful prospect of the corpse being sold to a surgeon for dissection. The realities of body snatching were grim enough to make the surgeon a man to be feared. Henry Lonsdale recorded a series of incidents that took place in the 1830s when "a man was hanged in Carlisle; and the friends of the culprit determined to revenge themselves on the doctors who engaged in the post-mortem examination. All the medical men sustained personal injuries, and of a severe kind. Mr Anderson . . . was shot in the face. . . . Another surgeon was found dead by the side of a lofty bridge, over the parapet of which, it was believed, he had been thrown."[24] The surgeon (and he was felt to be quite different from the physician) was loathed by the working class. John Nichols and John Ireland in the biography of Hogarth observed with approval that "our legislators, considering how unfit such men are to determine in cases of life and death, have judiciously excluded both surgeons and butchers from serving upon juries," the reason for this legal restriction being that "a frequent contemplation of sanguinary scenes, hardens the heart, deadens sensibility, and destroys every tender sensation."[25]

A corpse was watched until it was laid in the ground, for it was not only competing undertakers who snatched bodies from coffins. Men like Jerry Cruncher, who ill-treated his wife when not stealing corpses, were thought to be lurking around every cemetery. One of the entrances to Battersea Park is an Elizabethan-style cottage which was designed by Charles Newnham, a self-made man who struggled up from poverty to become a successful carpenter and builder. When he retired he wrote his autobiography that others might emulate his rise to prosperity. He told of a plasterer's laborer who fell from a great height onto the spikes of some iron railings:

> When his mates carried him to the nearest doctor, he pronounced him as quite dead. He was a single man, and they carried him to his lodgings. An hour or two afterwards, two men went. Claiming to be the relations, they were allowed to take him away.
>
> By and by, the real relations came. Finding the body had been surreptitiously moved, they proceeded to the Bow Street Police Office. Obtaining the assistance of a 'runner', they went in pursuit of the 'body-snatchers' as they were called. They escaped but the body was found at the dissecting room of the celebrated Dr Brooks, near Blenheim Steps, Oxford Street. The body was reconveyed to the place where it was stolen from to await the coroner's verdict, the relatives locking the door, and taking away the key to make sure of the body being safe.[26]

Those who died in the workhouse or the hospital and had neither friends nor family to claim the body were regularly handed over to the surgeons, and the quartering of a traitor's corpse after it had been drawn and hanged now seemed remarkably similar to what was being done to the cadavers of the poor. However, to this fear was now added another, that it was not simply the bodies of the poor dead which were being claimed by doctors. The tales of the "resurrection men" lived on in melodrama and popular folklore. Robert Louis Stevenson's short story "The Body-Snatcher" was published at the time of the Brown Dog Riots and promptly dramatized. The counsel of the surgeon Macfarlane to his shuddering associate when the corpse of their friend is laid out on the slab was hardly comforting to the less successful members of society: "Why, man, do you know what this life is? There are two squads of us—the lions and the lambs. If you're a lamb, you'll come to lie upon these tables like Gray or Jane Galbraith; if you're a lion, you'll live and drive a horse like me."[27]

The working class firmly believed that surgeons were vivisecting dogs, cats, and rabbits because they could not vivisect human beings. When the latter were available, they would be used. In response to this conviction a number of hospitals in working-class areas became declared antivivisection institutions: the Battersea General—the "Old Anti," as it was affectionately known to the residents—was the last of its kind in England, the place where Battersea children went on Fridays to have teeth pulled for a shilling or have their tonsils removed. The fêtes and raffles in support of this hospital were remembered by many Battersea folk: "Once yearly the parade came through the main streets, floats, horse and carts, walkers and bands. What a treat it was for us children. Once my sister was dressed up and sat in a cart. What a honour for our family! The collecting boxes went round for our 'mouldy coppers.'"[28]

Robert Tressell shared the resentment of his workmates when they were called on to put twopence in a hospital collecting box as they were paid their wages:

> Of course, it was not compulsory to do so, but they all did, because they felt that any man who omitted to contribute might be 'marked'. They did not all agree with contributing to the Hospital, for several reasons. They knew that the doctors at the Hospital made a practice of using the free patients to make experiments upon, and they also knew that the so-called 'free' patients who contribute so very largely directly to the maintenance of such institutions, get scant consideration when they apply for 'free' treatment, and are plainly given to understand that they are receiving 'charity'. (Chap. 22)

The fear of being vivisected or made the subject of experiment was not simply superstition and folklore. Many doctors did indeed regard their right to research as being more important than the care of patients. In 1883, William Murrell and Sidney Ringer administered large doses of sodium nitrate to hospital outpatients at the Westminster Hospital before they had conducted any experiments on animals. The eighteen outpatients became ill, suffering frightful pain, and subsequent tests upon animals proved quite conclusively that sodium nitrate was poisonous. The whole affair was publicized in the press, but Ringer and Murrell were exonerated by the Censor's Board of the

Royal College of Physicians. There was considerable criticism of the doctors and Royal College of Physicians in the popular press; then Dr. A. De Watteville published his support of Ringer and Murrell in a letter to the *Standard* in which he referred to the working class as *corpora vilia*, insisting that the few must suffer for the benefit of future generations. No one was left in any doubt that "the few" were to be charity patients: "So far from there being a reason why moral and pecuniary support should be refused to hospitals on the ground that the inmates are made use of otherwise than for treatment, there is ground why more and more should be given to them, in order to compensate by every possible comfort for the discomforts necessarily entailed by the education of succeeding generations of medical men, and the improvements in our methods of coping with disease."[29]

Naturally, a letter like this was seized upon by the antivivisectionists. Edward Berdoe used it in *Dying Scientifically: A Key to St. Bernard's*, which was published as a sequel to his immensely popular *St. Bernard's: The Romance of a Medical Student* (1888), a novel that described the surgical practices of a contemporary hospital. In *Dying Scientifically*, Berdoe cited several instances where the healing of patients in charity wards was deliberately retarded for the purpose of clinical study. Quite simply his conclusion was that "in our great general hospitals to which medical schools are attached the healing of patients is made subordinate to the professional advantage of the medical staff and the students."[30] The patients concerned were always the working and lower-middle classes, for it was still the privilege of those with means to be nursed at home.

The effect upon the working class was that doctors were now regarded with the deepest suspicion, and hospitals came to have as unsavory a reputation as the workhouse. If medical advice was needed, it was first sought at the local chemist shop, and patent medicines were always preferred to a doctor's prescription. It was not only Robert Louis Stevenson who felt that the soul of a ravening, amoral monster could be found in the breast of a kindly man of medicine like Dr. Jekyll.

When Edward Ford took himself over to Battersea to inspect the statue of the brown dog, he asked a young lad to show him where it could be found:

"Our dorg, sir; I should think I know. I helped to fight the stoodents, and if they're comin' again we'll give 'em wot for". "But why are you so interested in that dog?" I asked, as we turned down a side street. "Oh, I should think I am. I wouldn't 'ave my Bill cut open alive an' kept in a cage for two months and 'anded over from one cutter to another, no, not if I knows it; and as for them stuck-up chaps who yell and shriek 'cause they wants more hanimals to cut up, dad said last night he'd sooner die in peace than have them doctorin' 'im". "But, my dear boy, when your father is ill I am sure he is glad enough to be helped by doctors?" "Not by them doctors, though. We don't trust them 'ere in Battersea. We've got an 'orspital of our own, where the doctors don't believe in cutting hanimals up alive, it's called the Anti-Vivisection 'Orspital, and we always goes there when we're ill, mother and dad and Nellie and me".[31]

Allowing for the partiality of a journalist who was a convinced anti-vivisectionist, the passage does evoke the attitudes of the Battersea people. They objected to animals being tortured in the name of research, for it was not difficult to see those animals as images of themselves, the *corpora vilia* of De Watteville's statement. Country folk who tried to protect a hunted stag instead of joining in the chase were not engaged in a class war with the gentry; they were genuinely moved by the plight of the animal. The unremitting work of humane societies had been effective to such an extent that working-class people often tended to think of themselves as animals.

This compassion could even be found among the workers in a slaughterhouse, who saw no harm in killing animals but objected violently to those same animals being tormented. Joseph Lister had never shown any regard for the pain of his animal subjects, and he recorded angrily an incident which took place when he conducted an experiment in 1861 upon sheep at the Glasgow slaughterhouse. Lister was observing the effect of chloroform on the larynx of a sheep, and wrote in his diary: "I had just got so far with my observations when the inspector of the slaughter house walked up and told me he would not allow such brutality . . . and forthwith ordered me off the premises. Thus I had a taste of what has since been alas! experienced so largely by our profession, viz. how ignorant prejudice with good intentions may obstruct legitimate scientific inquiry."[32]

Workingmen jeered at the suffragettes in order to protect their own livelihood and restricted sphere of social influence, and when they turned out in Battersea to defend the brown dog, they were protecting themselves against the vivisector's knife. Like Thackeray, they too had learned to abhor the savage pursuits of the past. Football and horse-racing had become substitutes for bullbaiting and cockfights, and even that time-honored pursuit of drowning stray dogs was now frowned upon.

Dogs had been traditionally whipped in Yorkshire on St. Luke's Day, and one of the most popular village sports was to catch a stray dog and slowly drown it.[33] John Brown recorded a typical instance in the first half of the nineteenth century, when his brother rescued a sagacious small terrier: "My brother William found him the centre of attraction to a multitude of small black-guards who were drowning him slowly in Lochend Loch, doing their best to lengthen out the process, and se-cure the greatest amount of fun with the nearest approach to death."[34] Later, when this sport was being prosecuted as a crime, there was al-ways the excuse that a panting dog in summer was rabid and should be stoned or drowned.[35] The Band of Mercy tracts paid particular at-tention to this minor atrocity and told the cautionary tale of the boy who drowned a dog and was later drowned himself, slowly and hor-ribly, in a stormy sea. By the end of the century, a passion for dogs was not confined to the middle class, and an extraordinary number of popular ballads declared that canine love was purer and less selfish than the human variety.

Yet at the Royal Commission on Vivisection in 1907 Dr. Edward Schafer of University College, London, justified research in which he had drowned over fifty dogs: "He claimed that as the result of thirty-six experiments, two without and thirty-four with anaesthetics, he had discovered a more fruitful method of resuscitating the drowned."[36] The popular press exploded with indignation, and Edward Schafer was compared unfavorably with Bill Sikes, while a journal like the *Tribune* seriously questioned the results of his research.[37] To a workingman it must have seemed that the sport he had once enjoyed as a boy and had subsequently learned to deplore was now the pursuit of a cele-brated doctor. It was not simply that the working class had changed in its attitude to animals, but that it was increasingly identifying with these oppressed and ill-treated creatures. If Schafer was drowning dogs, then it seemed quite possible that he would want to drown people in order to refine his research, and if he insisted in calling his experiments scientific, there were many who saw them as mischievous and cruel. Joseph Lister saw the interference with his research motivated by "ignorant prejudice," but when animals were tormented, the shadowy presence of William Hogarth was felt, and his icons of cruelty gave substance to people's feelings. In teaching people to pity animals it became possible for those animals to embody the subjection and suffering of women and workers.

4

Black Beauty and Other Horses

If middle-class feminist women and trades unionists were drawn together in Battersea by the accident of a particular circumstance, there
were deeper bonds between them than either consciously imagined.
These affinities can be found first in Hogarth's second stage of cruelty,
where Tom Nero, the hackney coachman, is flogging an emaciated
horse which has collapsed on its knees in the shafts. Generally, in the
nineteenth century, if people were asked for the most obvious instance
of cruelty to animals, then this spectacle of a beaten and exhausted
horse would have answered. Many of the old residents of Battersea remembered the horses straining up the icy Rise in winter, and one old
lady of eighty wrote: "I can still see the very bedraggled horse that was
kept at the bottom of Broomwood Road. It was there to be hired by
anyone who wanted extra strength to get their load to the top of the
hill."[1] Too often a driver chose to save the money and whip his horse
up this hill or any other.

The idea of working-class cruelty to animals was personified by
Tom Nero of St. Giles' Charity School and confirmed whenever a cabman was seen belaboring his horse. Like Miss Evans of Battersea, William Howitt lived on high ground, Highgate West Hill in Kentish Town,
and he too wrote of the suffering horses being lashed to the top of the
hill.[2] It was a scene that could have been witnessed any day in most
English towns, but by the middle of the century there were concerned
observers like Howitt everywhere, and some were not content merely
to express feelings of dismay and compassion for the horses; they
were quite prepared to bring charges against the drivers. Children

63

were encouraged by the Band of Mercy to be on the lookout for drunken cabmen and to report them, like young Joe Green in *Black Beauty*. And, as we have already seen, the fines and the terms of imprisonment meted out to offenders were very harsh indeed.

The work which served to crystallize the way people saw themselves and horses was *Black Beauty* (1877), written by Anna Sewell as the declared autobiography of a horse. In its first year of publication in England it sold over 12,000 copies, and by 1894 Jarrolds, the publisher, estimated the sales to be more than 192,000 annually. But it was in America, which did not acknowledge English copyrights, that the book achieved its most spectacular success. George Angell was the founder of the Massachusetts Society for the Prevention of Cruelty to Animals, the American Humane Society, the Band of Mercy, and the SPCA magazine *Our Dumb Animals*. As a young man he had worked for the abolition of slavery, and he now looked for a book that would help horses in the way that *Uncle Tom's Cabin* had slaves. Within twelve days of receiving a copy of *Black Beauty* in 1890, he was soliciting funds for an American edition, and by the end of the year he had sold 216,000 copies. The sales continued at the rate of a quarter of a million copies a year.[3]

Black Beauty was not simply a juvenile classic of the order of Charles Kingsley's *Water Babies* (1863). The work became an approved school reader, and was energetically promoted by the RSPCA, the Band of Mercy, the Women's Christian Temperance Union, and a great many humane and antivivisection societies. It had the same fervor and passionate conviction as Bunyan's *Pilgrim's Progress*, which was written not to entertain but to change the hearts and minds of all who read it. From the start it found its audience among children and adolescents, who wept and anguished over the story of a black horse. *Black Beauty* is a strange work which most of us can recall but never quite remember. Generally, what comes to mind is the almost unendurable grief when we first read it. Yet, when we take it up again years later, we can recognize the driving homiletic force but not why it should once have stirred us to such tears and anger. Nonetheless, it remains in the mind like a buried landscape, and if we think about it at all, it is to wonder why we should once have wept so bitterly over the fate of a horse.

Anna Sewell was a most unlikely author for a popular classic: she was fifty-seven and dying when she dictated the chapters of *Black Beauty* to her mother, Mary Sewell. In a sense, the story was her last will and testament, composed when she was preparing with daily prayer and self-examination to meet her God. Perhaps it was the occasion of its creation which gave the work such urgent authority and allowed so many imperious voices to cry out from the text, voices which grieved for more than the plight of horses. Within the formal structure of a simple narrative, Anna Sewell raged against cruelty and injustice, against the nature of work, and the condition of women.

As a Quaker, Anna had been educated by those humane traditions which abhorred violence against people and animals, and her mother, Mary Sewell, preached this message in some of the most popular children's ballads of the day. Jarrolds had published *Mother's Last Words*, Mary Sewell's famous cautionary poem in 1860, and its success was astonishing. In stirring rhymed verse Mary told the story of a dying mother who implores her two young sons to follow her precepts of honesty and truth. The two lads are mindful of her message as they struggle to survive as crossing sweepers, with more than one reference to Jo in Dickens' *Bleak House* (1853). There is the chance of easy money if they turn to theft, but they refuse and continue to sweep and starve. Chris falls ill and John steals a pair of boots to warm his frozen feet; then, as he is about to give them to his brother, his mother's last words ring in his head and he promptly returns them. Chris dies of cold in the night, and the story ends with John seeing his little brother's spirit swept high above the soot and smoke of London and into the waiting arms of his smiling mother. John is rewarded for his honesty and grows up to become a prosperous tradesman.

In all of Mary Sewell's tales, and in the religious tracts issued by Jarrolds and the Band of Mercy, the links are drawn between kindness to animals, salvation, and economic success. One of the first precepts Mary Sewell insists upon in *The Children of Summerbrook* (1859) is kindness to all living creatures, even a butterfly: "I never thought that it would feel, / Or suffer any pain; / But if you really think it will, / I won't do so again."[4] The message is always starkly authoritarian, declaring that it is better to starve than to steal, and to die rather than challenge the established order of society. Tracts and tales like these roused Robert Tressell to fury because he appreciated their hold upon the imagination of his fellow workers—not for them a socialist manifesto when they could read parables of acceptance and patient fortitude. But even as he denounced the purveyors of "pie in the sky," the resolution of his own novel took on the configurations of the moral tracts he despised.

Tressell's work, like the tracts, is haunted by the vision of a regulated, paternalistic society—the England of William Windham, but without bloodsports.

Jean Ingelow's *Mopsa the Fairy* (1869) and George MacDonald's *At the Back of the North Wind* (1871) were the fictional sources for Anna Sewell's loquacious horses, discussing their own and the world's affairs. As an inspiration for them all was Swift's *Gulliver's Travels* (1726) and his sagacious Houyhnhnms, but whereas Gulliver soon acknowledged the horse as his master, MacDonald and Sewell saw it as the perfect servant. In MacDonald's novel Diamond is the name both of the little boy and the cab horse, and one evening the child overhears his namesake reproaching his stablemate, Ruby:

"Look how fat you are, Ruby!" said old Diamond. "You are so plump and your skin shines so, you ought to be ashamed of yourself."

"There's no harm in being fat," said Ruby in a deprecating tone. "No, nor in being sleek. I may as well shine as not."

"No harm?" retorted Diamond. "Is it no harm to go eating up all poor master's oats, and taking up so much of his time grooming you, when you only work six hours—no, not six hours a day, and, as I hear, get along no faster than a big dray-horse with two tons behind him? So they tell me."

"Your master's not mine," said Ruby. "I must attend to my own master's interests, and eat all that is given me, and be as sleek and fat as I can, and go no faster than I need."

"Now really if the rest of the horses weren't all asleep, poor things—*they* work till they're tired—I do believe they would get up and kick you out of the stable. You make me ashamed of being a horse. You dare to say my master ain't your master! That's your gratitude for the way he feeds you and spares you! Pray where would your carcase be if it weren't for him?"

"He doesn't do it for my sake. If I were his own horse, he would work me as hard as he does you."

"And I'm proud to be so worked. I wouldn't be as fat as you— not for all you're worth. You're a disgrace to the stable. Look at the horse next to you. *He's* something like a horse—all skin and bone. And his master ain't over kind to him either. He put a stinging lash on his whip last week. But that old horse know's he's got the wife and children to keep—as well as his drunken master—and he works *like* a horse." (Chap. 32)

Here is the gospel of work and the acceptance of class expressed through the symbol of the horse and the listening child, who shares both spirit and name with the old cab horse. They are diamonds, the most precious of jewels, because both are obedient and cheerful and good. The horse, patient and forbearing, is to become the model for workingmen, and when Diamond the boy takes his cab through the streets of London, he is like a small angel rebuking the cruel and drunken drivers by his mere presence. One of Diamond's missions on earth is to guide his fellow cabmen into the ways of temperance, and after he has comforted the wailing baby of the drunken cabman, the latter recognizes the boy as "one of God's messengers," and says to his wife with unconscious prophecy: "I do somehow believe that wur a angel just gone. Did you see him, wife? He warn't wery big, and he hadn't none o' them wingses, you know. It wur one o' them baby-angels you sees on the grave-stones, you know" (chap. 18).

The reward of such manifest goodness as Diamond's is not prosperity in this life, but heaven in the next. The North Wind, Diamond's friend and guide, is more than a darkly powerful and mysterious force of nature: she is death, and in the clouds of her hair there is both destruction and rest. Her ways are inscrutable, and Diamond must learn not to question her when ships are sunk and trees blown about like matches. The lesson of *At the Back of the North Wind* is obedience, as the narrator assures the reader on more than one occasion:

Diamond learned to drive all the sooner that he had been accustomed to do what he was told, and could obey the smallest hint in a moment. Nothing helps one to get on like that. Some people don't know how to do what they are told; they have not been used to it, and they neither understand quickly nor are able to turn what they do understand into action quickly. With an obedient mind one learns the rights of things fast enough; for it is the law of the universe, and to obey is to understand. (Chap. 16)

Just as Tressell could not resolve his novel without the assistance of the kindly Barrington, who plays Father Christmas to Owen and his family, the fortunes of Diamond and his friends are decided by Mr.

Raymond. But there are ambiguities of tone and language throughout the work: the North Wind is as terrifying as she is kind, and Mr.
Raymond's house, where Diamond becomes a pageboy, is called the
Mound, and the day comes when Diamond is found dead inside it. The
underlying thesis throughout so many stories written for children at
this time is a fatalistic pessimism that is in constant contention with the
bland assurances of the narrative voice. If the wages of virtue are
death, then what punishment should be accorded sin? Whenever metaphysical questions intrude so uncomfortably, the confident structures
of the homily begin to waver and blur, permitting ambivalent readings
and contrary images. Nonetheless, a solution was to be found in Mac-
Donald's work, for if the story was told about and by animals, then the
questions of reward and punishment could be defined in terms of sufficient oats, a dry bed, and a comfortable harness—surely all that anyone could possibly ask for when writing about the working class.

The language of horses and the dialogue of the stable became an
accepted mode for relating the concerns of workers and may be found
in any number of Band of Mercy and Band of Hope tracts. Tressell copies one of these little equine parables of conformity and obedience
when Crass produces a clipping from the *Obscurer*, handing it to
Harlow who then reads it aloud:

PROVE YOUR PRINCIPLES; OR LOOK AT BOTH SIDES

"I wish I could open your eyes to the true misery of our condition: injustice, tyranny and oppression!" said a discontented hack
to a weary-looking cob as they stood side by side in unhired cabs.

"I'd rather have them opened to something pleasant, thank
you," replied the cob.

"I'm sorry for you. If you could enter into the noble aspirations—" the hack began.

"Talk plain. What would you have?" said the cob, interrupt-
ing him.

"What would I have? Why, equality, and share and share alike
all over the world," said the hack.

"You *mean* that?" said the cob.

"Of course I do. What right have those sleek, pampered hunters and racers to their warm stables and high feed, their grooms
and jockeys? It is really heart-sickening to think of it," replied the
hack.

"I don't know but you may be right," said the cob, "and to
show I'm in earnest, as no doubt you are, let me have half the
good beans you have in your bag, and you shall have half the
musty oats and chaff I have in mine. There's nothing like proving
one's principles."

Original Parables. By Mrs. Prosser.

"There you are!" cried several voices. (Chap. 25)

Owen argues passionately for a better understanding of socialism
than this, but his mates are convinced by Mrs. Prosser's horse sense—
a term that was to stand for everything practical and businesslike. As
William Windham once assured the House, "There is no grievance existing in this country which we cannot correct, without calling in the
advice of a theorist."[5] Nothing less theoretical than a horse's imagination could be imagined, and equine reasoning was consequently preferred to the higher flights of human understanding. Moreover, when a
working man was seen as a horse, all the metaphysics of self could be
safely comprehended within the confines of the stable.

These horsey dialogues became an approved means of inculcating
docility in workers and in assertive women. The *Girl's Own Paper* conducted a running series of conversations between Pansy and Bob in
which the former must learn that rights are determined by the master,
not the horse: "Pansy, the mare, was a very different character. She held
strong views on the subject of equality, and now and then gave herself
very amusing airs. If she had lived at a time when the question of
women's rights and the extension of the suffrage were agitating the
feminine mind, one might have thought that Pansy had pondered the
matter in relation to horses."[6] Bob soon knocks some horse sense into
Pansy, who becomes a devoted servant to her master from that day forward. And in "The Maltese Cat" (1894), Kipling's sage little grey polo
pony is like a superior foreman, always eager to go the extra mile for
Lutyens, his master, and encourage the other horses to do the same. At
the end, the Maltese Cat is quite prepared to break his back in order to
save Lutyens from a fall, and for a horse "that was glory and honour
enough for the rest of his days."

Neither Anna Sewell nor her mother ever challenged the relationship between master and servant, but whereas Mary Sewell's social
philosophy was a bleak acceptance of the injustices of this world,
Anna never really acquired an obedient mind reflecting MacDonald's

"law of the universe." The choice of a horse as spokesman for the worker was itself a conservative gesture, for the horse could never aspire beyond its nature, it would always be a beast of burden carrying man or his belongings and asking only to be treated with a little kindness in return. Yet, despite this restrictive form, Anna Sewell contrived to make a number of subversive and radical statements about work as a condition of life.

From the first, Anna Sewell did not regard work as the natural avocation of man, despite the testimony to the contrary by Carlyle and Samuel Smiles. Black Beauty finds it far more enjoyable in the meadow with his mother, and his training, the breaking-in to a life of work, is a painful ordeal. He resents having a saddle thrown across his back and having his will broken to that of his master, even though he has been spared this particular ordeal until fully grown. There is a considerable degree of bitterness as Black Beauty describes the preparation for a life of work:

> Everyone may not know what breaking in is, therefore I will describe it. It means to teach a horse to wear a saddle and bridle, and to carry on his back a man, woman, or child; to go just the way they wish, and to go quietly. Besides this, he has to learn to wear a collar, a crupper, and a breeching, and to stand still whilst they are put on; then to have a cart or a chaise fixed behind, so that he cannot walk or trot without dragging it after him; and he must go fast or slow, just as his driver wishes. He must never start at what he sees, nor speak to other horses, nor bite, nor kick, nor have any will of his own, but always do his master's will, even though he may be very tired or hungry; but the worst of all is, when his harness is once on, he may neither jump for joy nor lie down for weariness. So you can see this breaking in is a great thing. (Chap. 3)

And when Owen in *The Ragged Trousered Philanthropists* contemplates the future that awaits his young son, a cold sweat breaks out upon him and his mouth fills with blood, for he knows that a workingman is broken like a horse and driven until he drops: "In a few years' time the boy would be like Bert White, in the clutches of some psalm-singing devil like Hunter or Rushton, who would use him as if he were a beast of burden. He imagined he could see him now as he would be then: worked, driven, and bullied, carrying loads, dragging carts, and running here and there, trying his best to satisfy the brutal tyrants, whose only thought would be to get a profit out of him for themselves" (Chap. 34).

His mates work like horses, but they refuse to question a society in which a few are dignified by the rank of master while the rest are servants. It is their subservience, their unfailing deference which makes them seem Owen's real enemy: "*They were the enemy.* Those who not only quietly submitted like so many cattle to the existing state of things, but defended it and opposed and ridiculed any suggestion to alter it. *They were the real oppressors*—the men who spoke of themselves as 'The likes of us,' who, having lived in poverty and degradation all their lives considered that what had been good enough for them was good enough for the children they had been the cause of bringing into existence" (Chap. 2). For Old Jack, Linden, and Newman, the cause of their poverty is new machines, foreigners, and women: "Thousands of 'em nowadays doin' work wot oughter be done by men" (Chap. 1). And the solution to all their problems is not reform, as Owen argues, but the luck to land in a job with a good master. Life is always a gamble, but they never expect more than Black Beauty's mother promised him:

> She told me the better I behaved the better I should be treated, and that it was wisest always to do my best to please my master; "But," said she, "there are a great many kinds of men; there are good, thoughtful men like our master, that any horse may be proud to serve; and there are bad, cruel men, who never ought to have a horse or a dog to call their own. Besides, there are a great many foolish men, vain, ignorant, and careless, who never trouble themselves to think; these spoil more horses than all, just for want of sense; they don't mean it, but they do it for all that. I hope you will fall into good hands; but a horse never knows who may buy him, or who may drive him; it is all a chance for us; but still I say, do your best wherever it is, and keep up your good name." (Chap. 3)

No matter how hard the painters work, they are always called on to do more by men like Misery and Hunter, and to Owen's fury, they are prepared to do it, because the only alternative is unemployment and starvation. Black Beauty and his friends go from place to place, sometimes to a good master, more often to a slave driver, and their condition is no different from that of Newman, Linden, and Old Jack. It is the knacker's yard for the worn-out horse, the workhouse and a pauper's grave for the worn-out worker.

Black Beauty ends on a note of perilous uncertainty; always working longer hours for less feed, the horse finds himself at last in the care of Miss Ellen and her sisters. He is recognized by Joe Green, his old name is restored to him, and he is cared for and groomed. All seems well except that we know how uncertain life can be for a horse, particularly one with broken knees and the weight of years upon him. So the concluding line carries with it an anxiety for the future which comes from knowing Black Beauty's past: "I have now lived in this happy place a whole year."

It is clear from the novel that a life of work is not to be welcomed with quite the glad enthusiasm enjoined by Samuel Smiles and his ilk, but also that to be out of work and to have no place is a worse fate yet. Black Beauty has been obedient, hardworking and eager to please, yet at the end his happiness is measured by the span of a year. Work is bad enough, but to be deprived of it is like a kind of death that can strike suddenly and without warning. It is the same for the ragged trousered philanthropists: "A few weeks with one firm, a few days with another, then out of a job, then on again for a month perhaps, and so on" (Chap. 3). And Owen can only shake his head in bemusement when his mates are not only treated like cattle; they begin to think like cattle: "The superior classes—those who do nothing—regarded them as a sort of lower animals. A letter appeared in the *Obscurer* one week from one of these well-dressed loafers, complaining of the annoyance caused to the better-class visitors by workmen walking on the pavement as they passed along the Grand Parade in the evening on their way home from work, and suggesting that they should walk in the roadway. When they heard of the letter a lot of the workmen adopted the suggestion and walked in the road so as to avoid contaminating the idlers" (chap. 43).

Olive Schreiner was convinced that if men were treated like animals, they would become something far worse than beasts: they would be made devils incarnate. In *The Story of an African Farm* (1883) Waldo first speaks of men who have been brutalized by the way they have been treated, first being changed into animals, and then devolving into fiends:

> "I think sometimes when we walked by my oxen I called to them in my sleep, for I know I thought of nothing; I was like an animal.

My body was strong and well to work, but my brain was dead. . . .
Now, when I see one of those evil-looking men that come from
Europe—navvies, with beast-like, sunken faces, different from any
Kaffir's—I know what brought that look into their eyes; and if I
have only one inch of tobacco I give them half. It is work, grind-
ing, mechanical work, that they or their ancestors have done, that
has made them into beasts. . . . You may work a man so that all
but the animal in him is gone; and that grows stronger with
physical labour. You may work a man till he is a devil. I know it,
because I have felt it." (Chap. 11)

Waldo then relates an incident that would have been familiar to all
his readers: an exhausted animal being flogged in the traces until it
drops. In this case it is not Tom Nero belaboring the fallen horse, but a
drunken carrier lashing "one ox, so thin that the ridge of his backbone
almost cut through his flesh" (chap. 11). Even as the ox lies dying, the
furious men whip it and drive their knives into it, for brandy and the
misery of work have made them devils. Again, a theme is sounded that
can be found in all these incidents: when a man is drunk he will beat
the animal in his charge to relieve the anger he feels towards his own
master. It is not a horse or an ox that is being flogged, but poverty, weari-
ness, and the unendurable emptiness of life. By this process of displacement and identification the image of the drunken cabman and
his suffering horse becomes a reproach to society, for the pain of the
animal is the pain of the man.

It was Anna Sewell who produced the emotive image between man
and horse when she wrote of Seedy Sam driving his horse until it was
ready to drop. Rather than denounce Sam for cruelty, Sewell condemned society for its callous disregard of any interest save its own.
When Sam is rebuked over the condition of the horse, he replies in a
"voice that sounded almost desperate" that when the horse is tired
only the whip will keep it going, just as the needs of his family are like
rods across his own back: "If the police have any business with the
matter, it ought to be with the masters who charge us so much, or with
the fares that are fixed so low. If a man has to pay eighteen shillings a
day for the use of a cab and two horses, as many of us have to do in the
season, and must make that up before we earn a penny for ourselves—
I say 'tis more than hard work; nine shillings a day to get out of each
horse, before you begin to get your own living; you know that's true,
and if the horses don't work we must starve" (chap. 39).

If cabmen drink and beat their horses, it is because their lives are unendurably wretched, and because they must work seven days a week for a pittance. Sewell is a fervent Sabbatarian for religious and social reasons, insisting that a day of rest is more in accord with Christ's teaching than a church service requiring the labor of the cabman and his horse. *Black Beauty* became a favorite text for temperance societies, as popular with working-class readers as it was with the rich, for the responsibility for brutality towards animals is not made the result of the innate callousness of the poor, but that of the insensitive and intemperate of all classes. The defining characteristic of the brute was not to be his income or his class, but the way he treated his animals. The man who got out and walked beside the coach to ease the horses' load was a gentleman; those who sat at their ease while the horses pulled their hearts out were bullies and cads. Seedy Sam was more of a gentleman than Lord George, who breaks Ginger's wind at a steeplechase, and Mr. Thoroughgood was closer to Christ than the earl who would not keep a horse with broken knees in his stable. If MacDonald regarded obedience as the law of the universe, Sewell saw it as love: "Cruelty was the Devil's own trade-mark, and if we saw anyone who took pleasure in cruelty, we might know who he belonged to, for the Devil was a murderer from the beginning, and a tormentor to the end."

In accordance with Anna Sewell's morality, people should be judged by the way they treated their animals, and by this rule, a well-groomed horse and a contented dog were visible proofs of a virtuous life. Since in Anna Sewell's opinion there is no afterlife for horses, she is careful to see that people should be rewarded and punished in this world like animals. Horses and humans live in the same spiritual universe, and there are no special privileges for the latter. Just as Hogarth showed the reward of cruelty to be the knife and a table in Surgeons' Hall, Anna Sewell relates the fate of Reuben Smith. Now Reuben was a first-rate driver and a good stableman with one failing: when drunk he turned into a madman and a devil. One night he rides Black Beauty at full gallop down a turnpike of freshly laid stones, not noticing that the horse has lost a shoe and is already beginning to stumble. Then in a passage of extraordinary eloquence Sewell relates the fate of Reuben Smith:

> This could not go on; no horse could keep his footing under such circumstances; the pain was too great. I stumbled, and fell with violence on both my knees, Smith was flung off by my fall, and,

owing to the speed I was going at, he must have fallen with great force. I soon recovered my feet and limped to the side of the road, where it was free from stones. The moon had just risen above the hedge, and by its light I could see Smith lying a few yards beyond me. He did not rise; he made one slight effort to do so, and then there was a heavy groan. I could have groaned too, for I was suffering intense pain both from my foot and knees; but horses are used to bear their pain in silence. I uttered no sound, but I stood there and listened. One more heavy groan from Smith; but though he now lay in the full moonlight, I could see no motion. I could do nothing for him nor myself, but, oh! how I listened for the sound of horse, or wheels, or footsteps! The road was not much frequented, and at this time of the night we might stay for hours before help came to us. I stood watching and listening. It was a calm, sweet April night; there were no sounds but a few low notes of a nightingale, and nothing moved but the white clouds near the moon and a brown owl that flitted over the hedge. It made me think of the summer nights long ago when I used to lie beside my mother in the green, pleasant meadow at Farmer Grey's." (Chap. 25)

Themes and images from *Black Beauty* are threaded through the literature and the consciousness of the age. They can be found in Battersea, where children suffered with the horses straining up a hill like the one where Black Beauty had once fallen, or in a work like Conrad's *The Secret Agent*, published in 1907. Conrad takes the character of Seedy Sam and translates him into the cabman and his horse, a vision of suffering that tears Stevie between compassion and rage.

At first Stevie is troubled by the sight of the horse, "whose hind quarters appeared unduly elevated by the effect of emaciation. The little stiff tail seemed to have been fitted in for a heartless joke; and at the other end the thin, flat neck, like a plank covered with an old horse-hide, drooped to the ground under the weight of an enormous bony head. The ears hung at different angles, negligently; and the macabre figure of that mute dweller on earth steamed straight up from ribs and backbone in the muggy stillness of the air" (chap. 8). The horse is an image of despairing endurance, and Stevie, the moral sensitive of the work, responds to the animal's suffering and begs the driver not to use the whip because "it hurts."

The night cabby uses the same arguments as Seedy Sam, speaking of the same needs, and the long nights when he has to work till three or four in the morning with cold and hunger as companions on the box beside him. At first all Stevie can say is that it is bad, to which the cabby replies that it is "'ard on 'osses, but dam 'sight 'arder on poor chaps like me." Straightway Stevie's pity embraces both horse and man in one gesture of convulsive sympathy, for the plight of both is the same: "The desire to make the horse happy and the cabman happy, had reached the point of a bizarre longing to take them to bed with him. And that, he knew, was impossible. For Stevie was not mad. It was, as it were, a symbolic longing; and at the same time it was very distinct, because springing from experience, the mother of wisdom" (chap. 8).

Conrad, like Sewell, was not preaching a gospel of radical change when he described the working class as beasts of burden, but simply that the middle and upper class should be more considerate and caring of the beasts in their charge. The message was profoundly conservative, as old as William Windham's presenting the House of Commons with that model of landlord and master, "an ancient Roman Catholic gentleman in the midst of his people, exercising the virtues of beneficence, humanity, and hospitality."[7] Or, as Sewell described John's receipt for curing the most vicious of horses, "patience and gentleness, firmness and petting, one pound of each to be mixed up with a pint of common sense, and given to the horse every day" (chap. 8).

Black Beauty became part of the social consciousness of the age with a multitude of literary imitations: autobiographies of animals from dogs to canaries proliferated, and all carried the same cautionary warnings against disobedience and the assurance that the cruel master would always be punished. The greatest of all human virtues in these works is kindness to animals. Unlike the animals depicted in American fiction, these English creatures yearned for good homes and considerate owners: not for them the call of the wild.[8] Tractable and docile, they are patterns for servants and workers, requiring only fairminded and responsible owners to make them models of cheerful gratitude. Just as Black Beauty is blissfully happy when his kind master Jerry Barker takes him to the country and lets him roll about in a field for a day, Tressell's philanthropists are overjoyed and full of thanks to Mr Rushton when he organizes a beano in the country. This single day of pleasure is enough to set them singing choruses in his praise while Owen weeps with rage over his mates, who ask only "to be allowed to work like brutes for the benefit of other people" (chap. 44).

The philanthropists are taken by brakes to a pub in the country, and it is as if they are being carried back to a world they have lost but never quite forgotten; for these city workers the country is now the place of rest and pleasure:

> The mean streets of Windley were soon left far behind and they found themselves journeying along a sunlit, winding road, bordered with hedges of hawthorn, holly and briar, past rich, brown fields of standing corn, shimmering with gleams of gold, past apple-orchards where bending boughs were heavily loaded with mellow fruits exhaling fragrant odours, through the cool shades of lofty avenues of venerable oaks, whose overarched and interlacing branches formed a roof of green, gilt and illuminated with quivering spots of sunlight that filtered through the trembling leaves; over old mossy stone bridges, spanning limpid streams that duplicated the blue sky and the fleecy clouds; and then again, stretching away to the horizon on every side over more fields, some rich with harvest, others filled with drowsing cattle or with flocks of timid sheep that scampered away at the sound of passing carriages. Several times they saw merry little companies of rabbits frisking gaily in and out of the hedges or in the fields beside the sheep and cattle. At intervals, away in the distance, nestling in the hollows or amid sheltering trees, groups of farm buildings and stacks of hay; and further on, the square ivy-clad tower of an ancient church, or perhaps a solitary windmill with its revolving sails alternately flashing and darkening in the rays of the sun. Past thatched way-side cottages whose inhabitants came out to wave their hands in friendly greeting. (Chap. 44)

It is a remarkable passage, overwritten and deliberately poetic, less an actual landscape than an arcadian paradise, a place to nestle and shelter, where all is gilt and gold with sweet fruits on every branch. Here is the peaceable kingdom where men and animals live happily together, and the people welcome strangers like the legion of the Shining Ones who served the King in the Celestial Country and guided pilgrims into the promised land. For Owen's companions it is a country without work: windmills turn, sheep and cattle browse in rich pastures, and everything is fixed forever in their minds like Sally Plornish's painted cottage. Maudlin with beer and gratitude the philanthropists sing their own hymns of praise to the master:

His clothes may be ragged, his hands may be soiled.
But where's the disgrace if for bread he has toiled.
His 'art is in the right place, deny it no one can
The backbone of Old England is the honest workin' man.

(Chap. 44)

The aspirations of Black Beauty and the workingmen are the same: good food, a comfortable bed and a green field on holiday. When Black Beauty comes at last to "a pretty, low house, with a lawn and shrubbery at the front, and a drive up to the door" (chap. 49), he has come to the promised land where the work is easy and the employer considerate. Authoritarian and conservative the message may have been, but it was nonetheless a powerful social influence: Robert Tressell and those radicals of like mind were in a minority and knew it. When Geoffrey Gorer set out to explore the English character in the early 1950s he was puzzled to account for the change that had taken place in a society which had been characterized by lawless violence at the beginning of the nineteenth century, with considerable pleasure being taken "in fighting and in witnessing the pain and humiliation of others, and the gratuitous suffering of animals."[9] Gorer accepts that "cruelty and aggression are English preoccupations," and then wonders where this passion for cruelty had gone. Had it been removed indoors and kept in the heart of the home and family, or had it been internalized into a form of self-punishment? Gorer is quite clearly as dissatisfied with his own conclusions at this point as we should be. We could perhaps point to the increasing popularity of sport, to the crowds shouting their lungs out at football or cheering on a favorite horse, and this again does not really answer. Reluctantly, we must say a little about aggression without taking refuge in a forest of footnotes, and aggression, whether thought to be innate or learned, is a subject that produces inflammatory opinions from the most reticent and circumspect. At this point in our journey we can guarantee disagreement.

With a variety of directions available to us, I think we should take Edward O. Wilson as guide and see if we can follow him to a satisfactory conclusion:

The clear perception of human aggressive behavior as a structured, predictable pattern of interaction between genes and environment is consistent with evolutionary theory. It should satisfy both camps in the venerable nature-nurture controversy. On the one hand it is true that aggressive behavior, especially in its more dangerous forms of military action and criminal assault, is learned. But the learning is prepared . . . we are strongly predisposed to slide into deep, irrational hostility under certain definable conditions. With dangerous ease hostility feeds on itself and ignites runaway reactions that can swiftly progress to alienation and violence. Aggression does not resemble a fluid that continuously builds pressure against the walls of its containers, nor is it like a set of active ingredients poured into an empty vessel. It is more accurately compared to a preexisting mix of chemicals ready to be transformed by specific catalysts that are added, heated, and stirred at some later time.[10]

What Wilson sees as a counteragent to aggression is "a confusion of cross-binding loyalties," a tangle of identifications that bond people so closely that distinctions become increasingly difficult to observe and define. Very likely something like this was occurring between animals and people throughout the nineteenth century. Aesop and La Fontaine had taught moral precepts by means of animals with human characteristics, but this ancient mode had now been reversed with particular groups of people consistently being defined as animals to the considerable advantage of the human animals. What we find throughout this period are not simply didactic fables but complex and emotional bondings between people and animals. Just as it is possible for an Aboriginal tribesman of Australia to shun the killing and eating of possums because they both belong to the same totemic family, whereas the rest of the tribe will hunt them most zealously, so it is conceivable that the English working class had come to feel a particular affinity with horses, dogs and other domestic animals. They had so often been made to see themselves as animals that this responsive vision became second nature to them; and to identify with an animal so inherently noble as the horse did not involve any measure of disesteem. Indeed, a workingman could regard the horse and the dog as the embodiment of his own better self without any loss of self respect. This sympathy frequently extended to those animals ritually hunted and killed by other classes, and it was not unknown for the farm laborer's wife to shelter the fox and point the hunt in the opposite direction.

The prohibition against cruelty to animals became dogma in working class morality: Gorer found that it was regarded as a cardinal sin for which a child deserved to be punished most severely, and it could even affect a person's existence in the next life. Admittedly, there was considerable doubt about the nature of heaven and hell, but one lower-class married man from Newent stated firmly: "Well I think if a man's been cruel to an animal or some other creature I mean cruel to a great extent knowing full well he had been cruel I think he will come back and suffer like such."[11] In 1869 in *Mopsa the Fairy* there was the refrain found in a multitude of religious tracts, as Jean Ingelow's fairy guardian of the old broken-down horses said darkly: "I wonder what will be done to all your people for driving, and working, and beating so many beautiful creatures to death every year that comes? They'll have to pay for it some day, you may depend" (chap. 3). What surprised Gorer was the belief in reincarnation, and the idea that people and animals could slip in and out of each other's skins. One young man wrote: "I think that if everyone has lived a good life, they will be some animals with daylight activities, to enjoy the sunshine and like, but if they have been bad they will be like mice and rates [*sic*] and other nocturnal animals, so under cover of darkness they can hide their shame and not enjoy the beauty of Gods world."[12] Here is Tressell's arcadian landscape with its frisking rabbits and happy people—a vision of paradise where animal and man lived in harmony and shared the same spirit.

What the evangelical reformers and the humane societies had unwittingly accomplished was a reinforcement of beliefs that ran quite counter to Christian doctrine. Foreshadowed in the fictional relationships of animals and men in the nineteenth century was the recreation of a magical world where all living things were members of the same family. The pervasive influence of Spiritualism played its part here, but in the main, the Band of Mercy tracts and writers like Ingelow and Sewell were drawing their fictional images from a very ancient well wher? there were no set boundaries between animal and human. The morality of human existence was made dependent upon the way one behaved towards animals: kindness would be rewarded and cruelty punished. But whereas Sewell saw the judgment of heaven meted out in this world, Gorer's young workingman could cheerfully contemplate the virtuous soul taking flight as a bird.

Historians have noted the decline of organized Christianity among the working class in England throughout the nineteenth and twentieth centuries. It was not an active, violent antagonism towards religion, so much as a passive indifference, a dwindling of attendance on Sundays, a general apathy. However, this is not the same thing as saying that these people lacked religion. Old folk traditions still existed but were now given a new direction, just as a place like Lavender Hill carries the past in its name while to the passerby it offers only brick and cement. The ritual of burning a cat alive had once been thought to be a sure means of exorcising evil spirits and averting misfortune in most rural areas in England, but by the end of the nineteenth century, the same act was regarded as one of the worst sins, meriting punishment in this world and damnation in the next. The act had not lost its gravity and import: it had simply come to be interpreted differently, and for some, it was of the same order as murder. When asked to give an example of the worst possible behavior among children, a working-class mother from Barnes, Surrey, wrote: "Push another child in the river etc. shut the cat puppy in the oven."[13] Margaret Hale would have regarded this woman as a most satisfactory tribute to her reforming zeal; what would have disconcerted her was that this morality was not dependent upon Christian faith but upon a revised version of pagan custom.

One result of this was a class of people that became known for its love of pets and its decency, in the full Orwellian sense of that word: people who believed that kindness to animals was an aspect of consideration for people, and that both were essential if a person were to live a moral life and be ensured of a reward in the next. Animals, whether tortured or misused, had always been part of the rituals of folklore and rural custom; now, by means of tracts and fictions, arrests and fines, animals were restored to their old significance, but with a changed prescription: they were still a fount of magical power, bringing luck in this world and a happy life in the next, not by means of their death, but as a result of the love and care bestowed on them. The cricket on the hearth brought happiness to the home as long as it sang; misfortune ensued when it had been crushed by a cruel or thoughtless foot.

Here then was one reason why people responded with such a sense of bewilderment and outrage when vivisectors began roasting live animals in ovens after the approved method of Claude Bernard, or drowning dogs in the London laboratories of Professor Schafer. There is no anger like that of the convert for the unreformed and backslider, and to many, the vivisectors seemed like magicians of a dark age ritually condemning animals to fearful tortures. When those tortures resembled those that working-class people had eschewed, the sense of revulsion was enormous. And then it was not simply animals which were being used, as Berdoe and the popular press assured its readers, but human beings like themselves who were experimental subjects in charity wards. For this reason the "Old Anti" in Battersea had a special place in the memory of those who supported it in preference to more modern institutions. Quite simply, people felt safe there.

Animals as victims, and the worker as society's victim, became interchangeable images. In Lewis Grassic Gibbon's *Cloud Howe* (1933), Jim the carthorse dies slowly with a broken shaft in his entrails, and with him dies a whole class of farm laborers. Boxer, the drayhorse in Orwell's *Animal Farm* (1934), is not too bright, but he is "universally respected for his steadiness of character, and tremendous power of work" (chap. 1). But when Boxer is too old and sick to work, he is sold off to a knackery, just as old Jack Linden is sent off to the workhouse to die in *The Ragged Trousered Philanthropists*. It was a powerful image continually reinforced by writers and reformers who saw workers and animals sharing the same fate. But a feeling of oppression was not unique to the working class; it was a condition that women shared in full. Although working men had only derisive contempt for suffragettes and feminists, they found common ground over the plight of vivisected animals. Women were to be the strength of the antivivisection movement, and every flogged and beaten horse, every dog or cat strapped down for the vivisector's knife, reminded them of their own condition in society.

5

Horrible and Indecent Exposure

By the early 1900s medical students and a great many other people were convinced that the antivivisectionists and the suffragettes belonged to the same objectionable movement, despite the fact that members of each group frequently had no sympathy, and in some cases, a positive dislike for each other. Lady Bathurst had been a friend and supporter of Frances Cobbe, but in 1913 she stated publicly that when "a suffragette has been convicted, first have her well birched by women, then shave off her hair, and finally deport her to New Zealand or Australia."[1] Anna Kingsford and Ouida were both opposed to women's suffrage, and both were dedicated antivivisectionists. On the other hand, we have already met Charlotte Despard, who was a vegetarian and antivivisectionist and also went to prison for her suffrage activities. The description of antivivisectionists by the French physiologist Élie de Cyon is certainly incorrect: "Is it necessary to repeat that women—or rather, old maids—form the most numerous contingent of this group? Let my adversaries contradict me, if they can show among the leaders of the agitation one young girl, rich, beautiful, and beloved, or some young wife who has found in her home the full satisfaction of her affections."[2] The belief that compassion for animals was a manifestation of sexual frustration was long held to be a medical fact, and like a great many other convictions of similar bias it lacked both logic and sense.[3]

Historians of the antivivisection movement have always observed that women supported the cause in numbers exceeded only by the suffrage societies.[4] Richard French stresses the influence of Frances

Cobbe and sees her undertaking the same role with regard to anti-vivisection that Florence Nightingale played with nursing. James Turner argues that a prosperous middle class, uneasy with the consequences of industrialism and feeling pangs of remorse and guilt when it saw the wretched poverty of workers, made animals a surrogate subject of concern.[5] This is an ingenious argument, although it is questionable whether guilt was as pervasive in Victorian society as it is with us to-day; the fact that people *should* have felt guilty about social inequities is no reason for assuming that they actually did. The real difficulty for Turner is that so many antivivisectionist women were active social re-formers: the Baroness Burdett Coutts, the Countess of Camperdown, Charlotte Despard, Lady Battersea, and Frances Cobbe come immedi-ately to mind. The puzzling question involves the great many women who cared passionately for animals and nothing for children and the poor, and in particular, why these women should have involved them-selves so passionately with the antivivisection movement to the exclu-sion of issues of social reform. The resolution of this question may well lead us down to a particularly dark and deeply buried river.

What we first discover with women and animals in the nineteenth century is the same degree of identification that we have found with workers. Women saw themselves as horses being flogged and beaten, and many saw their own condition hideously and accurately embod-ied in the figure of an animal bound to a table by straps with the vivi-sector's knife at work on its flesh. It was a sight that evoked anger and despair in women. When Frances Cobbe lectured about the experi-ments being conducted upon dogs, the women in her audience would often sob and become hysterical, to the delight of the jeering medical students, who saw this as another example of women's volatile sympa-thies and unstable temperament.[6] It was considered to be softheaded sentimentality when women persisted in seeing themselves as animals hunted, trapped, and tortured.

Some women doctors were dedicated antivivisectionists. Their con-victions were neither sentimental nor unreasoned, but a direct conse-quence of what they had seen done to poor women in the charity wards of public hospitals. Elizabeth Blackwell considered Dr. James Webster to be one of her strongest allies and best teachers at the Geneva Medi-cal College in Western New York where she studied medicine. Even so, in her diary of 1847 she recorded an incident that disturbed and troubled her: "Dr. Webster sent for me to examine a case of a poor woman at his rooms. 'Twas a horrible exposure; indecent for any poor woman to be subjected to such torture; she seemed to feel it, poor and ignorant as she was."[7] For the purposes of examination, the woman would have been strapped to a frame which raised her pelvis while her feet were held in stirrups or footrests, and in this position a group of medical students would have been invited to inspect her genitalia. This was standard gynaecological practice at the time, but Elizabeth Blackwell was appalled by the woman's plight.[8]

Far worse sights could be found in the charity wards of some of the large Paris hospitals, and here Blackwell recorded instances of "degrading cruelty." What could occasionally take place was described by Anna Kingsford, the first Englishwoman to graduate with a medical degree from the Faculté de Médecine of Paris:

> It is the same in the medical wards. On entering one devoted to diseases of the chest, the students are to be found regarding the patients simply as subjects for practice. . . . A woman is dying of consumption. She is in the last stage. Both lungs are destroyed, and the chest is filled with liquid. She has been almost insensible for several hours. If left alone she will die in comparative ease, without returning to consciousness. But this must not be. She must afford yet another lesson in return for the charity she has received, and as a penalty for being a pauper. Bending over her, the physician shouts at her to make her open her eyes. She tries in vain to obey him. Taking a pin from his coat, he thrusts it into the under surface of each lid. She utters a cry, and he withdraws the pin, saying, "You feel that, do you? Why don't you open your eyes, then?" He then pricks her hands and legs, each puncture eliciting a faint cry and effort at resistance. Then with the aid of a student he lifts her up in the bed; for she is dying, and is utterly unable to move herself. Putting his ear to her back, he shakes her violently with both hands, in order to hear the fluctuations of the liquid in the chest, an operation which has already been repeated daily for the same purpose. At each shake the patient puts out her emaciated hands, and cries piteously in a feeble voice, "Oh, sir! oh, sir!"[9]

At a time when modesty prevailed in women's dress and the working class wore combinations and drawers like the rest of society, a poor woman requiring gynaecological attention could expect to be trussed and exposed before a circle of students never known for their delicacy of manner. Sir James Paget recalled that on such occasions the presiding surgeon would often tell stories "some of which were obscene, some very nasty," for the operating theatre was a place for robust humor as well as surgery, and "that some of even the most distinguished members of the profession would commonly tell utterly indecent and dirty stories."[10] If the patient was a working-class woman, it was assumed that she was so well versed in the rougher ways of the world that courtesy was wasted upon her. Working-class men might dread the thought of becoming a patient in the charity ward of a large teaching hospital, but it was far worse for his womenfolk, who could expect to find themselves bound to an elevated saddle or table, ankles in stirrups, while a group of ebullient medical students examined their "private parts," to use the phrase familiar to all classes of women at this time. There were no refinements for poor women, and although the practice of medicine improved, the attitude of doctors towards such patients did not.

Working-class outrage towards the medical profession was fired by memories of the Contagious Diseases Acts and the movement to repeal them in the 1870s. It was not middle-class women who were being dragged off the streets then and examined to see if they had venereal disease, the workers were told, but their own wives and daughters. The propaganda of the day gave lurid accounts of innocent factory girls being seized by lustful police and forced to submit to lewd examinations by depraved doctors. Josephine Butler and the advocates of repeal had spoken directly to working-class audiences using pamphlets and lectures to demonstrate the horrors that awaited any suspected prostitute taken up for examination by the doctors. They could expect to be roughly handled and abused with worse to follow: "The attitude they push us into first is so disgusting and so painful, and then these monstrous instruments—often they use several. They seem to tear us open first with their hands, and examine us, and then they thrust in instruments, and they pull them out and push them in, and they turn and twist them about; and if you cry out they stifle you."[11] To a working-class woman undergoing a gynaecological examination at the turn of the century, it would seem that she was being treated like a prostitute, with no more consideration for her sense of modesty than if she had been taken from a whorehouse.

Anna Kingsford was horrified by the practice of conducting some surgical operations on poor patients without any kind of anaesthetic: "Paupers are thus classed with animals as fitting subjects for painful experiment, and no regard is shown to the feelings of either, it is not surprising that the use of anaesthetics for the benefit of the patient is wholly rejected. Even the excruciating operation of cautery with a red-hot iron is performed without the alleviation of an anaesthetic."[12]

When a young doctor like Somerset Maugham had working-class women in his care, he could always find a number of defenses ready-made to protect him from the reality of so much suffering. One of the most effective was a stereotype of the working-class woman as a raucous vocal animal: Arthur Morrison created such a fiction in Lizerunt of *Down Mean Streets* (1895), and in Maugham's first novel, *Liza of Lambeth* (1897), the heroine is clearly derived from Lizerunt. Maugham was persuaded to accept the fiction of the working-class woman as a species of animal after he became an obstetrical clerk at St. Thomas' Hospital in the 1890s. Of course there was another fiction of the working-class girl, and Shaw delighted his audiences in 1914 with young Liza Doolittle, who was so abashed by the reflection of her naked body in a bathroom mirror that she cried out to Mrs. Pearce, the housekeeper: "Ive never took off all me clothes before. It's not right: it's not decent." This perception of a young working-class woman might well have made a doctor like Maugham, and a great many others, feel most uncomfortable, and consequently it never became part of general medical practice.

Besides stereotyping women charity patients as animals, another defense against compassion was cynicism. The quality which was to characterize all of Maugham's writing can first be discerned in the aphorisms about women and pain he jotted down in his notebook at this time. Genially, he observed: "If women exhibit less emotion at pain, it does not prove that they bear it better but rather that they feel it less." Maugham was not singular at this time when he put his faith in a shallow determinism and the new science of physiology: "An acquaintance with the rudiments of physiology will teach you more about feminine character than all the philosophy and wise-saws."[13]

Manuals of physiology and gynaecology taught that women were incomplete males, with the clitoris and hymen as an undeveloped penis.[14] Women doctors like Anna Kingsford and Elizabeth Blackwell refused to accept this theory and others like it, but they had already discovered that the treatment of women was an area from which they were being specifically excluded. When Elizabeth Blackwell was admitted to Sir James Paget's institution, St. Bartholomew's Hospital in London, she wrote that "every department was cordially opened to me, *except the department for female diseases.*"[15] It was argued that women, by nature unstable, were incapable of caring for each other, and that the naturally nervous and excitable condition of women required the calm presence of a male to effect a cure.

A number of distinguished doctors and surgeons were appalled by current gynaecological practice. In 1895 Sir William Priestley, consulting physician to King's College Hospital, deplored what he chose to call "Over-operating in Gynaecology":

> Looking back on forty years of gynaecological practice I can recollect what has been termed a craze for inflammation and ulceration of the os and cervix uteri. During its prevalence it was said of some devotees that every woman of a household was apt to be regarded as suffering from these affections, and locally treated accordingly. Shortly afterwards came a brief and not very creditable period when "clitoridectomy" was strongly advocated as a remedy for numerous ills. . . . Then followed a time in which displacement of the uterus held the field, and every back-ache, every pelvic discomfort, every general neurosis was attributed to mechanical causes, and must needs be treated by uterine pessaries. . . . Lastly, we have had what has been described as an epidemic of operations for excision of the uterine appendages.[16]

Clifford Allbutt, consulting physician to the Leeds Hospital for Women and Children, stated in the Gulstonian Lecture of 1884 that women were being systematically induced into sickness:

> She is tangled in the net of the gynaecologist, who finds her uterus, like her nose, is a little on one side; or again, like that organ, is running a little, or it is as flabby as her biceps, so that the unhappy viscus is impaled upon a stem, or perched upon a prop, or is painted with carbolic acid every week in the year, except during the long vacation when the gynaecologist is grouse-shooting, or salmon-catching, or leading the fashion in the Upper Engadine. Her mind thus fastened to a more or less nasty mystery, becomes newly apprehensive and physically introspective, and the morbid chains are rivetted more strongly than ever. Arraign the uterus, and you fix in the woman the arrow of hypochondria, it may be for life.[17]

Allbutt voiced the opinion of a great many doctors when he complained that women were being induced into a state of hypochondria by gynaecologists and was widely quoted when he wrote of women as the subject of "medical fashion," being "visited almost daily for uterine disease, *their brave and active spirits broken under a false belief* in the presence of a secret and overmastering local malady, and the best years of their lives honoured only by a distressful victory over pain."[18] These "endless examinations" always required a woman to be fastened to a chair or table, while the gynaecologist inspected and painted the offending organ. The response to such treatment was not always gratitude on the part of the patient, who came to resent her body and its failings, and the doctor who had such authority over it.

Neither the *British Medical Journal* nor the *Lancet* was a supporter of women's rights. Both were opposed to women's suffrage and the opening of the medical profession to women. In 1876 the *Lancet* stated bluntly: "We believe women's work is to console and support man, not to usurp his functions."[19] Yet both deplored the gynaecologist's usurpation of female medicine, particularly surgery. "Trifling maladies" magnified into chronic disease were bad enough in Elizabeth Blackwell's opinion, but what roused her to a fury of indignation was the sexual surgery being practiced by a number of gynaecologists. In 1876, Dr. Robert Battey urged the removal of healthy ovaries as the most effective treatment for menstrual difficulties and those other ailments generally grouped under the heading of "mania."[20]

Elizabeth Blackwell characterized Battey's work as "the castration of women," and it is true that a number of gynaecological textbooks of this period refer to this and similar operations as "spaying." Like Anna Kingsford, Blackwell saw such surgery as an extension of vivisection, with doctors using women in place of dogs and cats. She had seen poor women made ready for operations and never failed to denounce the way they were treated as cruel and indecent. However, she never described what she had actually seen, for Blackwell was restrained by the contemporary reticence of language, but when Maxence Van der meersch walked through the wards of a number of Paris hospitals in the 1940s, including La Charité, where Anna Kingsford had studied, he was not subject to the same linguistic code. Van der meersch wrote of the operation which Blackwell had deplored: "Michel never forgot that poor woman, dangling upside down with her thin hair thrown back, her face seen from above in a tragic foreshortening; that woman dis-

embowelled like an animal hanging on a hook in a butcher's and tell-
ing her story while Géraudin bent over her, tearing out the ovaries and
sponging blood from the bottom of the pelvic cavity, as though from a
bucket of flesh lined with muscles."[21]

The image of a woman like a vivisected animal haunted Elizabeth
Blackwell, who recognized that increasingly women were being used
as subjects for medical research; the only difference between the rich
and the poor woman was that the latter could not always expect the
solace of chloroform and the comfort of her own home when she was
examined or operated upon. Those women who could afford the gynaecologist's fees were frequently operated on in the privacy of their
homes with a nurse in attendance. In the 1930s Sir Comyns Berkeley
insisted that the gynaecologist must equip himself with a portable operating table, since the test of a good surgeon was his ability to operate
anywhere, and he would, moreover, find a number of his patients refusing to enter a hospital.[22]

Blackwell's opposition to vivisection was confirmed in Paris when
she witnessed the experiments of Claude Bernard and his students,
knowing that those same students would soon become surgeons. She
set out the case with her customary vigor, arguing that "torture is not
only unsuited to laboratory work, but is an inevitable source of error in
results."[23] Apart from the suffering of the animals, what troubled her,
as it did a number of doctors, was the margin of error between animal
and human experimentation. Berdoe cited a number of instances
when doctors had conducted experiments upon patients which had
proved fatal to animals. In one case, "Codeia makes dogs or rabbits
move in a circle or backwards, and later it produces convulsions and
death. Robiquet, having made these observations, proceeded to ad-
minister it to children, 'in whom it caused very alarming symptoms'.
Either he must have taken it for granted that the poison would act differently upon animals and man, or he concluded that its action in
both cases would be similar; in any case the poor children had a narrow escape from 'dying scientifically'."[24]

When Blackwell saw "Senn of Philadelphia, setting fire to a dog that
he had pumped full of hydrogen gas, before the Medical Congress of
Berlin in 1890," she immediately wondered when this particular experiment would be made upon some unfortunate patient.[25] Her concern was always for the poor who were the subjects for research, and
she continually stated that vivisection "tends to make us less scru-
pulous in our treatment of the sick and helpless poor. It increases that

disposition to regard the poor as 'clinical material', which has become, alas! not without reason, a widespread reproach to many of the young members of our most honourable and merciful profession."[26]

Like Frances Cobbe, Blackwell was disturbed by the effect such experiments had upon those who conducted and observed them. Cobbe argued that vivisectors had fallen victim to *Schadenfreude*, that most insidious form of wickedness, a delight in the spectacle of pain.[27] The students watching an animal contorted with agony in the laboratory were responding in the same fashion as the crowd around the cockpit or the bullring, and it was disingenuous to claim otherwise. Blackwell wrote that "such demonstration may justify that instinct of curiosity which always exists in youthful human nature, or it may pander to that craving for excitement which makes the spectacle of a surgical operation so much more attractive to the undeveloped mind than careful clinical study—a tendency which is also seen in gambling, watching executions, bull-fights, etc.—but these are tendencies to be repressed in serious and responsible study, not encouraged."[28]

In response to charges like these, the vivisectors declared with Lord Lister that "an act is cruel or otherwise, not according to the pain which it involves, but according to the mind and object of the actor."[29] The social consequences of such a peremptory assumption of moral authority by a small group of men were not lost upon the general public, and when Sir T. Lauder Brunton was giving evidence before the Royal Commission on Vivisection in 1906, he observed: "There were no grounds for saying that the witnessing, or the performance of experiments on living animals in any way affected the character of the spectator or the operator."[30] But having said this, Brunton added thoughtfully that in his considered opinion it was always advisable to restrict the audience for such experiments.

Although Frances Cobbe and Elizabeth Blackwell were prepared to argue with a considerable degree of common sense against vivisection, this was hardly the case with Anna Kingsford. She was everything Frances Cobbe detested: a mystic and visionary who had prophetic dreams and claimed supernatural powers. Yet in Kingsford's writings we can see most clearly those "cross-binding loyalties," to use Wilson's phrase, that led women to become identified with animals. It was a remarkable tribute to the force of Anna Kingsford's beliefs and her personality that she gained her degree in medicine while persistently refusing to allow her professors to vivisect at her lessons. Other women complained quietly, or remained silent, Anna Kingsford professed her visions throughout the course of her study. One morning she re-corded a particular dream that was to provide a recurring motif in her philosophy:

> I went in my sleep last night from one torture-chamber to an-other in the underground vaults of a vivisector's laboratory, and in all were men at work lacerating, dissecting, and burning the living flesh of their victims. But these were no longer mere horses or dogs or rabbits; for in each I saw a human shape, the shape of a man, with limbs and lineaments resembling those of their tor-mentors, hidden within the outward form. And so, when they bound down a horse, and gathering round him, cut into him with knives, I saw the human shape within him writhe and moan as if it were a babe in its mother's womb. And I cried aloud, "Wretches! you are torturing an unborn man!" But they only mocked at me, for with *their* eyes, they could not see that which I saw. Then they brought a rabbit and thrust its eyes through with hot irons. And the rabbit seemed to me, as I gazed, like the tiniest infant, with human face, and hands which stretched appealingly towards me, and lips which tried to cry for help in human accents. And again I cried to them, "O blind! blind! do ye not see that your victim is of your own kind, a child that is human." But they only laughed and jeered at me, and in the agony of my despair I woke.[31]

Kingsford saw humanity in animals, and she suffered intolerable pain when others did not share her vision. How was it possible, she cried, to teach children morality from animal stories and then to kill and eat those very same animals, or subject them to cruel torture? And when she saw an animal strapped to a table, convulsed with fear and struggling to escape, she saw herself. Frequently she declared that she was prepared to offer her own body for vivisection rather than see an animal suffer for her, and in Kingsford's case this was not mere rheto-ric. Robert Browning, who wrote the poem "Tray" as a protest against Schafer's drowning of dogs, had said, "I would rather submit to the worst of deaths, so far as pain goes, than have a single dog or cat tor-tured on the pretence of sparing me a twinge or two."[32] But Kingsford's agony was of a different order as she beheld the vivisectors leading hu-manity through a torture chamber in the name of progress and health. Her anguish became a passionate hatred for the men she termed devils, and her struggle against them was not simply a contest of ideas but a metaphysical duel.

Practical, genial, and diplomatic, Frances Cobbe was aghast when Anna Kingsford—armed, as she believed, with occult powers—declared war against the vivisectors, a war conducted from astral planes where the force of her will would bring death to her enemies. Cobbe had no quarrel with Theosophists and Spiritualists, but she drew the line at behavior like this. All her life she had tried to make antivivisection a rational cause with its philosophy drawn, in her case, from Kantian ethics and Benthamite utilitarianism. Now she was confronted with a woman who had a degree in medicine from a school where animal experimentation was part of the curriculum, a woman whose eloquence and physical beauty were remarkable and who invoked "Hermes, Son of God, slayer of Argus, Archangel," to destroy the vivisectors. It was all the more embarrassing because she seemed to be remarkably successful, or lucky, in her campaign against the enemy. Why could not Anna Kingsford write and lecture scientifically like her good friend Elizabeth Blackwell, and not as a mystic and seer? And why did Anna Kingsford's friend and acolyte Edward Maitland go out of his way to publicize the results of Kingsford's deathly powers? In her diary, Anna Kingsford had written:

> *Paris, November 12. "Mort de M. Paul Bert."* "La nouvelle de sa mort, arrivée Jeudi soir à quatre heures, n'à surpris personne." Yesterday, November 11, at eleven at night, I knew that my will had smitten another vivisector! Ah, but this man has cost me more toil than his master, the fiend Claude Bernard. For months I have been compassing the death of Paul Bert, and have but just succeeded. But I *have* succeeded; the demonstration of the power is complete. The will *can* and *does* kill, but not always with the same rapidity. Claude Bernard died *foudroyé*; but Paul Bert has wasted to death. Now only one remains on hand—Pasteur, who is certainly doomed, and must, or I should think, succumb in a few months at the utmost. Oh, how I have longed for those words— "Mort de M. Paul Bert!" And now—there they actually are, gazing at me as if it were in the first column of the *Figaro*,—complimenting, congratulating, felicitating me. *I* have killed Paul Bert, as I killed Claude Bernard; as I will kill Louis Pasteur, and after him the whole tribe of vivisectors.[33]

The rift between Frances Cobbe and Anna Kingsford was to create yet another division in an already fragmented movement, even though Anna Kingsford was voicing moods and responses that spoke to a new consciousness among women. It was as if animals, and particularly the vivisected animal, embodied all the fears of sexual surgery: images of women strapped to chairs or tables, feet held high in stirrups, and the gynaecologist standing over them with a knife. As Elizabeth Browning wrote in *Aurora Leigh*, Book 1 (1857), "The works of women are symbolical," and the symbols we find here are all the more potent because they are drawn from a muffled context of reticence and silence. Little can be understood of this process of displacement and substitution without reference to a linguistic code among women wherein bodily functions were indicated by delicate ellipses, and contrary to the fictions of Maugham and Morrison, working-class women were as eager to adopt this speech of respectability as any middle-class matron.

Learning to "speak nicely," like a lady, was the aspiration of more young working-class girls than Liza Doolittle. Old Miss Mason of Tyneham Close in Battersea had worked at Morgan's Crucibles for forty years, and in her eighties she wrote:

> I live alone and often think of these things now and think how different things are now. I remember Dr. Oatman, he lived near the Square and he and his wife used to walk their two big sheep dogs and to me they seemed like the King and Queen they were always dressed so nice. They had children and I used to follow them because they spoke so nicely. They had a nurse who used to take them to the Park and I would sit near just to hear them talk,—that has stayed with me. I still like to hear people speak nicely, I am afraid I don't have a very nice speaking voice, and that is one thing I would love to have.[34]

Women spoke of their ailments in euphemisms. Menstruation was "the curse," or, more delicately, "unwell" ("All's well that ends unwell!" was the favorite quip of a famous gynaecologist in the 1920s), and a working-class girl might reluctantly admit that she was feeling "poorly." Pregnancy among the well-to-do was always *enceinte*, or in a "delicate condition," while those of less exalted rank might admit to "being in the family way," leaving coarser expressions—"pudding club" and so forth—to the lower orders. Any medical problem below the waist and above the thighs was always referred to vaguely as "trouble downstairs," with all the social connotations of that particular place. More jocularly, the phrase "below decks" might be used, and again, a concept of class would be invoked to deflect question or comment. George Russell in the 1890s observed that the language people used in public had changed radically since the beginning of the century, and women had been more affected than men: "I have been told by one who heard it from an eye-witness that a great Whig duchess, who figures brilliantly in the social and political memoirs of the last century, turned to the footman who was waiting on her at dinner, exclaimed, 'I wish to God that you wouldn't keep rubbing your great greasy belly against the back of my chair.'"[35] Russell then noted the refinement of women's language in his own day, pausing to wonder if their vocabulary even contained the words that were everyday usage with their grandmothers. George Bernard Shaw observed in *Pygmalion* that whereas a duchess might permit herself an extraordinary degree of license in her speech, working girls like Liza Doolittle yearned for refined speech as the passport to respectability and improved social status.

It is not until the 1940s that we have the description of a working-class woman undergoing an ovariotomy, and yet it was this operation which made a passionate antivivisectionist of Elizabeth Blackwell. For all her courage and power of language, Anna Kingsford could never bring herself to record this particular operation. Nonetheless, women were not silenced, and their despair and anger were projected into the figures of animals, captured and tortured at the hands of the vivisectionist.

6

Riding Masters and Young Mares

In *Aurora Leigh* Elizabeth Browning used animals as a means of defining the bounds and restraints that confined women to a special sphere. Aurora always sees herself as a bird condemned to be a prisoner of her aunt ("a wild bird scarcely fledged, was brought to her cage"), and this image of the caged bird was to become the symbol of middle-class women, employed so often that it became an habitual trope. Even Trollope, never a writer to fashion an exotic or unusual metaphor where the tried and ordinary will serve, has Ayala say to her sister in *Ayala's Angel* (1881): "We are like two tame birds, who have to be moved from one cage into another just as the owner pleases." And in the music hall, variations on the theme of the sparrow that spurned a golden cage for a leafless tree were always sure to produce a few sobs from the gallery. However, if Aurora, educated and blessed with a private income, described herself as a bird, Marian Erle, the laborer's daughter, whose life became entwined with Aurora's, was seen as a hunted animal. When her mother is about to sell her to the squire, a man with "beast's eyes," she rushes headlong down the mountainside: "They yelled at her, / As famished hounds at a hare. She heard them yell; / She felt her name hiss after her from the hills, / Like shot from guns." And when she flees from London she uses another image to describe herself: "I think they let me go when I was mad, / They feared my eyes and loosed me, as boys might / A mad dog which they had tortured."

Marian has been a prostitute, used by men and despised by them, and if Elizabeth Browning found her plight embodied in the tortured dog and the hunted hare, another writer, Jean Ingelow, saw woman as a certain kind of horse, not MacDonald's Diamond, strong and ready to pull the heaviest load, but a more delicate and spirited animal. When Jack arrives in fairyland in *Mopsa the Fairy* (1869), he sees a beautiful brown mare lying under the trees. Her groom whispers to Jack that this is Lady Betty and then tells her story in the world of men: "She was a beautiful fleet creature, of the race-horse breed, . . . and she won silver cups for her master, and then they made her run a steeple-chase, which frightened her, but still she won it; and then they made her run another, and she cleared some terribly high hurdles, and many gates and ditches, till she came to an awful one, and at first she would not take it, but her rider spurred and beat her till she tried. It was beyond her powers, and she fell and broke both her forelegs. Then they shot her" (chap. 3).

Lady Betty, like Diamond, is a literary forebear of Black Beauty and his carriage partner, that desperate and tragic animal Ginger. In many ways, *Black Beauty* has always been a woman's book, and I would venture to say, without recourse to statistics or computerized studies, that its effect upon adolescent girls has always been one of unbearable anguish. Generally read at the perilously emotional time when a child crosses the threshold to adult life, *Black Beauty* is a work of inconsolable grief. It is read obsessively, as though it contained lessons which must be learned, no matter how painful. I can speak only from my own experience and those of many other women who have read the book with the same feelings of anger and loss. Over and over again I would turn to the passage where Ginger, the proud, high-spirited Ginger, is dragged past in a cart: "A short time after this a cart with a dead horse in it passed our cabstand. The head hung out of the cart tail, the lifeless tongue was slowly dropping with blood; and the sunken eyes! but I can't speak of them, the sight was too dreadful. It was a chestnut horse with a long, thin neck. I saw a white streak down the forehead. I believe it was Ginger; I hoped it was, for then her troubles would be over. Oh! if men were more merciful, they would shoot us before we came to such misery" (chap. 40).

The lesson that Black Beauty must learn from Ginger's death is that it is useless to strive for independence, for happiness and justice in this world, "for, as poor Ginger said, it was no use; men are the strongest" (chap. 47). Like her mother's poems and plays, Anna Sewell's story is a cautionary tale, but with many differences of tone and intention. If Mary Sewell preached resignation and contentment, there are a number of voices in *Black Beauty* which contend with each other for the reader's attention, and often rage against the existing social order. Quite clearly, what Anna Sewell saw around her was a world without justice, where merit went unrewarded and virtue was of no more account in the order of things than crime. Captain, that fine old soldier, has a splintered shaft run into his side by a drunken drayman, "and a sad sight it was to see the blood soaking into his white coat, and dropping from his side and shoulder" (chap. 44). Merrylegs, the cheerful "little fat gray pony, with a thick mane and tail, a very pretty head, and a pert little nose" (chap. 4) ends pulling a "heavy cart, while a strong, rough boy was cutting him under the belly with his whip, and chucking cruelly at his little mouth" (chap. 41). And the source of all this inhumanity and cruelty can be found in man's authority over society; for every man who shows compassion and kindness, there are ten others who abuse and ill-treat any creature in their charge. One voice in the text speaks for Christian charity and hope, but there is another, more insistent, that says life is capricious, uncertain, and tragic.

Ruth Padel has written perceptively about the sexual ambiguities of Black Beauty, who is clearly not a stallion, so must be a gelding, although there is no explicit reference to castration in the novel.[1] We do have Susan Chitty's assurance that the model for Black Beauty was the Black Bess which Anna Sewell's brother rode to their house every day.[2] On the frontispiece, the novel is declared to be the autobiography of a horse, but it is more certainly that of a woman. Possibly because the persona chosen was not human, Anna Sewell felt free to speak her mind and feelings in ways that would have been consciously censored had she written as a woman. What can be heard in the text is the cadence of an unmediated voice, which is the special quality of autobiography and the sense of absolute honesty that has been known to affect people when they stand at the edge of their own graves. Anna Sewell was preparing herself to make a good death when she dictated the novel to her mother.

If Black Beauty can be seen as the model workingman, it is also possible to see the horse as a woman, graceful, charming, dutiful, and obedient. The horse is described as a regular beauty: "I was now beginning to grow handsome, my coat had grown fine and soft, and was bright black. I had one white foot, and a pretty white star on my forehead. I was thought very handsome" (chap. 3). Merrylegs is another kind of beauty with a pretty head and pert nose, and Ginger rather more aristocratic: "a tall chestnut mare, with a long handsome neck" (chap. 5). Black Beauty has no vices, no failings of character or appearance, and yet he is broken and beaten by men. Now, what is apparent to any adult reader of *Black Beauty* is that the language used to describe the breaking in of the horse is the special terminology of pornography, and of much gynaecological practice.

Gynaecologists strapped women to chairs and tables for the purposes of examination and operation, while footrests, always referred to as "stirrups," were in general use after 1860.[3] And in Victorian pornography, women are "broken to the bit," to use the phrase which John Cleland made popular in *Fanny Hill* (1750). The language of pornography is the language of the stable, with women being made to "show their paces" and "present themselves" at the command of the riding master, who flogs and seduces them into submission. When Dickens describes Lady Dedlock in *Bleak House* (1853), he captures both the character of the speaker and a whole world of sexual innuendo in the space of a few lines: "Her figure is elegant and has the effect of being tall. Not that she is so, but that 'the most is made,' as the Honourable Bob Stables has frequently asserted upon oath, 'of all her points.' The same authority observes that she is perfectly got up and remarks in commendation of her hair especially that she is the best-groomed woman in the whole stud" (chap. 2).

Women are subdued and held by straps so they can be mounted and flogged more easily, and they always end as grateful victims, trained to enjoy the whip and the straps, proud to provide pleasure for their masters. There is an uneasy similarity between the devices made to hold women for sexual pleasure and those tables and chairs, replete with stirrups and straps, which made women ready for the surgeon's knife. When Elizabeth Blackwell saw a woman exposed in this fashion she was appalled, and her sense of outrage was deepened by its unconscious reference to the darkest male fantasies. It is quite possible that Elizabeth Blackwell and Frances Cobbe were familiar with the nature and forms of contemporary pornography; certainly doctors like Blackwell and Kingsford were aware of the implications of the strapped postures imposed upon women in the operating theatre. The same could not be said of the many women who flocked to join the antivivisection movement, women who were moved to tears and anger when they stood in front of a poster showing a dog strapped to an operating table with terror in its eyes. For them, to protest against vivisection (often hysterically, as men frequently noted with considerable satisfaction) was to revolt against a world of male sexual authority which they sensed, even if they had not actually experienced it. With many women the displacement of image and concept was unconscious and all the more powerful because it was never brought into the light of day.

There is surely no need here to rehearse the Victorian admonishments to women that called for obedience and cheerful compliance with the will of men: they can be found in the advice of Black Beauty's mother and iterated at length throughout the book. In Charlotte Brontë's *Shirley* (1849) Caroline Helstone rejects the idea that women should be confined to a sphere of service:

> Certain sets of human beings are very apt to maintain that other sets should give up their lives to them and their service, and then they requite them by praise: they call them devoted and virtuous. Is this enough? Is this to live? Is there not a terrible hollowness, mockery, want, craving, in that existence which is given away to others, for want of something of your own to bestow it on? I suspect there is. Does virtue lie in the abnegation of self? I do not believe it. Undue humility makes tyranny; weak concession creates selfishness. (Chap. 10)

This is precisely the lesson which Black Beauty must learn: to have no will of his own, "but always to do his master's will." And as the author of *The Way of a Man with a Maid* writes, whenever a man encounters a woman, his intention is "to master, to break in, to conquer and to teach." Now in *Shirley*, the heroine, Shirley Keeldar, has an exalted view of her sex which soars far beyond Caroline's plea for freedom; nonetheless she ends being subdued by her teacher, Louis Moore, who expresses his ideal relationship with a woman in this fashion:

> I wish I could find such a one: pretty enough for me to love, with something of the mind and heart suited to my taste: not uneducated—honest and modest. I care nothing for attainments; but I would fain have the germ of those sweet natural powers which nothing can rival: any temper Fate wills—I can manage the hottest. To such a creature as this, I should like to be first tutor and then husband. I would teach her my language, my habits, and my principles, and then I would reward her with my love. (Chap. 36)

If Shirley had rejected Louis out of hand and told him that his principles were better suited to the kennel or the stable, there would not be quite so many unresolved difficulties in the novel. However, Shirley accepts her role as pupil, acknowledging her inferiority with a pitiful appeal to Louis, and calls upon him to "teach me and help me to be good." No wonder that Jenni Calder writes that neither of the heroines, Caroline or Shirley, ever becomes a fully developed personality, for they are nipped in the bud by marriage and the writer's desire to conform to contemporary sexual attitudes.[4] Both women accept subjection, and because the men they choose to marry are so deficient, they are in consequence diminished as women in the reader's esteem. The theme pervades the Victorian novel: Dorothea chooses to marry Dr. Casaubon in *Middlemarch* (1872) and discovers that marriage becomes a mockery once the teacher's inadequacies are revealed to the student; Sylvia marries her tutor Philip Hepburn in Elizabeth Gaskell's *Sylvia's Lovers* (1863) and finds herself "a prisoner in the house; a prisoner in her room."

Even Black Beauty, tractable and loving, regrets the lost freedom that is the price to be paid for breaking in:

> I was quite happy in my new place, and if there was one thing I missed, it must not be thought I was discontented; all who had to do with me were very good, and I had a light airy stable and the best of food. What more could I want? Why, liberty! For three years and a half of my life I had had all the liberty I could wish for; but now, week after week, month after month, and no doubt year after year, I must stand up in the stable night and day except when I am wanted, and then I must be just as steady and quiet as any old horse who has worked twenty years. Straps here and straps there, a bit in my mouth, and blinkers over my eyes. Now I am not complaining, for I know it must be so, I only mean to say that for a young horse full of strength and spirits, who has been used to some large field or plain, where he can fling up his head, and toss up his tail and gallop away at full speed, then round and back again with a snort to his companions—I say it is hard never to have a bit more liberty to do as you like. (Chap 6)

Most painful of all for Black Beauty is the day when he is forced to take the bit in his mouth, and Sewell's language echoes John Cleland indulging himself with female fears of "the bit" and a woman's doubt about "accommodating that capital part of man . . . which does not appear . . . less than a wrist and at least three of my handfuls long" (*Fanny Hill* [1750]). References to "the bit" are a constant in Victorian pornography, used in Cleland's sense, or more literally when a woman must learn to take it in her mouth. And it should be noted that in the fantasies of pornography no woman—unlike Ginger—ever bites. Black Beauty is horrified when the bit is forced into his mouth: "Those who have never had a bit in their mouths cannot think how bad it feels; a great piece of cold hard steel as thick as a man's finger to be pushed into one's mouth, between one's teeth, and over one's tongue, with the ends coming out at the corner of your mouth, and held fast there by straps over your head, under your throat, round your nose, and under your chin; so that no way in the world can you get rid of the nasty hard thing; it is very bad! yes, very bad!" (chap. 3).

Elizabeth Blackwell was affronted by the "indecent exposure" imposed upon a poor woman in the presence of doctors, and Black Beauty felt only horror as the bit was forced upon him, but this is not the attitude of the pornographer as he describes the breaking in of a young woman. Typically, Jack, the riding master, undertakes the task in a stable:

> "Oh! the horse!" Victoria declared in her softly modulated voice when she perceived what stood before her.
>
> "It would not do for you to be thrown by a live one," I observed solemnly while she gazed with some wonder, though not unpleased, at the grey-dappled rocking horse which stood in waiting. . . . It was the largest I had been able to secure and stood glossy in its new paint on its rockers, with a fine saddle and steel and leather stirrups.
>
> Victoria gave a little start. . . .
>
> "Here, of course, we do not ride sidesaddle, for it is considered quite rightly by Miss Hotspur to be unsafe. Young ladies are prone to slide off their mounts in that way, Victoria. If you care to raise your dress and place your left foot in the saddle, I will assist you over," I said smoothly. . . .
>
> "B . . . but sir, I will need to raise my dress too high—oh, pray do not. Oh!" For . . . I had swiftly bent, gathered up the hem of her dress and swept it over her hips, thereby revealing anew to my eyes the lovely lines of her legs. . . . Her round bottom was naked. . . . Giving the horse a further push so that its rocking became for a moment even more violent, I then moved to its head and quickly clipped Victoria's wrist to a pair of manacles. . . .

"Sir, sir, sir, I beg you!" Victoria howled, her voice rising up to a startled shriek as my palm cracked smartly against her bottom.

"*Quiet*, Victoria!" I commanded sternly, "or you will stay thus all afternoon, my girl. . . . So saying, I reached down to her feet, which were gripped uneasily in the stirrups, and drew down upon the toes of her shoes two adjustable metal bars, which in turn served to lock her feet into position so that she could not withdraw them from the stirrups. . . . Giving her no respite. . . . I attended next to the most ingenious of my devices which appertained to the saddle . . . by pressing a button which released a strong spring at the rear of the saddle, that part of it was caused to rise. With its movement . . . Victoria's delightful bottom was lifted upward a good foot off the back of the horse while the pommel in front prevented her from being tipped forward.[5]

Screaming in protest, Victoria is first flogged and then sodomized by the riding master; she ends politely asking for more. Again—and it cannot be emphasized too strongly—this is a male fantasy which is repeated endlessly in later Victorian pornography, and what must horrify any sane reader is its lack of eroticism and its emphasis on cruelty. Straps, ropes, and whips signify the victim's loss of freedom. All that is left for the young woman is to accept gratefully the domination of man and learn to like it, just as Black Beauty must accept the bit without complaining, for "it must be so," as Ginger says: "Men are strongest, and if they are cruel and have no feeling, there is nothing that we can do, but just bear it—bear it on and on to the end" (chap. 40).

When a woman is found to be particularly intractable in Victorian pornography, there is nothing more efficacious than a gang rape, for it is important that she must learn to submit willingly to all men, just as a horse must stand for every rider who seeks to mount it. The lesson is one of obedience, the law of the universe, as the workingman is told in *At the Back of the North Wind*. In *The Way of a Man with a Maid* the imperious Maude is seized on her wedding night and raped by a group of the guests, and when the fourth man has taken her, "Maude it seemed had become quite converted." The effect is always the same: from "rising cries of shame, embarrassment and horror" to "langourous acceptance," the victim submits to pain and authority and is "converted."

The same scene occurs with dreary regularity, generally in a stable, always with the language of horse training. In *Birch in the Boudoir* (1895?) the stable boys at Greystones School regularly flog and rape young women under the narrator's delighted gaze. But in this work, as in so many others, the consummation of masculine pleasure comes when women are bridled and harnessed like horses, and in that fashion seduced. Such brutal intercourse requires a new term, and perhaps it may be more appropriate if it is described as *coitus atrox*, for seduction, and even rape, do not quite carry the ferocity and degradation implicit in these acts of violence. Charles the narrator is enchanted one hot summer afternoon when he finds that the grooms have devised a new mode of *coitus atrox*:

> As I had surmised, the stable was silent and deserted. I wondered where the two grooms might be, and whether they had taken Jackie and Maggie with them. It seemed a day of midsummer madness, when lechery was enthroned in men's minds—and women's too! I remembered that there was a hundred-yard length of chain, stretching down the cliff to a buoy in the shallows, which had to be wound onto the spool of the old mill wheel. The grooms had been told by Miss M. to see it done that afternoon. I went down almost as far as the old miller's grinding wheel, unused for many a day, and stopped short. Nothing I had seen so far on this midsummer day equalled the present spectacle.
>
> The grooms had devised an ingenious scheme for drawing the long chain up the cliff and 'round the grinding wheel, to which one end was already attached. The wheel had a yoke across it, protruding at either side, to which beasts of burden had once been attached. Some means must be found to turn it now, in a heavy two-hour labour. What ingenious fellows they were!
>
> The blond bell of Jackie's hair was clearly seen threshing to and fro as she struggled in their grip. But they bent her forward, leather wrist cuffs and collar holding her down on the yoke bar on one side of the wheel. Once she was bent over so tightly and helplessly, they fondled the fattened seat of her bronze-toned riding jeans only briefly before taking those pants right off her and baring her below the waist. . . . I was delighted to see that they were still not quite satisfied with her predicament. The groom took a false pony-tail of hair, which matched Jackie's own blond colour. Its base was a leather butt, two inches long, and thick as a thumb. Grinning at the young blonde, he showed her a jar of vase-

line, took a blob on his finger, and smeared it thickly on Jackie's arse-hole! Even so, she gave a gasp as he forced the butt in her anus. The tail was drawn up her buttock-crack, under her belt, and then arched in a charming curve, its ends just sweeping the top of her buttocks.

Fifteen-year-old Mandy was strapped bending to the yoke bar on the other side in the same way. . . . The grooms can be rascals, of course, but only in a softly suggestive way. The harnessing apparatus included a thin bridle strap between each girl's teeth, which could not be detached from the rest. To prevent chafing, it was necessary to pad the thin leather.

So it goes on, hour after hour, stung by flies and flogged incessantly, but at the end they are both "squirming piteously with longing over the bar," and the grooms obligingly satisfy their desire. Charlie's account is immediately eclipsed by another of a young school girl, bitted and harnessed, pulling a Turkish pasha in a pony chaise, trotting and stopping at his command and farting in lieu of a post horn. The triumph is complete when women have been reduced to the condition of mares by means of the whip and the penis, and the full satisfaction of this victory is relished only when they acknowledge their degradation. Thus in *The Yellow Room* (1891)—a later edition of 1896 bore the subtitle of *A Problem in Modern Ethics*—young Alice Darvell finds herself the prisoner of her uncle, who begins by flogging her and then straps her to a padded table where the girl involuntarily urinates. This gives Sir Edward Bosmere the opportunity to train his ward in the proper use of language:

> "You are Miss Alice Darvell, and this is your handwriting and signature?" asked he severely, showing the papers to her.
> "Oh yes, uncle; they are," answered the girl, trembling with fright.
> "You pea'd like a mare before your uncle, eh, miss?"
> "I—I—I couldn't help it."
> "Did you?"
> "Y—ye—yes!"
> "Well, you shall be flogged like a mare. Strip yourself." . . .
> At last, raising his whip, as he stood at her left, he said: —"So we 'pea'd like a mare before uncle,' and are now going to be flogged like a mare."

Pornography requires that the victim never retaliate: none of these young women ever really tries to escape, and no one seeks revenge upon the riding master. Ruth Padel argues that the suffering imposed upon women by men in pornography ennobles them, and she takes as her thesis those lines of Wordsworth from *The Excursion* in which the poet moves from a sense of outrage at "nature's violated rights" to an exultation at "a soul / Imparted—to brute matter."[6] This attempt to read a subtext into pornography is strained beyond the point of credibility; what is clear in these novels is the change after the 1870s from earlier pornographic modes wherein a customary trope relates the violated woman's quest for revenge. Certainly, spirituality is hardly the consequence of male aggression in pornography, where the desired effect is to corrupt and debase, nor is it the result in *Black Beauty* as Ginger cries out against her treatment at the hands of men. What amazes Black Beauty is that Ginger can have endured so much and yet still retain a measure of pride and independence. Like the proud beauties of pornography she is broken in by a gang: "But when it came to breaking in, that was a bad time for me; several men came to catch me, and when at last they closed me in at one corner of the field, one caught me by the forelock, another caught me by the nose and held it so tight I could hardly draw my breath; then another took my under-jaw in his hard hand and wrenched my mouth open, and so by force they got on the halter and bar into my mouth; then one dragged me along by the halter, another flogging me behind, and this was the first experience I had of men's kindness; it was all force" (chap. 7). The bitterness of this passage continues as Ginger speaks of her next master: "'A strong bold man; they called him Samson, and he used to boast that he had never found a horse that could throw him. There was no gentleness in him, as there was in his father, but only hardness, a hard voice, a hard eye, a hard hand; and I felt from the first that what he wanted was to wear all the spirit out of me, and just make me into a quiet, humble, obedient piece of horse-flesh! Yes, that is all that he thought about,' and Ginger stamped her foot as if the very thought of him made her angry" (chap. 7).

No woman in pornography ever reacts like this. The riding master flogs his victim into "perfect submission," and her wails and pleas always end in obedience. But poor Ginger is "ruined by hard riding," sold like Black Beauty from one rough master to the next until she breaks down. The two horses meet for the last time at a cab rank in one of the most pitiful scenes of the whole work:

One day, whilst our cab and many others were waiting outside one of the parks where music was playing, a shabby old cab drove up beside ours. The horse was an old worn-out chestnut, with an ill-kept coat, and bones that showed plainly through it, the knees knuckled over, and the forelegs very unsteady. I had been eating some hay, and the wind rolled a little lock of it that way, and the poor creature put out her long thin neck and picked it up, and then turned round and looked about for more. There was a hope-less look in the dull eye that I could not help noticing, and then, as I was thinking where I had seen that horse before, she looked full at me and said, "Black Beauty, is that you?"

It was Ginger! but how changed! the beautifully arched and glossy neck was now straight, and lank, and fallen in; the clean, straight legs and delicate fetlocks were swelled; the joints were grown out of shape with hard work; the face that was once so full of spirit and life was now full of suffering, and I could tell by the heaving of her sides, and her frequent cough, how bad her breath was. . . .

I said, "You used to stand up for yourself if you were ill-used."

"Ah!" she said, "I did once, but it's no use; men are strongest, and if they are cruel and have no feeling, there is nothing that we can do, but just bear it—bear it on and on to the end. I wish the end was come, I wish I was dead. I have seen dead horses, and I am sure they do not suffer pain; I wish I may drop down dead at my work, and not be sent off to the knacker's." (Chap. 40)

Suffering does not ennoble Ginger: she ends as a carcass in the back of a dray, and the reader is left with the despairing knowledge that the authority of men cannot be overcome and that only by death can their tyranny be escaped. An abiding terror remains as the reader is made to understand that it is not really the subjection of women which is desired, but their continued suffering as the ubiquitous Jack makes clear in *The Way of Man with a Maid*.

Pending Alice's re-appearance, I debated with myself the im-portant question, what next should I do to her? There was no doubt that I had succeeded in taming her, that I had now only to state my wishes and she would comply with them! But this very knowledge seemed to destroy the pleasure I had anticipated in having her in such utter subjection, the spice of the proceedings

up to now undoubtedly lay in my forcing her to endure my sala-
cious and licentious caprices, in spite of the most determined
and desperate resistance she could make! And once she became a
dull passive representative of a proud and voluptuous girl, I
should practically be flogging a dead horse were I to continue my
programme.

Jack does indeed contrive new torments for Alice until she is incapable of either resistance or complaint, and then he finds other game.
As for Ginger, she is saved by death, but Merrylegs is last seen being
cut under the belly with a whip as he pulls a heavy cart, his mouth
dragged and torn by the bit. The image of woman as horse becomes
one of the most powerful icons in literature, capable of translation to a
subversive mode of protest against male sexual authority. Thomas
Hardy used it with symbolic import in *Tess of the d'Urbervilles* (1892)
when Tess sets out for Casterbridge with the beehives in the back of
the cart and Prince between the shafts. The old horse plods patiently
through the night, and "Tess fell more deeply into reverie than ever,
her back leaning back against the hives. The mute procession of trees
and hedges became attached to fantastic scenes, outside reality, and
the occasional heave of the wind became the sigh of some immense
sad soul, conterminous with the universe in space, and with history in
time" (chap. 4).

All natural things find their own affinity in this world of dream.
Suddenly the lantern goes out and Tess wakes to a prophetic reality:

In consternation Tess jumped down, and discovered the
dreadful truth. The groan had proceeded from her father's poor
horse Prince. The morning mail-cart, with its two noiseless
wheels, speeding along these lanes like an arrow, as it always did,
had driven into her slow and unlighted equipage. The pointed
shaft of the cart had entered the breast of the unhappy Prince like
a sword, and from the wound his life's blood was spouting in a
stream, and falling with a hiss into the road.

In her despair Tess sprang forward and put her hand upon
the hole, with the only result that she became splashed from face
to skirt with the crimson drops. Then she stood helplessly looking on. Prince also stood firm and motionless as long as he could,
till he suddenly sank down in a heap. (Chap. 4)

The horse speaks for Tess, for her violation while sleeping in the dark woods, for the blood she will shed in revenge, and for her own life. Animal and human are part of the same evolutionary web in Hardy's mind, and all belong to the same "whole conscious world," where pain affects every living thing. Because he understood women so well, Hardy sets Tess and Prince into an imaginative crucible where events in the natural world and human destiny are fused into the same prophetic whole. Animals become reflections and manifestations of people in Hardy's writing, and the horse embodies the plight of both women and working men.[7]

The icon of the suffering and beaten horse remains a constant in the description of women, oscillating between the jubilant metaphors of male authority in pornography and the despairing outrage of imaginative fiction. The realities of social existence were modulated by this perception, and several old Battersea women, when looking back to the time of their childhood, recalled as one of their most poignant and vivid memories, the horses straining up Battersea Rise in the winter with whips cracking at their heads. But when they voiced their remembered pain, were they speaking of horses or themselves? The ambivalence of the symbol did not diffuse its capacity to hold and express the creative impulse, and it continued through into the twentieth century, with a writer like Dorothy Parker using it as an alternative mode of reference for personal grief in several of her short stories.

When Hazel Morse, Parker's "Big Blonde" (1929), sees a carter flogging his horse, which stands with its head down, patiently accepting the blows, she knows that she is watching herself. In "Just a Little One" (1927) the woman sprawled across the bar pours out her loneliness and fear and wants to adopt a horse, "a little horse," like "the little drink" that has become her life and being, and if Fred, her casual acquaintance, cannot care for her, then he will surely help her to care for the horse, which is the only part of herself that she can find to love. Frequently, a couple unable to endure each other or themselves will live compatibly together by transferring their affection to a dog, and in "Just a Little One," with mordant irony, the woman catalogues all the available pets, then settles on a horse as the animal which best embodies herself:

"Do you realize, Fred, what a rare thing a friend is, when you think of all the terrible people there are in this world? Animals are much better than people. God, I love animals. That's what I like about you, Fred. You're so fond of animals."

"Look, I'll tell you what let's do, after we've had just a little highball. Let's go out and pick up a lot of stray dogs. I never had enough dogs in my life, did you? We ought to have more dogs. And maybe there'd be some cats around, if we looked. And a horse, I've never had one single horse, Fred. Isn't that rotten? Not a single horse. Ah, I'd like a nice old cart-horse, Fred. Wouldn't you? I'd like to take care of it and comb its hair and everything. Ah, don't be stuffy about it, Fred, please don't. I need a horse, honestly I do. Wouldn't you like one? I would be so sweet and kind. Let's have a drink and then let's you and I go out and get a horsie, Freddie—just a little one, darling, just a little one."

However, if women pitied horses, and in the case of the lost soul in "Just a Little One," wanted to take one home, there was also a sense of outrage against the riding masters who used women like horses. Anger continually breaks through Anna Sewell's *Black Beauty* and cries out for justice and humanity. The ensuing subgenre of "pony novels" was consumed by adolescent girls with insatiable voracity, and in these stories the image of the horse is used to protest the power of men. Enid Bagnold in *National Velvet* (1935) put a young girl astride the horse and sent her off to win the Grand National, and a flood of novels followed that pattern. If there must be a horse and riders, then the pony novel tells young women that Ginger's acceptance of masculine authority is no longer necessary, and that it is possible for women to assert their own independence and ride the symbols of their subjection to victory.

Just as the horse reflected the condition of women, another image reflected her suffering and the control which doctors had over her body. The vivisector, like the riding master, was to become a recurring figure in pornography and in women's fiction, but with a number of differences. Woman as horse was a creature to be trained and made obedient, but as a vivisected animal, woman was made to satisfy a delight in the spectacle of pain.

Antivivisectionists were appalled by the popularity of those demonstrations which called for animals to be vivisected: "The physiological theatre offers plays that are as exciting, thrilling, and entertaining as any others; there is quite enough of murderous attempts and of struggle for life, and the manager is anxious to bring the best performers on stage. Not a few are rivals, and try to overthrow each other, but that does not make the drama less exciting."[8] When observers like Frances Cobbe and Louise Lind-af-Hageby witnessed these demonstrations, they felt as though they were in the presence of a new pornography, and all the animals stretched out writhing on boards were like women on the gynaecologist's table or bound to some chair devised by the riding master. Why did the language of gynaecology with its stirrups, saddles, and straps, resemble that of pornography? And why were the writers of popular fiction now seeing women as the next experimental subject after cats and dogs? In order to answer those questions we must explore further the course of that subterranean landscape of pornography.

7

A Woman Is Being Beaten

When Victorian pornography is read through a Freudian glass, as Steven Marcus has encouraged us to do, the result is rather like reading Shakespeare retold by Bowdler: most of the original text remains, but the whole is cast into another frame of mind that obscures and distorts more than it illuminates. Marcus emasculates the nature of these pornographic novels by assuring us that they are "a compromise with and a defence against homosexuality" and "nothing more than a representation of the fantasies of infantile sexual life, as these fantasies are edited and reorganized in the masturbatory day-dreams of adolescence."[1] Their harmlessness and essential triviality are assured by their resolution into unconscious patterns of behavior which can be reconstructed only in the course of analysis.

All of us today live in the house that Freud built, even though we may complain about the plumbing and the leaks in the roof. As Gillian Beer states, "It is impossible, in our culture, to live a life which is not charged with Freudian assumptions, patterns for apprehending experience, ways of perceiving relationships, even if we have not read a word of Freud, even—to take the case to its extreme—if we have no Freudian terms in either our active or passive vocabulary."[2] Indeed it would be difficult to deny that our whole mental climate was irrevocably altered by Freud and that we still see the world through his eyes. Freud's perceptions of the sexual and emotional passions of childhood; the reality of the unconscious; the nature of transference and resistance, repression, and unconscious fantasies; and the need to repeat early sorrows are admitted by his severest critics. Even Jeffrey Masson in his recent freewheeling attack on Freud is at pains to indicate these as areas of genuine discovery.[3] And it should be noted that there have been far more stringent criticisms of Freud than Masson's—by Frank Cioffi, for example, who has recently stated: "It has long been apparent to a few free and discerning spirits that Freud's account of his transition from the thesis that at the root of every psychoneurosis was the patient's memory of sexual abuse in infancy to the view that it was rather to be found in their infantile incestuous fantasizing is a farrago."[4]

However, many of Freud's most devoted admirers would admit that when it came to analyzing the nature of women, Freud was as much the spokesman for contemporary sexual attitudes as any other conventional Victorian, to the extent that he was prepared to support the sexual surgery of Wilhelm Fliess, who believed that masturbation in women could be cured by operating upon the left middle turbinate bone of the nose![5] It is not the eccentricity of Freud's views on women which startle a modern reader but their pervasiveness among writers and thinkers of his day. Thus Marie Jahoda, a convinced Freudian, is forced to admit:

> Inevitably one must ask what went wrong in Freud's essay on femininity, and why. Nothing in Freud's life experience, as far as he saw fit to communicate it, points to a personal bias against women. . . . What happened, one must assume, is that Freud unwittingly succumbed to the prevailing cultural stereotype of women, mistaking their historical roles for the essence of femininity. He thought he understood the beginning of their development; he saw in the social stereotype what he regarded as the inevitable outcome; he therefore felt justified in seeking for psychological processes only to the extent that they confirmed the inevitable.[6]

Unfortunately, Freud's hypothesis of penis envy (to the extent that a woman's desire for an intellectual profession is a sublimated modification of the repressed wish for a penis) provided a psychological straitjacket from which women did not free themselves until the middle years of the twentieth century.[7] And when it came to the analysis of sadism and masochism, Freud argued that "sadism has a more intimate relation with masculinity and masochism with femininity, as though there were a secret kindship present."[8] When translated into popular opinion, as all of Freud's theories were, a statement like this can have dangerous social consequences: women enjoyed being slapped and beaten and went out in provocative clothing inviting rape. The difficulty with this part of Freud's thought is that it devolved so easily into the generally accepted prejudices against women, providing satisfactory and seemingly scientific justification for treating them as social inferiors.

Much in Freud's theory of women can be traced to the days when he studied physiology at the Brücke Institute in Vienna, where vivisection was practiced and the unity of science was the goal of doctors who explored the anatomy of animals with scalpel and probe. In his early years as a medical student, Freud had been inspired by Goethe and passed through a brief period of pantheistic monism, a mystical philosophy loosely defined as *Naturphilosophie*, in which the universe and nature were conceived as one vast organism generated from eternal basic conflicts, with conscious mind as the emanation of this turmoil.[9] But *Naturphilosophie* was cast aside in favor of a determinist view of nature and the human personality founded in physiology. Freud accepted the current belief that the formation of the clitoris was evidence of women being immature and undeveloped men, and more importantly, that truth from an emotionally disturbed patient could be elicted only as a result of considerable effort on the part of the doctor.[10] Before a woman could be successfully analyzed, she had to acknowledge her concealed desire for the penis and the futility of her desire to become a man. Woman was inferior because biology had determined her status, and the clitoris was the emblem of her lowly status, living evidence that she was a castrated male. Implicit in Freud's theory of women is the establishment of an authoritarian hierarchy, with the psychiatrist assuming the dominant role of doctor, teacher, and adversary in the battle to reveal the buried truths of the psyche.

Accordingly, Steven Marcus reads Victorian pornography as a form of repressed homosexuality in which infantile masturbatory fantasies bind writer to reader in an endless round of adolescent daydream. But the material does not respond to this mode of interpretation, and all too often Marcus finds himself in the role of the psychiatrist searching for the truths which he himself has buried. We have already seen that this pornography can be defined as *coitus atrox*, a mode of intercourse that is extraordinarily violent and sadistic, employing the birch and the whip, straps and knives, to break in the victim. Marcus states unequivocally that "the figure being beaten is originally, finally, and al-

ways a boy. . . . What has happened in the fantasy to which this literature gives expression is that the erotic zone has been shifted away
from the genitals and onto the area of the buttocks. This literal regres-
sion of interest helps to account for the fact that in this literature,
which was after all written to arouse its readers, the genitals are vir-
tually never mentioned, nor are the usual tabooed words used—these
latter being of course ordinarily associated with genital activity." [11] The
conclusions of Marcus's argument are drawn directly from Freud's essay "A Child Is Being Beaten," in which the following statement is
found: "The children who are being beaten are almost invariably boys,
in the phantasies of boys just as much as in those of girls." [12]

The stumbling block here is that there are conspicuously few pornographic novels in which the main theme is homosexuality. Charles
Reginald Dawes in his study of these writings regards the first pornographic homosexual novel as *The Sins of the Plain; or, The Recollections of a Mary-Ann*, of 1881, and notes the comparative infrequency of
other works of this type. [13] The recurring theme which dominates the
novels after 1870 is the birching and beating of women. It is not uncommon to find works that clearly imitate *Fanny Hill*—for example,
*Eveline; or, The Amours and Adventures of a Lady of Fashion Written by
Herself* (1904), but the narrative voice of a woman gives way in the later
years of the century to someone who can best be described as a riding
master. The eponymous hero of *My Secret Life* uses money to control
and dominate women, often buying an "animal" in the form of a street
woman, and concluding: "Women are all bought in the market—from
the whore to the Princess. The price alone is different, and the highest
price, in money or rank, obtains the woman." [14] But whereas Walter
pursues his obsession with a guinea in his hand, the riding master
uses the whip, and the passion which drives him to frenzies of exer-
tion is not sexual desire, but the lust to dominate, to assert his authority, to control and subdue.

Frances Cobbe located the source of sadism in English life in the
systematic flogging of children. Boys, and occasionally girls, were routinely birched, and Cobbe shrewdly felt that a great deal more than
discipline was involved in this activity. "That odious and abominable
Rod, with its double sting of pain and shame, what a curse it has been
to humanity all down the ages! If it had given no more pleasure to parents and teachers to flog a boy or girl than to dust a bookshelf, and if
no hidden and abominable gusto accompanied the indecent and cruel

act, it is certain there would not have been one whipping for ten thousand which have been actually inflicted." She then appended an illuminating footnote:

> A ludicrous example of unintentional confession of the real feelings of the whipper occurred some years ago in Dublin. A lady told me that she had reason to believe that her little girl was threatened with a whipping at the school which she attended. The lady accordingly wrote to the schoolmistress forbidding the punishment. She received a reply in which the mistress sadly complained that she had "snatched the cup of pleasure from her lips!"[15]

Nothing titillates the riding masters more than the spectacle of a woman being flogged, and they will even travel as far as China for the pleasure of seeing a woman stripped and beaten. The *frisson* of flogging in a boarding school atmosphere of male eroticism could and did lead to homosexuality, but there was an added thrill when the approved disciplinary punishment for a boy was imposed upon a woman. It was not customary to birch a girl across her bare buttocks, but this becomes the inevitable introduction to *coitus atrox* in the pornographic novel and is always described in more salivating detail than the actual penetration. In the following pasage it can be seen that Marcus has misread the content of these novels: forbidden words are freely used, the genitals are mentioned, the victim is unquestionably female, and the import of the action is not homosexual but authority and obedience:

> Getting up he went to a chest of drawers, and, opening one, took out a riding whip. Silently, and notwithstanding her violent resistance, he again got the refractory girl over his knee, with his arm round her, her dress up, and her bottom as bare as her drawers would admit. Across the linen and the bare part he gave her a vigorous cut, making the whip whistle through the air. It fell, leaving a livid mark across the delicate white flesh, and caused a yell of pain. Again he raised it and brought it down—another yell and desperate contortions.
>
> "Oh, uncle, don't! Oh! no more! no more! Oh! I can't bear it. I will be good. I will obey!"
>
> Sir Edward paid no attention, and raising the whip, made it whistle a third time through the air. A more piercing shriek.

"It is not enough for you to promise to obey; you must be punished, and cured of your obstinacy. And you called me a wretch and monster. . . . You shall have your dozen, miss"—swish. "So you liked my tickling your clitoris, did you, better than"—swish—"tickling your bottom with this whip, eh?" . . .

Sir Edward was carried away by the passions excited by punishing this lovely girl, and her yell as the whip again cut into her delicate flesh he did not hear, so beside himself was he. (*The Yellow Room*)

The riding master must first have proof of his authority in the form of a whip and a bound woman before he can pleasurably enjoy intercourse with her. Certainly, he finds no particular delight in women other than as victims. Interestingly enough, before embarking on the longest and most detailed rape in Victorian pornography, Jack in *The Way of a Man with a Maid* provides a rationale for his action, and he cheerfully admits that it has nothing to do with love or desire. His motive is hatred and revenge:

I, the Man, will not take up the time of readers by detailing the circumstances under which Alice, the Maid, roused in me the desire for vengeance which resulted in the Way I adopted and which I am about to relate. Suffice it then to say that Alice cruelly and unjustifiably jilted me! In my bitterness of spirit, I swore that if ever I had an opportunity of getting hold of her, I would make her voluptuous person recompense me for my disappointment and that I would snatch from her by force the bridegroom's privileges that I so ardently coveted. But I had to dissemble.

There are a number of curious evasions and statements in this brief passage: the characters are not individuals but types defined by status; the maid is not only a virgin but a servant who is duty-bound to obey her master and who merits punishment for her disobedience. And, of course, dissembling describes the way in which the narrator will control his reader's response by implying that he is justified in his project. The social implications are evident, for it is not merely the subjection of a woman which Jack seeks, but authority over a whole class.

The incident of a woman being beaten into submission is given added *frisson* when the victim is seemingly a boy who inadvertently is revealed to be a woman. Marcus has written of the ambivalent naming of many of these figures, the Frankies, Willies, Bobbies, and so forth, but the impulse in these cases is not latent homosexuality but overt misogynistic sadism. It was permissible to flog an adolescent boy's bottom, but girls were customarily caned on the hand. So, when a boy is discovered to be a woman as she writhes under the whip, the riding master is immediately absolved from any accusation of brutality, since flogging of schoolboys was considered by many to be the routine duty of a conscientious teacher.

This is the theme of one of the most popular Victorian pornographic novels, *Frank and I,* in which the hero befriends a young waif who calls himself Frank. There is no deep emotional bond between the two as the narrator goes about his duty of training the well-spoken lad; when the latter refuses to copy a manuscript, the narrator decides that a birching is in order. At this point there is only a flicker of narrative excitement as Frank is told that the birch will determine whether he is a coward. The narrator is pleased to note: "He winced at each cut, twisted his hips from side to side, and cried with pain, the tears rolling down his cheeks; but he clenched his teeth, and never once bawled out, nor did he attempt to shield his bottom with his hands. In fact he took his punishment in a plucky manner, considering it was the first time he had felt the sharp sting of a birch. He was not a coward after all." It is this fact which satisfies the narrator, and casually over dinner that night he tells Frank: "You are not the first boy who has had a birching. Most boys get a birching occasionally. They require it. I was often birched when I was a boy. It is nothing when you are used to it."

But what is nothing more than a trifling incident of necessary duty involving a dilatory and rebellious boy is rapture of the highest order when that boy is revealed as a woman. The narrator has set about flogging Frank with his usual stolid satisfaction in a good deed well done:

> I tucked his shirt up and began to apply the rod, and as I was angry with him, I laid on the cuts smartly, raising long, red weals all over the surface of his white bottom. He wriggled, writhed, and cried as the stinging strokes of the birch fell . . . at last he could no longer suppress his cries, and he began to scream in a shrill tone, at the same time putting both his hands over his bottom. I seized his wrists and held them with my left hand, while I continued to apply the rod with a little more force, extorting from him louder screams, as well as piteous appeals for mercy and entreating to me not to flog him so hard . . . I saw the front part of

his naked body. And what I saw paralyzed me with astonishment, causing my uplifted arm to drop to my side, and the rod to slip from my grasp. In that momentary glimpse, I had caught sight of a little pink-lipped cunt, shaded at the upper part with a slight growth of curly, golden down.

'Frank' was a girl! . . . And as I realized the fact that I had just been birching, and that I was at that moment looking at the naked bottom and thighs of a young female, I got a most tremendous cockstand. What a sensitive thing is the sexual feeling, and how quickly it is excited!

In explanation of his remarkable response the narrator blandly assures the reader at various points throughout the novel that "in every one, male or female, there is more or less, a 'lust of cruelty', which shows itself in different ways, in different people." *Schadenfreude*, as Frances Cobbe observed with the verbal reticence of the day, could take many different forms, from flogging children and wife beating to tormenting animals in the name of science. Nonetheless, in "Wife-Torture in England" (1878), Cobbe saw the abuse of children and animals as a less pervasive social crime than the beating of women, and the term she coined to describe the frenzy and anger excited by the spectacle of pain was "heteropathy."[16] However, if the crimes of violence between working-class men and women were declining in the later years of the nineteenth century (and this must be set in the context of a decline in all crimes against the person), there was an extraordinary growth and change in the nature of pornography.[17] In novels like *The Way of a Man with a Maid* the heteropath was able to declare his passion without fear of social restraint, and women existed only to be violated and subdued. We should not forget at this point that pornography was read by the middle- and upper-class male: the price of the pornographic novel, privately printed and circulated, removed it from the hands of working-class men. Just as certain bloodsports had been made the privilege of the few, pornography became the leisure reading of those men with the means to pay for it.

If the abuse of women was now deplored as a social crime to be indulged in only by brutes and bullies, those same men could find vicarious satisfaction in pornography. And that cruelty can be extraordinarily satisfying cannot be denied, for cruelty is the magnifier of identity, a simplifier of social function, and the temporary resolution of insecurity and doubt. It is characteristic of the riding master that he is a self-admitted heteropath and never questions his actions beyond reference to the principle of cruelty: "When you were fastened down on your back with legs tied widely apart, I must confess that the pleasure was the pleasure of cruelty!" Cruelty relies upon a rigid observance of the categorical distance between victim and oppressor, and in the later novels of the nineteenth and early twentieth centuries, the social distinctions are rigidly observed. In earlier novels, servants are always hoodwinking their employers, just as violated women will seek revenge upon their seducers, but this is never the case in these later works. Maids and menservants exist to cook, clean, and pleasure their masters without any sign of insubordination. For example, when the narrator of the 1904 edition of *Eveline* has intercourse with a groom, the language is still that of the stable, but she takes care to address her partner in terms that define their status: "Stop it, Lurkins! You may service me, that is all!" And this at a time when everyone in society seemed to be complaining about the lack of servants, and their general deficiencies, as it became easier for young women to find jobs in factories and offices. By contrast, in the pornographic novels, servants remained obedient and well trained and were never corrupted by democracy, or "ergophobia" (fear of work), as *Punch* generally described it. Indeed, in these fantasies servants are always the first to surrender every part of their anatomy to the employer, as eager to oblige in the bedroom as in the kitchen.

One of the myths arising from this pornography and perpetuated by historians and critics from a feminist like Beatrice Faust to Peter Gay is that the woman is always a willing victim. Faust describes the world of pornography as one in which "women are presented as approaching sexual activity in exactly the same way as men do, living up to masculine fantasies of the sexually assertive, instantly aroused."[18] In listing the components of the Victorian pornographic novel, Peter Gay notes that the woman is always as sexually eager as the male, a willing accomplice.[19] Even such balanced critics as Eberhard and Phyllis Kronhausen characterize the women of pornographic fantasy as "predatory females ever on the prowl for a new sexual partner or a new sexual experience."[20] The myth prescribes a natural progress from willing to grateful victim, but this is not what we find in the riding master's stable. There, by contrast, the excitement of the male is a direct response to the woman's frantic efforts to escape from her manacles and straps. When she is subdued—and subjection is inevitable—the riding master no longer derives any real pleasure from her and uses her instead as a "stalking horse" to search out other victims. Cruelty, according to Jack, is a constant in human nature, and therefore a woman has only to be given a taste for it in order to enlist her in the company of male oppressors. Once a woman has been broken in, she becomes the willing ally of men in trapping and violating other women, beating and birching them as she had been taught. At a time when women were beginning to band together in a sisterhood of common causes, these novels show women eager to become surrogate men in the service of cruelty. Nothing can be more frightful than these surrogates, women who have assumed the role and function of men, and who exist only to subdue and persecute their own sex.

After she has become a grateful victim, Helen asks Jack in *The Way of a Man with a Maid* a question for which he has a fluent answer:

> "And so it really gave you pleasure to torture me, Jack?" she asked almost cheerfully, adding before I could reply: "I was very angry with my maid this morning and it would have delighted me to have spanked her severely. Now, would such delight arise from satisfied revenge or from being cruel?"
>
> "Undoubtedly from being cruel," I replied, "the infliction of the punishment is what would have given you the pleasure, and behind it would come the feeling that you were revenging yourself. Here's another instance—you women delight in saying nasty cutting things to each other in the politest of ways; why? Not from revenge, but from the satisfaction afforded by the shot going home. If you had given your maid this morning a box on the ears you would have satisfied your revenge without any pleasure whatever; but if I had been there and held your maid down while you spanked her bottom, your pleasure would have arisen from the infliction of the punishment. Do you follow me, dear?"
>
> "Yes, I see it now," Alice replied.

The pornographic novel establishes a confederation of male oppression in which women are released to become a Helen Hotspur, a Miss Martinet, Lady Tickle, or Pamela Rumple. Not only do these grateful victims accept a code of sexual sadism, but, like trusties in a prison, or Dracula's vampires, they are the most savage in enforcing it. They live by this code and its language of primitive sexual definition, which they delight in teaching others. Part of the breaking in of a recalcitrant young woman is always to force her to use a language of brute simplicity that restricts sexuality to particular physical actions devoid of emotion or imagination. It is ironic that one aspect of women's liberation in the 1960s was denoted by the use of those same terms which the riding masters taught their reluctant victims by means of the whip and the birch. Pornography, as distinct from erotic writing, exists in the space of restricted language that denies feeling and rational commentary. Essentially it is fantasy that sets up its own reality against the bands of women marching for the vote, militant, assertive women who were challenging male political and social supremacy.

Women who had already secured control of their own earnings and inheritances were now demanding the same political rights as men. The "New Woman" was a frightening aberration in the opinion of a great many men, particularly when a number of their own sex were openly deserting them for the cause of women. The Victorian pornographic novel is an assertion of male authority directed against assertive women and those men like Shaw, Gissing, Galsworthy, Ibsen, and Wells who seemed to have enlisted under a feminist banner. It is the obscenity in prose that was shouted at the suffragettes when they attempted to speak, the abuse that charged feminists with being sexstarved old maids who needed a stick to keep them happy, and in these novels the penis is always another manifestation of the whip or the scalpel. When suffragettes were seized and beaten by police to the approval of a jeering crowd, when they were bound to a stretcher and force-fed through a tube pushed down their throats by a wardress and attending doctor, the fantasies of pornography became fact. Far from being the expressions of infantile sexuality that Marcus would have us believe, these novels challenge feminist demands with the most savage insistence on male dominance. For all humane people, and for women in particular, these are serious and dangerous works.

A recurring figure in the later novels is the doctor who purports to treat his women patients on a couch or table equipped with straps and restraining cords. And in a number of works like *The Amatory Experiences of a Surgeon* (1881) the prose instantly accelerates from its turgid recapitulations when the narrator describes the purpose and function of his couch and the writhings of his patient-victim under the straps. In this area, where the riding master assumes the role of doctor, certain affinities can be seen between the practice of gynaecology and the literature of the antivivisection movement. Jack the riding master is never so ebullient as when constructing a device to hold and restrain his female victims. Not only does he invent these contrivances, he even constructs them himself. So we have him offering the interested reader a model which can be adapted to serve a number of purposes:

> Thus heartened, and whilst Helen settled to her letters, I began my carpentry. . . . By six that evening I had my 'cornering' device installed. It consisted first of a hinged piece of timber some six inches wide by three and a half feet long which could be lifted up and outward from the corner to whatever height was desired. This I afixed to the further right-hand corner of my new Snuggery and therewith attached to the free end of the timber a curved piece in the shape of an outward-reaching half-moon.
>
> The next step was to provide footholds, and these were no less easy to devise. Each comprised two pieces, which, when placed close together, formed the mould of a female foot. The toepieces were secured to the floor some three feet out from the corner. To the rear of these, but sliding in grooves, I fixed the heelpieces, which were thus perfectly adjustable to small- or medium-size feet. The final touches were to add a stout piece of strap on either side of the hinged piece—one of the lengths being buckled— and then wall rings with attendant wrist manacles to the walls themselves.

Having constructed this cornering device, Jack then knocks together an ingenious chair which elevates the victim to any required position by means of levers and straps. With his stable and Snuggery well furnished, Jack is ready to break in any unsuspecting young female.

At this time the trade catalogues for physicians and surgeons were replete with descriptions for the new gynaecological operating chairs and tables, illustrated with line drawings or photographs showing a woman strapped into the position that Elizabeth Blackwell had found horrible and indecent. Johnson's operating chair of 1860, widely used in England and America, is described as "a frame supported on four legs, a shallow stuffed seat and a stuffed back which was maneuverable to various angles by means of a frame and ratchet. It had two attached bars ending in stirrups or footrests, which could slide in and out of a groove, or be removed entirely."[21] A dismountable examining chair of 1878 was even more ingeniously designed with a saddle, stirrups and back support which could be moved to any desired angle. No one would deny the utility of these couches and chairs, but it is also quite apparent that they bear a striking resemblance to the devices of the pornographic novel, not only in design but in the terms used to describe the various parts.

Lautenschlager's *Trade Catalogues of Vivisectional Apparatus* were the major source of equipment for physiologists, and they showed photographs and drawings of animals fixed to boards with straps and cords, together with an array of scalpels and ovens, vices and saws. A photograph of Sir Victor Horsley and Professor Gotch's experiment upon the spine shows a cat stretched out on a table as it is stimulated by an electrical shock.[22] The animal is extended, its legs outstretched like one of the riding master's victims, and it is bound fast by thin leather straps. If the operating methods of the gynaecologist and the contents of the pornographic novel were unknown to middle-class women, they could not have been unaware of these photographs and drawings of vivisected animals. The major antivivisection poster of the 1890s showed a dog stretched out on an operating table, staring pitifully and with terror at the vivisector's hand and the scalpel about to cut into its flesh. This poster was displayed on railway stations and in the journals of the antivivisection societies. When Louise Lind-af-Hageby opened her shop in Oxford Street, she had the model of a dog with its stomach laid open in the window, and an array of similar photographs. There was always a crowd in front of the glass (the scene Patrick White depicts in *The Vivisector*), and occasionally there were demonstrations.

Cruelty is incapable of development; it operates within a closed circle which permits of variation but not change. One quality characterizes the structure and language of the pornographic novel, and that is its monotony. The end is always submission to the will of the oppressor; there may be spirited resistance at first, but inevitably the victim identifies with the riding master and becomes an oppressor in turn. The cycles meet and lock in a succession of orgies where every orifice is entered until the work collapses from inanition. The language is restricted to mechanistic, simple forms with limited connotations, and when metaphors are employed, they are of the most trite and banal kind derived from the kennel or the stable. The pornographic novel creates a linguistic cell—a Snuggery, to use Jack's term—from which light, air, and imagination are excluded as the final act of submission is followed by obsequious gratitude and pleasure on the part of the victim. The structure is always a series of discrete incidents in which a Polly, Jane, Marian, or Victoria is trapped, tormented, and violated. Character exists only in a brief reference to class and age and a slightly more elaborate description of physical and genital characteristics. Color of eyes may not be mentioned, but the tone and texture of pubic hair always merits an adjective or two. Within that enclosed circle the riding master puts one unwilling woman after another through her paces until she rises and stands at his side, a whip in her hand, the shadow of his own self.

When the antivivisectionists began to describe the experiments being conducted upon animals, they found themselves confined to the same circular mode: a dog, cat, or rabbit is strapped to a frame or table, and then it proceeds to suffer. But whereas the riding master's victim screams first with pain and then with delight, the animal is released from its agony only by death. Jack never fails to invite the reader to enjoy the spectacle of the trapped victim: "There, arrayed on the bed, was a truly voluptuous young creature, her arms bound to her sides by two heavy luggage straps. A pink silk chemise enfolded her waist, being wreathed there prettily, the shoulder straps having been loosed and drawn down and the lacy hem well turned up above her naked buttocks. Save for black silk stockings, she was otherwise naked." This is the icon of pornography, the image varying only by name in a cycle of obsessive repetition. Throughout her flogging, the woman does not scream: she howls, mews, screeches, and yelps, for the pornographic novelist is careful to limit the amount of human feeling permitted his victim in her suffering, confining his animal subject in a net of language.

In Louise Lind-af-Hageby's book *The Shambles of Science* there is an unconscious transference between the modes of pornography and narrative exposition. Like the novels, it is a series of vignettes, not of Lucy, Amelia, Emma or Jane, but of a grey striped cat, a rabbit, or a brown dog:

> To-day's lecture will include a repetition of a demonstration
> which failed last time. A large dog, stretched on its back on an
> operation board, is carried into the lecture-room by the demon-
> strator and the laboratory attendant. Its legs are fixed to the
> board, its head is firmly held in the usual manner, and it is tightly
> muzzled.
>
> There is a large incision in the side of the neck, exposing the
> gland. The animal exhibits all signs of intense suffering; in his
> struggles he again and again lifts up his body from the board, and

makes powerful attempts to get free. . . . The lecturer has gone out of the room, the apparatus is ready, the dog will not run away nor will he offend our ears by any loud yelps; besides, if he did try both it would only be rather amusing. It is so ridiculous to see him trying to tear off the strings and to get loose; why, he looks as if he wanted to fly, working his shoulders as if they were wings. . . .

When the lecturer re-enters, the dog's struggles are changed into convulsive trembling of the whole body. This is nothing unusual; the animals seem to realise the presence of their tormentors long before these touch them. Dogs whose heads are covered so that they cannot see will nevertheless show signs of the utmost terror when their vivisectors approach them.[23]

In accounts like these the writer struggles with her anguish as she tries and fails to record dispassionately the scene before her. The language is clumsy but urgent as her rage and compassion contend with the desire to maintain a scientific distance from the subject. And in *The Way of a Man with a Maid* another victim is being flogged:

"*Ooooh-aaah!! Ooooh-aaah!*" she howled at the end of her first gritting screech whilst her hips waved more wildly than ever. "*No-oh! Don't!*"

It was a long, long moment before her hips subsided in part, at least, her hips waggling as do the hindquarters of dogs when they shake off water.

Throughout the antivivisection literature there is a continuing emphasis upon an operating table, and all the devices necessary to restrain and hold the victim. Louise Lind-af-Hageby describes in detail the means used to hold an experimental animal immobile: "An operation-table is carried into the room, on which a grey rabbit has been stretched on its back. Its four feet are tied with strings which are drawn down into slits in the table. The head is partly fixed by some screws, but not sufficiently to prevent the animal from moving it. The throat has been opened, the jugular vein exposed, and a cannula inserted."[24] And Jack giving instructions for another piece of equipment: "I had not finished and went on to explain the rest of my invention which I deemed quite as ingenious as my chair which ensnared and rendered helpless all who sat in it. This device, needing no concealing upholstery, would be rather quicker to make."

Jack describes his "devices" with the same jokey quality that many physiologists reserved for characterizing animal responses in their experiments. This disregard for animal suffering had horrified a great many readers of Frances Cobbe's *The Nine Circles; or, The Torture of the Innocent* (1892), a work in which experimenters could be found describing a dog which had had part of its brain removed as a "Jack Pudding," and a monkey's behavior after its left angular gyrus had been exposed and cauterized and its left eye "secured": "At the end of half-an-hour it was evidently wide awake but would not move unless touched. At this time it was removed from its cage and placed on the floor, where it began to grope about in a sprawling manner, knocking its head against every article in its path."[25] Or here is Louise Lind-af-Hageby recording the roars of laughter and footstamping when an experiment failed: "'I am afraid this experiment is not very successful,' says the lecturer with a sigh, after various other forms of 'stimulation.' Laughter and applause. . . . The dog is shaking the board in his efforts to escape. During the stimulation these efforts have been redoubled. The brute is the only one of the party who is lacking in true humour. But then—he is only a dog."[26] Then there is the humor of the pornographic novel when Dr. Jacobus has "an educated young wife, emancipated and self-possessed," strapped to a table before an interested audience: "'Indeed, gentlemen, in so distinguished an audience as this, there may be scholars who wish to see the performance of such curious acts. It is prudent, then, to have Lesley in a state where she can display any function of her rear anatomy commanded by you.' He then responded to a ripple of amusement." (*Birch in the Boudoir* [1897]). Every indignity is imposed upon this woman to recurring laughter and applause: she is flogged and sodomized and finally taken off to have her clitoris excised to the wild applause of the audience.

The distinction between the vivisector's experiments and the episodes of the pornographic novel is that in the latter there is never any question of failure, for the victims of the riding master always end as lascivious, demonic servants of the whip, but the animals resist to the bitter moment when they are released by death. No woman in these novels ever seeks revenge or death, but the animals claw at their boards until they are chloroformed or dead.

What disturbed Frances Cobbe and Bernard Shaw was the likeli-

hood that some women were being drawn into the antivivisection movement from a masochistic desire to be subdued and made to suffer like
the animals they saw bound to operating tables. And there was the uneasy realization that for some antivivisectionists, male and female, the
contemplation of such material engendered sensations both of gratification and guilt. Peter Gay, in considering pornography, raises "the
vexed question of whether reading is a stimulus inviting imitation or a
catharsis making imitation unnecessary."[27] Certainly, Frances Cobbe
was always seeking to restrain some of the more emotional responses
of women like Anna Kingsford and her spiritualist admirers, suspect-
ing that they were seeking vicarious immolation rather than the release of tortured animals. Bernard Shaw wrote of attending an antivivisection rally at the Queen's Hall in London where "the ladies among
us wore hats and cloaks and head-dresses obtained by wholesale mas-
sacres, ruthless trappings, callous extermination of our fellow creatures," and marvelled that they could be quite so selective in their condemnation of cruelty.[28] For critics like Shaw, Edward Carpenter, and
Henry S. Salt, the claim of being an antivivisectionist without also being
a vegetarian, for example, was to lay oneself open to those charges
of hypocrisy and inconsistency that William Windham had levelled
against the opponents of bullbaiting.

The "grateful victim" was unhappily a social reality, and there were
innumerable women who expected to be beaten by men and who regarded abuse as the price which must be paid for being female. For
women like these, the antivivisection movement was a means whereby
they could gratify impulses they would not have been able to recognize in themselves, or even have wished to acknowledge. They declared themselves to be outraged by the experiments they read about
and saw illustrated in the voluminous publications of the antivivisection societies, but all too often it was not the plight of the animals
which stirred them to such anger, but their own. The issue of women's
rights and antivivisection had blended at a level which was beyond
conscious awareness, and continually animals were seen as surrogates for women who read their own misery into the vivisector's victims.

It is most unlikely that the women, and a great many of the men,
who joined the antivivisection movement or who sympathized with it
had ever seen a pornographic novel of the kind we have just examined.
Pornography was reserved for the rich; the working-class bawdry so
familiar in the earlier years of the century had been driven from the
streets by Vagrancy Acts and the Vice Society.[29] As we have observed,

the twenty-guinea pornographic novel was expensive and difficult to purchase; nonetheless, pornography is our buried river subtly changing the landscape above it. It cannot be described as a collective unconscious, for that is to give it too generalized a sense; rather it is a climate of opinion that is felt without being consciously observed. Wilhelm Reich wrote of the impossibility of changing an ideological superstructure without first altering the psychic structure, but in this case the condition of women and that of vivisected animals was like a conditioned reflex, one image evoking the other even when they served contradictory ends.[30]

Frances Cobbe was always aware of the connections between vivisection, pornography, and the condition of women; so too was Elizabeth Blackwell. But most responded passionately for reasons that ran counter to the basic impulse. These were the women who could sit and applaud a lecturer denouncing the evils of vivisection with feather cloaks around their shoulders and the skin of some slaughtered beast on their feet. It was left for the writers of fiction to make disturbingly clear that when these women wept for tortured animals, they were crying for themselves.

8

The Truths of Fiction

When Emanuel Klein, Lecturer in Histology at St. Bartholomew's Hospital and assistant professor at the Brown Institution, gave his evidence in heavily accented English before the Royal Commission in 1875, the passage of the Cruelty to Animals Act of the following year was ensured. R. D. French is not exaggerating when he notes: "The impact of Klein's testimony upon opinion within the Commission and upon the public, after the minutes of evidence appeared, cannot be overestimated."[1] As late as 1927 Sir Edward Sharpey-Schafer, in the history of the Physiological Society, wrote that Klein's "evidence . . . was unfortunate, for as a foreigner he failed to appreciate the dignity of such a Commission and treated the enquiry with contempt."[2] Brusquely, Klein had told the commissioners that he used anaesthetics on animals to avoid being bitten or scratched, and never to alleviate their pain. Despite repeated appeals from the vivisectors present to qualify and moderate his opinions, he stated bluntly that "just as little as a sportsman or a cook goes inquiring into the detail of the whole business while the sportsman is hunting or the cook putting a lobster into boiling water, just as little as one may expect these persons to go inquiring into the detail of the feeling of the animal, just as little can the physiologist or the investigator be expected to devote time and thought to inquiring what the animal will feel while he is doing the experiment."[3]

The popular press exploded after Klein had given his evidence, and the figure of the archvivisector—a Dr. Benjulia or a Dr. Moreau—was born. Thomas Huxley wrote in fury to Darwin:

130

I have felt it my duty to act as counsel for Science, and was well satisfied with the way things were going. But on Thursday when I was absent at the Council of the Royal Society Klein was examined, and if what I hear is a correct account of the evidence he gave I may as well throw up my brief.

I am told that he openly professed the most entire indifference to animal suffering, and said he only gave anaesthetics to keep animals quiet!

I declare to you I did not believe the man lived who was such an unmitigated cynical brute as to profess and act upon such principle, and I would willingly agree to any law which would send him to the treadmill.[4]

Klein's evidence was to become a set piece in the antivivisectionist attack against the physiologists, but the war was not fought simply by means of pamphlet, poster, and essay; novelists used the special power of fiction to move the hearts of their readers. And at this point the ambiguities that Shaw had discerned in the response to vivisection were revealed with disturbing clarity in George MacDonald's *Paul Faber, Surgeon* (1878).[5] Juliet, the beautiful and romantically frail heroine, is a woman with a secret past: no one suspects that she was once seduced as a young girl. Paul Faber, the local doctor, seeks to make her his wife, but Juliet is reluctant until she sees him angrily drive a young assistant from the surgery for having vivisected a dog. The wretched animal rushes past Juliet in "an agony of soundless horror," and at that moment she decides to accept Paul Faber's proposal, feeling that a doctor who is so opposed to vivisection must be the very soul of honor and compassion.

The day comes when Juliet's secret is revealed, and Paul Faber reacts with a tirade of accusation and reproach. In an extraordinary scene, the prurience that Shaw suspected in some of the more passionate antivivisectionists is evoked by means of the riding whip. Begging forgiveness for having deceived him, Juliet takes up the whip, bares her back and begs Paul to beat her with it. MacDonald, who believed in obedience as the law of the universe, offers a rapturous and revealing commentary:

To me scarce anything is so utterly pathetic as the back. That of an animal even is full of sad suggestion. But the human back! —It is the other, the dark side of the human moon; the blind side of the being, defenceless, and exposed to everything; the ignorant side, turned towards the abyss of its unknown origin; the un-featured side, eyeless and dumb and helpless—the enduring animal of the marvellous commonwealth, to be given to the smiter, and to bend beneath the burden—lovely in its patience and the tender forms of its strength. (P. 242)

In an anguish of anticipation and guilt Juliet begs to be flogged, and all the images of pornography are adumbrated in MacDonald's precipitate language: "When she felt him take the whip, the poor lady's heart gave a great heave of hope; then her flesh quivered with fear. She closed her teeth hard, to welcome the blow without a cry. Would he give her many stripes? Then the last should be welcome as the first. Would it spoil her skin? What matter, if it was his own hand that did it!" (p. 246). Paul Faber disobligingly refuses his wife's request, breaks the whip, and leaves the narrator to lament his hero's pride and lack of feeling. Husband and wife are reconciled only when Faber confides to Juliet that he not only has a mistress of long standing in his own past but a child. Erratically MacDonald shifts between his compassion for the vivisected dog and his obvious desire to see a guilty woman flogged by her husband, between his passion for authority and his concern for the suffering of animals. The result is a work which expresses more by its contradictions than by any narrative statement.

Other novelists inspired by the furor over Klein's evidence found their plots falling inevitably into the moral sequence dictated by Hogarth: the man who could vivisect a dog would unquestionably find his next victim in his wife or sweetheart. In 1881 Leonard Graham published *The Professor's Wife*, in which a beautiful and childlike heiress, Beatrice Egerton, falls in love with Sir Eric Grant, a famous surgeon. Beatrice, who is not remarkable for her mental acumen, is startled when she discovers that Grant is an ardent feminist:

"I ought to tell you at once that I am a strenuous upholder of the rights and the powers of her sex," said Mr. Grant, in his challenging tones.

"You don't mean you are an advocate of women's rights!" cried Beatrice.

"Certainly I am. I shall not live to see it, probably; but if your life is prolonged to the average you will see the disabilities of women removed, and the professions open to them; as they ought to be." (P. 37)

Grant is presented to the readers as a rather chilly apostle of progress, and only slowly is it made clear that he combines his radical views with vivisection and mesmerism. Moreover, despite his public opinions on women's rights, what he wants in a wife is a pretty plaything who will sit on his knee in the evening and prattle. Beatrice is admirably suited to this role and perfectly happy until she finds herself puzzling over a remark Grant makes about his students, who have just given him some china to celebrate his knighthood. Casually, Grant tells Egerton, Beatrice's guardian: "I told them they had much better spend their money buying dogs" (p. 36).

As Lady Grant, Beatrice is blissfully content with her marriage until a stranger tells her of the nature of her husband's research. Horrified, she goes to his laboratory, and what she sees there induces an attack of brain fever and subsequent madness. Grant entrusts the care of his wife to Professor Golbig, a sinister German physiologist based upon Klein. Golbig keeps Beatrice drugged and hypnotized, and in that condition, she slowly dies. Sir Eric is disturbed by the death of his wife, but consoles himself with the thought that he expresses to Golbig: "Yes, we made use of our opportunities; the phenomena were most instructive. After all, the lower animals are unsatisfactory; you learn more by the human subject" (p. 156).

If the connections between sexuality and vivisection were intimated in these novels and others like them, they were made blindingly clear in Wilkie Collins' febrile and complex work *Heart and Science* (1883).⁶ Collins revived his reputation as a major novelist with *Heart and Science*, and we tend to forget that in his own day Collins was reviewed with more serious attention than Dickens. Dickens was the great entertainer, Collins was the critic of morals, often standing aside from the mainstream of popular opinion to castigate social conventions as false, and occasionally depraved. When, for example, people speak of the Victorian predilection for Thomas Hughes' variety of muscular Christianity, they tend to overlook Collins' *Man and Wife* (1870), which was written to denounce the new athleticism in the shape of Geoffrey Delamayn, premier Oxford athlete and dedicated wife-beater. As Sir Patrick Lundie says of Delamayn: "Your friend is the model young Briton of the present time. I don't like the model young Briton. I don't see the sense of crowing over him as a superb national production, because he is big and strong, and drinks beer with impunity, and takes a cold shower-bath all the year round. There is far too much glorification in England, just now, of the mere physical qualities which an Englishman shares with the savage and the brute" (chap. 3).

Like many others, Collins read Klein's evidence and recognized a brute, the intellectual counterpart of Delamayn, but whereas the latter simply got drunk and abused his wife, there was something far more dangerous about a man who publicly stated that he had the right, a scientific right, to inflict pain upon animals. What was denied people by law and public opinion was being demanded as a special privilege by physiologists like Klein, and Collins suspected that the impulses determining this mode of research had less to do with science than with sex. The title of Collins' work in a less inhibited age would possibly have been *Sex and Science*, but what was implied in the title was made quite explicit in the novel.

Collins came to this conjunction of ideas by a very different route from that of Elizabeth Blackwell and Frances Cobbe. Of all his literary contemporaries, Collins had the most extensive knowledge of brothels, pornography, and the seamier side of life. He was the guide of Dickens, a "vicious associate," leading him through an underworld where every vice was bought and sold.[7] Collins enjoyed a reputation for depravity that both offended and gratified his friends, and it was rumored that he secretly wrote pornography. Perhaps because he was so well acquainted with this nether world, Collins came to have a remarkable sympathy for women, and in Collins' novels women are never cardboard dolls but living beings endowed with intellect and passion. He is, above all else, a sexual psychologist of extraordinary insight, questioning accepted social conventions and adjusting traditional characters to reveal a new and frightening landscape of the mind.

Heart and Science was applauded in its own day but has been dismissed by modern critics, who have adopted the condescending manner towards antivivisection that was until comparatively recently a passport to approval among scientific colleagues in academic life. Dougald MacEachen, Kenneth Robinson, and William Marshall all charge Collins with being moved more by sentiment than understanding.[8] Robinson writes that "there is no awareness of the rapidly widening horizons of scientific discovery, only a spurious air of topicality which no doubt impressed the casual reader."[9] Marshall, like Mac-

Eachen, regards Collins as being past his prime at this time, and the general consensus is that "he ventured into an area of dispute, the controversy over vivisection, in which his opinions were based upon sentiment and inclination rather than upon understanding."[10]

Collins had corresponded with Frances Cobbe and received a great deal of material from her; he had also had his manuscript read by doctors of his acquaintance. But to the general charge of being unaware of the issues, Collins made the special plea of the novelist: history and science offer facts; fiction reveals truth. What he was determined to reveal in *Heart and Science* were the sexual imperatives directing the vivisector's hand, even as similar compulsions had led him to describe a Sir Percival Glyde and a Count Fosco. Collins has always been described as a "sensation novelist," but he does not belong to the common run of shudder-and-shriek practitioners. The special quality of melodrama is its vulgarity, its ability to translate action and thought into immediate and accessible emotion. Collins had refined this talent to a point where his characters assume a metaphorical urgency, as though a page of the police gazette were being used as the text for a discourse in moral philosophy. His men and women move mysteriously between startling contradictions and unsuspected coincidence, figures which impose their own shadows onto the clarity of the surrounding circumstances.

The mystery in a novel by Collins does not reside so much in the convolutions of the plot as in the dislocation that results from his characters' inability to read the import of their actions. If not actually drugged, they still contrive to conceal more from themselves than from each other. And this, of course, is the point Collins wanted to make about the vivisectors and a man like Klein: if he knew why he was driven to this form of scientific activity, he would be as horrified and remorseful as the kindly Dr. Jekyll when he found he was inhabited by the murderous Hyde. It is the awareness of the other self which constitutes the moment of discovery in Collins' novels, and in the case of Dr. Benjulia in *Heart and Science*, the man would sooner kill himself than acknowledge the truth.

Heart and Science has a plot constructed after the fashion of a ramshackle mansion, where the improbable is in constant danger of collapsing into the absurd, but the people who inhabit the mansion are more baffling than the secret cupboards and pots of poison. Carmina Graywell, accompanied by her old Italian nurse, Teresa, returns to England to live with her aunt, Mrs. Gallilee, who has a son, Ovid Vere, by her first marriage, and two young daughters, Maria and Zo, by her second. Ovid, a fine surgeon, is on the brink of collapse from nervous exhaustion as a result of his research into "brain disease," and he barely has time to become engaged to his cousin before he is packed off to Canada to recuperate. "Brain disease" was not an invention of the novelist, but an accepted medical ailment which doctors maintained could lead to madness or death. Mrs. Gallilee is a scientific amateur and has a wide circle of professional acquaintances which she cultivates more assiduously than her purse will permit; consequently, she is always on the lookout for a windfall and soon realizes that if her niece should die, Carmina's entire fortune would revert to her.

When Carmina does indeed fall ill, Mrs. Gallilee immediately summons her friend, Dr. Benjulia, a man who practices vivisection in the hope of finding a cure for brain disease. He is delighted to have a subject for research in Carmina and, instead of treating her, allows the disease to progress so that he can examine it. For her part Mrs. Gallilee is quite prepared to use poison if Carmina shows any sign of recovering; at the very least, she will exercise her powers as guardian and prevent the girl from marrying before she is twenty-one. Fortunately, Ovid returns in time to save Carmina with a remedy for brain disease that he had found among the papers of an old mulatto doctor, a man who was a convinced antivivisectionist.

Mrs. Gallilee's scientific interests are not inspired by curiosity, but by a furious envy of her younger sister, Susan. Long ago, when Susan and Maria Graywell were preparing to enter the marriage market, everyone assumed that Maria would make the best match. Instead, it was Susan who married a Scottish lord, while Maria had to content herself with a country gentleman and, after his death, with the amiable but ineffectual Mr. Gallilee. Susan had won first prize in the marriage stakes, and her sister was consumed with jealousy: "From the horrid day when Susan became Lady Northlake, Maria became a serious woman. All her earthly interests centered now in the cultivation of her intellect. She started on that glorious career, which associated her with the march of science. In only a year afterward—as an example of the progress which a resolute woman can make—she was familiar with zoophyte fossils, and had succeeded in dissecting the nervous system of a bee" (chap. 7).

Dr. Benjulia is another matter altogether; his secrets are more deeply buried than Mrs. Gallilee's mean obsessions. He seems a man devoid of feeling, a veritable savage in the opinion of those who know him, and yet he is driven by ambition and his love for little Zo Gallilee. This love is not a conventional affection, and Collins does not hesitate to intimate the precise nature of those feelings and Zo's equivocal response to her doctor friend. Zo is fascinated by the doctor's long, often blood-stained stick:

> Zo ran away with his bamboo stick. After a passing look of gloomy indifference at the duenna, he called to the child to come back.
>
> She obeyed him in an oddly indirect way, as if she had been returning against her will. At the same time she looked up in his face, with an absence of shyness which showed, like the snatching away of his stick, that she was familiarly acquainted with him, and accustomed to take liberties. And yet there was an expression of uneasy expectation in her round attentive eyes. . . .
>
> "Come here, child. Shall I tickle you?"
>
> "I knew you'd say that," Zo answered.
>
> When men in general thoroughly enjoy the pleasure of talking nonsense to children, they can no more help smiling than they can help breathing. The doctor was an extraordinary exception to this rule; his grim face never relaxed—not even when Zo reminded him that one of his favorite recreations was tickling her. She obeyed, however, with the curious appearance of reluctant submission showing itself once more. He put two of his soft big finger-tips on her spine, just below the back of her neck, and pressed on the place. Zo started and wriggled under his touch. He observed her with as serious an interest as if he had been conducting a medical experiment. "That's how you make our dog kick with his leg," said Zo, recalling her experience of the doctor in the society of the dog. "How do you do it?" (Chap. 12)

Typically Collins, it is not how the doctor does it which constitutes the real question, but why he does it. The sexual implications of his behavior are left for the reader to decipher. Even when Benjulia justifies his work to his brother, Lemuel, he cannot see the connection between his vivisections and his tickling of little Zo. The two brothers rehearse the arguments for and against vivisection, and Benjulia praises a man like Klein who has the courage to say that he enjoys his work. Then, with frenzied indignation, Benjulia defends what he does, but there are odd silences and omissions in the man's tirade:

> "Brother Lemuel, when you stole your way through my unlocked door, you found me travelling on the road to the grandest medical discovery of this century. You stupid ass, do you think I cared about what *you* could find out? I am in such perpetual terror of being forestalled by my colleagues, that I am not master of myself, even when such eyes as yours look at my work. In a month or two more—perhaps in a week or two I shall have solved the grand problem. I labor at it all day. I think of it, I dream of it, all night. It will kill me. Strong as I am, it will kill me. What do you say? Am I working myself into my grave, in the medical interests of humanity? *That* for humanity! I am working for my own satisfaction—for my own pride—for my own unutterable pleasure in beating other men—for the fame that will keep my name living hundreds of years hence. Humanity! I say with my foreign brethren—Knowledge for its own sake, is the one god I worship. Knowledge is its own justification and reward. The roaring mob follows us with its cry of Cruelty. We pity their ignorance. Knowledge sanctifies cruelty." (Chap. 32)

Pride and lust govern Benjulia, just as covetousness and spite direct Mrs. Gallilee's actions. His words will find tongue again when Dr. Moreau justifies his experiments to Edward Prendrick.

Animals and their relationship with people are a continuing figure in the novel. At the beginning, when Carmina and Teresa have just arrived in London, there is an instance of casual brutality to a dog. Carmina is followed by the starving animal, and just as she is about to buy it something to eat, it is killed: "The dog, accustomed to kicks and curses, was ignorant of kindness. Following close behind her, when she checked herself, he darted away in terror into the road. A cab was driven by rapidly at the same moment. The wheel passed over the dog's neck. And there was an end, as a man remarked looking on, of the troubles of a cur" (chap. 4).

The suffering of the dog is momentary by comparison with the protracted agony of Benjulia's animals. And it is not only animals and little girls which are the subjects for his research. In one extraordinary scene, Benjulia questions his cook, a handsome woman with a taste for romantic novels, who has conceived the notion that her employer is going to propose to her. She tells Benjulia that she has been reading *Pamela; or, Virtue Rewarded,* a work to raise the hopes of any ambitious servant. Benjulia proceeds to tell her a story about a master and a maid, a Mr. A. and a Miss B., and the cook's hopes rise like dough in a warm kitchen: "If she had seen the doctor at his secret work in the laboratory, the change in him might have put her on her guard. He was now looking (experimentally) at the inferior creature seated before him in the chair, as he looked (experimentally) at the other inferior creatures stretched under him on the table" (chap. 37).

Benjulia's story is a familiar one, and the cook is enraptured. At the very climax of the story, anticipating the proposal, she flings her arms around Benjulia, but he continues with his story as though nothing untoward had happened:

> "And what did Mr. A. do next?" he repeated. "He put his hand in his pocket—he gave Miss B. a month's wages—and he turned her out of the house. You impudent hussy, you have delayed my dinner, spoiled my mutton, and hugged me round the neck! There is your money. Go."
>
> With glaring eyes and gaping mouth, the cook stood looking at him, like a woman struck to stone. In a moment more, the rage burst out of her in a furious scream. She turned to the table, and snatched up a knife. Benjulia wrenched it out of her hand, and dropped back into his chair completely overpowered by the success of his little joke. (Chap. 37)

No pornographer could have written this scene, or portrayed the aftermath when the cook's fury changes to terror as she senses something "superhuman in the doctor's diabolical joy. Even *he* felt the wild horror in the woman's eyes as they rested on him." The riding master's victims never reach for a knife or fly from his presence as though from a devil. But the cook recognizes that Benjulia is a man who can derive pleasure only from inflicting pain upon others. He is a sadist whose sexual drive manifests itself in the calculated ferocities of torture.

At the end, Benjulia realizes that the cure he has sought is now Ovid Vere's: all his work, all the pain and suffering, have been for nothing. Collins then gives us two related scenes: Benjulia has decided to take his own life, but first he goes to the Gallilee house to see Zo. She has gone, and the schoolroom is empty. He takes a single memento from her desk, the torn cover of one of her school books:

> The ragged paper cover of one of these last bore on its inner side a grotesquely imperfect inscription: *my cop book zo*. He tore off the cover, and put it in the breast-pocket of his coat.
> "I should have liked to tickle her once more," he thought, as he went downstairs again. (Chap. 42)

Tickling, in the language of pornography, is a synonym for flogging or sexual intercourse, and we have met the stick before in all its manifestations of whip and male organ.

Having regretfully said farewell to one aspect of his sexual life, Benjulia returns home to its public and conscious form—his laboratory. In the following scene, Collins takes an incident from MacDonald's novel and uses it to express the horror of Benjulia's research and the deeper tragedy of its futility. Benjulia's manservant has followed his master to the laboratory and watches secretly, close to one of the side walls:

> Now and then, he heard—what had reached his ears when he had been listening on former occasions—the faint whining cries of animals. These were followed by new sounds. Three smothered shrieks, succeeding each other at irregular intervals, made his blood run cold. Had three death-strokes been dealt on some suffering creatures, with the same sudden and terrible certainty? Silence, horrible silence, was all that answered. In the distant railway there was an interval of peace.
> The door was opened again; the flood of light streamed out on the darkness. Suddenly the yellow glare was spotted by the black figures of small swiftly-running creatures—perhaps cats, perhaps rabbits—escaping from the laboratory. The tall form of the master followed slowly, and he stood revealed watching the flight of the animals. In a moment more, the last of the liberated creatures came out—a large dog, limping as if one of its legs was injured. It stopped as it passed the master, and tried to fawn on him. He threatened it with his hand. "Be off with you, like the rest!" he said. The dog slowly crossed the flow of light, and was swallowed up in darkness. (Chap. 42)

The manservant returns to the house, but cannot sleep. He continually thinks of the dog and wonders where it can find shelter on a bitterly cold night. He dresses himself, goes downstairs and opens the door.

> Out of the darkness on the step, there rose something dark. He put out his hand. A persuasive tongue, gently licking it, pleaded for a word of welcome. The crippled animal could only have got to the door in one way; the gate which protected the house-inclosure must have been left open. First giving the dog a refuge in the kitchen, the footman—rigidly performing his last duties—went to close the gate. (Ibid.)

Terrified, he steps back as the laboratory explodes in roaring flame and a shower of sparks. Benjulia is dead, and his will leaves everything to Zo, his favorite subject for research.

Patrick Brantlinger has argued that "the sensation novel never challenged the dominance of more serious, more realistic fiction, and sensation authors and narrators seem forever to be backing away from the deepest truths in their stories, abdicating or undermining their own authority."[11] This is not quite the case with Collins in *Heart and Science*. What he accomplishes is a translation of the general repugnance people felt towards vivisection into an abhorrence for the illicit sexual gratification that the vivisector derived from his work. It is not a reasoned argument against using animals for experimental purposes—other novelists were to attempt that in laborious and statistical detail—but a delineation of feeling. Few had actually witnessed the experiments in a physiology laboratory, although many suspected them to be horrors of unimaginable cruelty. Collins is careful never to describe an experiment, deflecting the existing emotional response from the subject to the figure of the vivisector—and it is not what the vivisector does that is so appalling, but what he is as a man.

The real terror in *Heart and Science* is not in the locked and secret laboratory but in the mind of Benjulia, a man who tickles little girls and tortures animals. This is the psychological truth elicited from emotion which Collins valued more than the profit-and-loss arguments of the antivivisectionists. Certainly, Benjulia took his place in popular consciousness, and he can be found in Dr. Moreau and the popular belief in 1888 that Jack the Ripper was a vivisecting surgeon of London University who had extended his research from dogs to prostitutes.

When the curator of the Medical Museum of London University received a kidney in the post which was almost certainly removed from
one of the murdered victims of Jack the Ripper, there were sporadic
riots outside the hospital, and doctors were jostled. The working-class
fear of vivisection was inflamed by rumors that the murderer was a
surgeon taking out his revenge on prostitutes for having infected his
son with venereal disease.[12] And there was a long working-class tradition for regarding doctors as enemies "who preyed, for personal profit
and success, on their helplessness and destitution."[13] What could be
found in these demonstrations was the feeling that the vivisector had
links with sexuality and death, a point that Edward Berdoe stressed in
his romans à clef, St. Bernard's: The Romance of a Medical Student
(1887) and Dying Scientifically: A Key to St. Bernard's (1888).

Berdoe was a doctor with impeccable credentials: he was a Member of the Royal College of Surgeons, Licentiate of the Society of
Apothecaries, Member of the British Medical Association, and a Gold
Medallist in Medicine and Medical Scholar of the London Hospital—
but he belonged to the old school which maintained that clinical observation was more important than animal research. In his later years
Berdoe was to write that "in our great general hospitals to which medical schools are attached, the healing of the patients is made subordinate to the professional advantage of the medical staff and the students."[14] James Turner says that Berdoe "lived mentally in the first half
of the century"; at best he was regarded by his younger colleagues as a
blethering old idiot.[15] Nonetheless, Berdoe acquired a small reputation
as a novelist with the popular St. Bernard's—and Berdoe's delination
of that grisly institution became the prototype for all those hospitals
where medicine serves doctors at the expense of the patients.[16]

Harrowby Elsworth, an idealistic young man, has distinguished
himself at Oxford and becomes a medical student at St. Bernard's, a
large metropolitan hospital. There he soon encounters the sinister
Dr. Malthus Crowe, lecturer in physiology, who embodies Sir Astley
Cooper's remark that "the art of medicine is founded on conjecture and
improved by murder" (p. 333). His porters are accomplished dog stealers and no less malefic than their master: "They were scarred and fur-
rered about the hands and arms with bites, cuts, and scratches, which
had healed badly, and to the skilled observer sufficiently stamped them
with the trade mark of the hospital" (p. 199). Crowe's assistant and de-
monstrator is Mr. Mole, a suspicious and ambitious young physiologist
who yearns for the day when he will have Crowe's position.

The plot moves into an Hogarthian configuration that will be repeated in all the fictional studies of vivisection. It is not enough that Crowe tortures dogs and uses charity patients for experimental research; he is also, like Tom Nero, a murderer whose victim is his hapless but wealthy wife. Slowly Crowe distills a poison from toadstools (having first made sure of its lethal potency on some dogs and a couple of old patients) and then prescribes it as a tonic for his wife's "nerves." She dies in agony, but the crime does not go undetected, for Mole has made it his business to become friendly with the maid, Janet Sprigg, and from her he discovers the truth. He sets out the evidence before his master and blackmails him into retiring after he has recommended Mole for the position of lecturer in physiology. Always it is the wife who is the vivisector's unsuspecting victim, a narrative progression which becomes an inevitable trope in works of this kind. *St. Bernard's* enjoyed a tremendous success with its revelations of medical malfeasance, and it was helped too by the publicity of Jack the Ripper and the Whitechapel murders. Harrowby, of course, forsakes St. Bernard's and founds a Nightingale hospital in Spain with a young nurse who has also left London in despair of being able to change the way patients are treated at St. Bernard's. So influential was Berdoe's novel and its sequel that a Society for the Protection of Hospital Patients was founded in 1897.

Novel followed novel with a similar theme: the vivisector's wife is first driven mad and then used for purposes of research. Barry Pain, a very prolific author indeed, provided a slight variation in 1897 with *The Octave of Claudius*. Dr. Lamb has already driven his wife, Hilda, insane when he proposes a particular experiment to Claudius Sandell: he will have eight days with a thousand pounds a day to spend; then he must submit to an experiment which will cost him fifty seconds of pain and his life. With a lot of luck and at the expense of a very fragile plot, Claudius manages to outwit the fiendish vivisector, keeping both the money and his life.

Hogarth's progression from cruelty to animals to the murder of women was consistently used as a theme by male novelists, however, there was a significant difference when the writer was female. Marie Daal's *Anna, the Professor's Daughter*, translated into English in 1885, included all the customary antivivisection themes, but Daal does not show her heroine succumbing to madness and death. The vivisector can be resisted: Anna helps to reform the brutish Herman, and only when he has renounced his callous attitude to animals does she agree to marry him.[17] This revision of the Hogarthian narrative becomes a dominant theme when the novelist is a feminist like Sarah Grand.

Sarah Grand, whose real name was Frances Elizabeth Clarke McFall, was born in 1854 and at sixteen married Surgeon-Major David Chambers McFall of the Royal Irish Fusiliers, a man twenty years her senior. That the marriage was a dismal experience for the young woman can be readily deduced from a succession of novels she wrote in which artless girls are married off to soldiers or doctors and suffer miserably. Like a handful of desperate young women she determined to achieve independence with her pen, and by 1898, when her husband died, and a year after the publication of *The Beth Book*, Sarah Grand was recognized as one of the most successful novelists of the day. "The Grand Sarah," as she was known, had written her autobiography in *The Beth Book*: the record of her victory over poverty, a scanty education, and marriage to a man of ineffable stupidity and selfishness.[18]

From the days of her childhood Beth is heir to the traditions of subservience and violence that afflicted so many women; she is regularly beaten by her mother, and a little money set aside for her education is used instead to provide her brother with an allowance. She knows at an early age what constitutes a woman's sphere, and the language that defines it: "She all but perceived that the woman's sphere is never home exclusively when man can make use of her for his own purposes elsewhere. The sphere is the stable he ties her up in when he does not want her, and takes from again to drag him out of a difficulty or up to some distinction, just as it suits himself" (p. 261).

Despite a toughness of mind and considerable shrewdness, Beth cannot avoid her fate, which is to be married off to the first man who can support her. This happens to be Dr. Daniel Maclure, a man more remarkable for the whiteness of his teeth than for any other attribute. From this point on, Beth unconsciously confounds all the rules of the riding master and the stable. As we have seen, one of the first and most humiliating burdens imposed on a woman is the language of the stable. In the later works of pornography, there is one set scene which seldom varies from novel to novel: a young girl is made to speak words which, if she hesitates to voice them, she will then be made to write out like a school lesson after a good birching. When Dan attempts to make Beth use this language she refuses angrily:

> He made remarks about the faces and figures of all the women they passed on the road, criticizing them as if they were cattle to be sold at so much a point.

"That little girl there," he said of one of them, whom he beamed upon and ogled as they passed, "reminds me of a fair-haired little devil I picked up one night in Paris. Gad! she *was* a bad un! up to more tricks than any other I ever knew. She used to—" (here followed a description of some of her peculiar practices).

"I wish you would not tell me these things," Beth remonstrated.

But he only laughed. "You know you're amused," he said. "It's just your conventional affectation that makes you pretend to object. That's the way women drive their husbands elsewhere for amusement; they won't take a proper intelligent interest in life, so there's nothing to talk to them about. I agree with the advanced party. They're always preaching that women should know the world. Women who *do* know the world have no nonsense about them, and are a jolly sight better company than your starched Puritans who pretend to know nothing. It's the most interesting side of life after all, and the most instructive; and I wonder at your lack of intelligence, Beth. You shouldn't be afraid to know the natural history of humanity."

"Nor am I," Beth answered quietly; "nor the natural—or unnatural—depravity either, which is what you really mean, I believe. But knowing it, and delighting in it as a subject of conversation, are two very different things. Jesting about that side of life affects me like mud on a clean coat." (Pp. 348–49)

Beth finds it difficult to tolerate her husband's position as superintendent of a lock-hospital—an institution for the confinement of women with venereal disease. Lock-hospitals had been denounced by the repealers of the Contagious Diseases Acts as squalid prisons where the inmates were treated more harshly than violent criminals, and any hospital which had once been a lock institution found it difficult to erase the obloquy attached to such a place. What finally convinces Beth that she must leave her husband or go mad is not his work as a lock doctor but the discovery that he is a vivisector. For weeks she has felt like an animal strapped to a frame, struggling to escape, wondering whether to confront her husband publicly with his philandering or simply take refuge in the irresponsibility of madness. And the attraction of the latter is strengthened by her realization that it would be socially acceptable for her to go mad; it was, after all, a condition that could befall any nervous and intelligent young woman chafing against domestic restraints:

The words, when they recurred to her, were a revelation. What had she been doing all day? Mad things! What was this sudden haunting horror that had seized upon her? Why, madness! Dan was just as he had always been. The change was in herself, and only madness could account for such a change. There was madness in the family. She remembered her father and the "moon-faced Bessie"—the familiarities with servants too; surely her mother had suffered, and doubtless this misery which had come upon her had been communicated to her before her birth. (P. 429)

Desperately Beth fights against the creeping affliction, but she can feel herself becoming more painfully bound than ever to a man whom she despises. Then one evening Dan arrives home with a small terrier that he says must have followed him in from the street. Beth remarks on its breeding and intelligence and thinks no more of it. Late that night she is reading when she hears what at first seems to be a human voice at the extremity of pain. It is coming from the surgery, and Beth immediately suspects that some sick person has been inadvertently locked in there. She goes downstairs, lights the candles, and at first she can see nothing untoward in the cluttered room except a table covered with a calico sheet.

> Beth, checked again in her search, was considering what to do next, when the horrid cry was once more repeated. It seemed to come from under the calico sheet. Beth lighted the gas, put down her candle, and saw a sight too sickening for description. The little black-and-tan terrier, the bonny wee thing which had been so blithe and greeted her so confidently only the evening before, lay there, fastened in a sort of frame in a position which alone must have been agonising. But that was not all.
> Beth had heard of these horrors before, but little suspected they were carried on under that very roof. She had turned sick at the sight, a low cry escaped her, and her great compassionate heart swelled with rage; but she acted without hesitation.
> Snatching up her candle, she went to the shelves where the bottles were, looked along the row of red labels, found what she wanted, went back to the table, and poured some drops down the poor little tortured creature's throat.
> In a moment its sufferings ceased.
> Then Beth covered the table with the calico sheet mechanically, put the bottle back in its place, turned out the gas, and left

the room, locking the door after her. Her eyes were haggard and her teeth were clenched, but she felt the stronger for a brave determination, and more herself than she had done for many months. (P. 437)

Beth has seen herself in the vivisected animal, but she does not suffer brain disease in consequence or collapse into incurable madness; rather, she knows that she must escape from the marriage even as she has given the dog its release from pain. Dan attempts to bluster, to justify his research, but Beth has seen too much: Dan the philanderer and Dan the vivisector are aspects of the same unsavory individual. It is not a man of science that Beth reviles, but the riding master who violates the pride and mutilates the bodies of women. At first Dan tries to play the traditional role of master in the house:

> "You killed that dog, then!" he exclaimed, turning on her savagely. "How dare you?"
> "How dare *you?*" she inquired.
> "How dare I, indeed, in my own house!" he bawled. "Now, look here, madam, I'm not going to have any of your damned interference, and so I tell you."
> "Please, I am not deaf," she remonstrated gently. "And now, look here, sir, I am not going to have any of your *damnable* cruelties going on under the same roof with me. I have endured your sensuality and your corrupt conversation weakly, partly because I knew no better, and partly because I was the only sufferer, as it seemed to me, in the narrow outlook I had on life until lately; but I know better now. I know that every woman who submits in such matters is not only a party to her own degradation, but connives at the degradation of her whole sex." (P. 439)

Dan tries to pose next as the man of science using experimental vivisection in a disinterested pursuit of knowledge, but this argument falters when he realizes that Beth is aware of the properties of curare. What she next charges him with is the observation made by Collins and writers like Cobbe and Kingsford: the vivisector enjoyed the pain he inflicted upon animals, and in Dan's case, since he would not dare try and beat a woman like Beth, he was venting his frustrated rage upon her surrogate. Beth knows this, but her awareness does not make her afraid of Dan, it merely convinces her that she is married to a moral delinquent who should be a social outcast:

"I cannot understand any but unsexed women associating with vivisectors. Don't pretend you pursue your experiments reluctantly—you delight in them. But, whatever the excuse for them, I am sure that the time is coming when the vivisector will be treated like the people who prepared the dead for embalming in ancient Egypt. You will be called in when there is no help for it; but your task accomplished, you will be driven out of all decent society, to consort with the hangman—if even he will associate with you." (P. 441)

After these passionate accusations an extraordinary change takes place in the marriage. Beth is already planning to leave Dan, but before she goes, it is as though she has become the vivisector, examining her husband with cool detachment as a subject for research. She does not need curare, straps, and scalpels to enable her to see the innermost workings of Dan's nature:

Now she knew him for what he was exactly—shallow, pretentious, plausible, vulgar-minded, without principle; a man of false pretensions and vain professions; utterly untrustworthy; saying what would suit himself at the moment, or just what occurred to him, not what he thought, but what he imagined he was expected to do. Beth had never heard him condemn a vice or habit which she did not afterwards find him practising himself. She used to wonder if he deceived himself, or was only intent on deceiving her; but from close observation of him at this period, she became convinced that, for the time being, he entered into whatever part he was playing, and hence his extreme plausibility. Beth found herself studying him continually with a curious sort of impersonal interest; he was a subject that repelled her, but from which, nevertheless, she could not tear herself away. His hands in particular, the handsome white hands, had a horrid sort of fascination for her. She had admired them while she thought of them as the healing hands of the physician, bringing hope and health; but now she knew them to be the cruel hands of the vivisector, associated with torture, from which humanity instinctively shrinks; and when he touched her, her delicate skin crisped with a shudder. She used to wonder how he could eat with hands so polluted, and once, at dessert, when he handed her a piece of orange in his fingers, she was obliged to leave it on her plate, she could not swallow it. (P. 445)

The Hogarthian association of vivisection and women was still explicit in works like *The Beth Book*, but the relationship was different: the wife no longer became the victim of inevitable madness but instead resisted her oppressor with intelligence and determination. John Galsworthy always saw the potential wife-beater in a vivisector and frequently described Irene Forsyte, "Soames' wife, in *The Man of Property* (1906), as a wounded animal. The marriage has broken, Irene is unfaithful, but Soames cannot let her go: "Many people, no doubt, including the editor of the 'Ultra Vivisectionist', then in the bloom of its first youth, would say that Soames was less than a man not to have removed the locks from his wife's doors, and after beating her soundly resumed wedded happiness" (pt. 3, chap. 1). Like Beth, Irene is prepared to risk poverty and disgrace rather than endure a wretched marriage, and because she will not submit to Soames' authority, she succeeds. This was the response to the pornography of the riding master and his victims, and increasingly it was to challenge the male fantasies of aggression and power.

The New Woman did not go mad and refused to become a victim, but it was H. G. Wells who gave the icon of woman and vivisected animal its most terrifying accent. This was all the more remarkable since, although Wells was a feminist, he was not opposed to vivisection. Indeed, he was a member of the Research Defence Society, but in the latter years of the nineteenth century he had been troubled by the nature of so much physiological research: animals were being subjected to bizarre transplants, extra tails implanted on rats, a cat's leg sewn onto the stump of a dog's limb. Then too, he had heard Thomas Huxley's Romanes Lecture of 1894, "Evolution and Ethics," in which Huxley had spoken of suffering as "the badge of all the tribe of sentient things, attaining to its highest level in man."[19] In consequence, ethical progress could only be made, not through an imitation of the cosmic process, still less by evading it, but by combating it with all the strength of man's moral energy.[20] Nature had decreed that pain should be the law of the universe, but man's noblest creation, ethics, imposed justice and order upon life. From this contest between nature and ethics Wells created *The Island of Dr. Moreau* (1896), and the Hogarthian icon was dramatically and irrevocably changed.

When Edward Prendrick is cast ashore on the strange island ruled by Dr. Moreau, he finds it inhabited by disturbing creatures which seem human and yet remind him of animals. Immediately his curiosity is aroused, for Prendrick is not the ordinary traveller but a biologist who had studied for some years under Huxley. He suspects that Moreau is the notorious physiologist who had been driven out of England some years previously because of his research into morbid growths. A pamphlet had been published about his activities, and on "the day of its publication, a wretched dog, flayed and otherwise mutilated, escaped from Moreau's house" (chap. 7). Even Moreau's fellow investigators had denounced him from amidst the public outcry, and the vivisector suddenly vanished from England. Prendrick now knew where Moreau had found refuge and a place to continue his research.

Montgomery, Moreau's assistant, has brought several animals to the island, including a puma, and now Prendrick hears this animal shrieking in pain from the laboratory. Its cries are so terrible that Prendrick takes refuge in the forest, where he finds the vivisector's creations, animals surgically transformed into the semblance of human beings. They have been taught to obey Moreau as a god, a god who presides over the antiseptic hell of his laboratory, the House of Pain. Several days pass, and the cries from the puma have begun to change; Prendrick recognizes the voice of a human being:

> After a long pause I resumed my meal, but with my ears still vigilant. Presently I heard something else very faint and low. I sat as if frozen in my attitude. Though it was faint and low, it moved me more profoundly than all that I had hitherto heard of the abominations behind the wall. There was no mistake this time in the quality of the dim broken sounds, no doubt at all of their source; for it was groaning, broken by sobs and gasps of anguish. It was no brute this time. It was a human being in torment!
>
> And as I realized this I rose, and in three steps had crossed the room, seized the handle of the door into the yard, and flung it open before me.
>
> "Prendrick, man! Stop!" cried Montgomery, intervening.
>
> A startled deerhound yelped and snarled. There was blood, I saw, in the sink, brown, and some scarlet, and I smelt the peculiar smell of carbolic acid. Then through an open doorway beyond, in the dim light of the shadow, I saw something bound painfully upon a framework, scarred, red, and bandaged. And then blotting this out appeared the face of old Moreau, white and terrible.
> (Chap. 10)

When Moreau sees fit to explain his research, it is as though he had taken Huxley's Romanes Lecture and turned it inside out, declaring that "to this day I have never troubled about the ethics of the matter.

The study of Nature makes a man at last as remorseless as Nature. I have gone on, not heeding anything but the question I was pursuing" (chap. 14).

There is an insidious appeal to Moreau's reasoning that begins to affect Prendrick, who finds that he is slowly accepting the research and its creations. Prendrick is proof of all the antivivisectionist arguments that people who are forced to participate in acts of cruelty or who watch scenes of torture will lose all sense of compassion and pity, becoming dead to feeling. It has even become possible for him to endure the daily tormented shrieks of the puma:

> So indurated was I at that time to the abomination of the place, that I heard without a touch of emotion the puma victim begin another day of torture. It met its persecutor with a shriek almost exactly like that of an angry virago.
>
> Then something happened. I do not know to this day what it was exactly. I heard a sharp cry behind me, a fall, and, turning, saw an awful face rushing upon me, not human, not animal, but hellish, brown, seamed with red branching scars, red drops starting out upon it, and the lidless eyes ablaze. I flung up my arm to defend myself from the blow that flung me headlong with a broken forearm, and the great monster, swathed in lint and with red-stained bandages fluttering about it, leapt over me and passed. (Chap. 17)

It is no ordinary woman who breaks her bonds and rages forth to destroy the vivisector, but a virago trailing bloody rags as proof of her sex. And the virago will not rest until she has killed the vivisector who has tortured and maimed her in the name of science. All the themes of women, vivisection, and animals are drawn together in this explosive and prophetic image of anger and revenge: in the realm of fiction, the victory clearly belonged to the woman and puma who destroyed Dr. Moreau. But even though fiction may reveal truths, those truths are often defined more by aspiration than actuality. We must now return to the world of known things and meet the real victors in this contest.

9

The New Priesthood

On the thirteenth of January 1908, Stephen Paget arrived at the Battersea Town Hall and roundly denounced the benighted sentimentality of those who had sanctioned an inflammatory and libellous inscription on the brown dog memorial fountain. He was met with jeers and groans from the audience, a fight broke out between the Battersea men and a group of students who had infiltrated the meeting, and his motion was ignominiously lost. Yet he stood there as a spokesman for the victorious party, the apostle of the new priesthood. The term was not used lightly at the time, for it was disturbingly clear to many that moral authority was passing from men of church and state to those who spoke for science and medicine.[1] A little more than thirty years before, in March 1876, Frances Cobbe had founded the Society for the Protection of Animals Liable to Vivisection (always known as the Victoria Street Society), and it seemed then as though the intellectual and aristocratic strength of England was standing with her. Tennyson, Carlyle, Manning, Browning, Jowett, Collins, Sir John Coleridge (the lord chief justice of England), the lord mayor of London, and the Earl of Shaftesbury led a splendid group of more than eighteen admirals and generals, seventeen bishops and archdeacons, forty-three peers and those of lesser rank, and twenty-six members of Parliament.[2] Now at the turn of the century, Frances Cobbe was dead, and the president of the Victoria Street Society, Stephen Coleridge, could not hope to muster such a magnificent assembly. As R. D. French has so ably demonstrated, the medical profession had become one of the most powerful groups in English society, and it was pledged to vivisection as a necessary part of scientific research. If faith in God and his Christian churches was waning throughout society, a fervent secular belief in science was rapidly taking its place.

Darwin and Huxley had both supported vivisection, and in its first years the Research Defence Society was able to number Arthur Conan Doyle and H. G. Wells among its members: as a doctor, Doyle was unwilling to oppose the members of his first profession even though he had a great love for animals. Not one writer of note had been in favor of vivisection fifty years earlier: G. H. Lewes was singular in his espousal of vivisection and was frequently criticized for his beliefs, publicly on one occasion by Matilda Tennyson.[3] It is true that George Eliot endowed a fellowship in physiology at Cambridge after Lewes' death, but she was never a proponent of vivisection, and the fellowship was more in honor of her husband than his subject. By 1900 the antivivisectionists were on the defensive and unable to deny that animal experimentation was providing one of the most significant modes of medical research. The attempts of writers like Edward Berdoe and Robert Hadwen to discredit the discoveries of Pasteur and Claude Bernard were not particularly successful. In many ways they sounded like voices from the past, recalling the efforts of Bishop Wilberforce and his followers to repudiate evolutionary theory by proving the historical and factual accuracy of Genesis. It was increasingly clear that the germ theory of disease had been proven by men like Pasteur, Villemin, Koch, and Cohn, who had all used animals experimentally. If proof were needed for the intellectual ascendance of the vivisectionist cause, it was apparent in the choice of Stephen Paget to write on that subject for the 1909 edition of the *Encyclopaedia Britannica*.[4]

Had the vivisectionists' findings alone been called upon to provide justification for the practice, their opponents would still have found it difficult to gainsay the evidence of improved methods in surgery and medical science. However, without any reference to the benefits involved, it was now clear that vivisection had a spokesman whose eloquence and moral fervor rivaled the philosophers and sages of the period. Claude Bernard was not only the foremost physiologist of the nineteenth century but also the founder of a new faith which promised mankind the paradise of perfect health. Faith in Christianity could give the believer everlasting life: Bernard maintained that by means of vivisection the day would come when men would have the power to alter and change the very process of life itself. "It is not given to man to alter the cosmic phenomena of the whole universe nor even those of the earth; but the advances of science enable him to alter the phenomena within his reach. Thus man has already gained a power over mineral nature which is brilliantly revealed in the applications of modern science, still at its dawn. The result of experimental science applied to living bodies must also be to alter vital phenomena, by acting solely on the condition of these phenomena" (p. 114).[5] Humanity would eventually be raised to the power of divinity, and men would be truly gods. Lewes, like many of his contemporaries, was enthralled by the soaring prophecies which he sensed in Bernard's writings and the promise that man would one day free himself from his evolutionary fate and set about "teaching nature a new lesson."[6]

What exhilarated Lewes and many others appalled some. The de Goncourt brothers recorded in their journal:

> Claude Bernard for his part was reported to have announced that after a hundred years of physiological science, one would be able to make laws for organisms and carry out human creation in competition with the Creator himself.
>
> We made no objection, but we do believe that when science has reached that point, the good Lord with the white beard will arrive on earth with his key-chain and tell mankind, just as they do at the Art Show at five o'clock: "Gentlemen, it is closing time!"[7]

It was not difficult to find a place for God in Darwin's universe, but this was unnecessary in Bernard's world laboratory; all man required was a little more time, and God would be as redundant as the dodo.

Darwin's *Origin of the Species* (1859) established man's place in the animal world, where, like his fellow creatures, he was regulated by an evolutionary process. It was obvious that humanity had fought its way to a place of eminence in the long struggle to survive on earth, but it was still bound by the inescapable laws of natural selection. Bernard's *Introduction to the Study of Experimental Medicine* (1865) did not expound any aspect of evolutionary theory; rather, it seemed as though Bernard had chosen to regard Darwin as an irrelevance. Bernard was convinced that the physiologist now had within his grasp the means to master and modify the animal kingdom, which included his own nature and destiny. Like Dr. Moreau he had only to learn the intricacies of the animal machine to be able to fabricate new and more complex machines from living tissue and become the creator of a second genesis.

More than just a working scientist, Bernard was the fabricator of dreams and fictions which captured the imagination of the age. For Frances Cobbe he was the most malefic of men, whereas scientists like Sir James Burdon Sanderson and Sir Victor Horsley regarded him as the founder of modern physiology: Sir Michael Foster, professor of physiology at Cambridge, wrote the first biography of Bernard in English.[8] Dostoevsky portrayed him as the embodiment of religious unbelief and intellectual arrogance in *The Brothers Karamazov* (1880); Emile Zola, on the other hand, maintained that his novels were the expression of Bernard's observational method.[9] No one now would question the part Darwin played in altering the contemporary vision of the world and mankind's place in it, but Bernard's role in the drama was just as important, if less obtrusive.[10] He was the mentor of Emanuel Klein and the shadowy foreign presence behind the demonic vivisectors of the novels, and his philosophical method was the inspiration for the *Handbook for the Physiological Laboratory* (1873), which became the standard English text for physiological research.[11] It was Bernard, not Darwin, who provided a new system by which nature should be examined and controlled. The schoolchild cutting up a frog or submitting it to electrical shock in a biology class was expressing Bernard's theory of observational vivisection. In the simplest terms, Darwin changed what men believed, Bernard what they did: but had it not been for the continuing excoriation of the antivivisectionists, Bernard's name and reputation might well have been confined to the society of scientists.

More than any scientific writer of his day, Bernard possessed a dramatic authority which gave his works a lucid and driving energy. Even in translation his language has a grace and excitement which captures the reader emotionally, for Bernard reaches out like a poet for metaphors to carry his meaning. His experiments were all quests for knowledge, but he described them as dramas of the human spirit confronting a brute world selfishly trying to conceal and defend its secrets. The paradox, of course, was that Bernard insisted throughout his life on the vivisector maintaining a calm and dispassionate attitude towards his experiments. When he exposed the nerves of a howling and struggling dog, the animal's cries were no more than the grating of gears in a machine, and it was mawkishly sentimental to place animal pain before the interests of science. What has always perplexed and disturbed his admirers is the contradiction between his delineation of the vivisector's attitude towards his experiments and his actual words. It is a problem that Frederic Holmes indicates but does not elucidate when he records Bernard's description and reaction to an experiment by the contemporary physiologist Réaumur:

> The emotion with which de Réaumur describes his anxiety while awaiting the end of his experiment rings true for all persons who have devoted themselves to experimental research and who have experienced similar feelings. In fact, at the time when one is in pursuit of a physiological phenomenon and one feels that he is at the point of wresting a secret from nature, the final experiments become decisive. At that moment the mind, made tense by the expectation of the result, awaits it with a mixture of resignation and a secret joy which one does not yet dare to confess to one-self. De Réaumur, seeing the tube returned by the bird of prey which he had forced to swallow, felt his emotion increase in pro-portion as he unwound the thread, and finally he looked at the bottom of the thread with timidity, but his eyes did not deceive him, he saw well; the meat had disappeared: it had been dis-solved by the gastric liquid, of which the remainder was still coat-ing the walls of the tube. There was, therefore, the gastric juice demonstrated. From then on de Réaumur's genius redoubled to imagine new ways to obtain that juice.[12]

Holmes is inclined to see a romantic youth with literary aspirations in a passage like this, not the "calmly rational scientist" which was al-ways Bernard's perception of himself. Indeed, Bernard had expressed this ideal in the *Introduction*: "The experimenter must now disappear or rather change himself instantly into an observer; and it is only after he has noted the results of an experiment exactly, like those of an ordi-nary observation, that his mind will come back, to reason, compare and decide whether his experimental hypothesis is verified or disap-proved by these very results" (p. 48). The tentative conclusion which Holmes draws from this paradox is that "Bernard reacted to his scien-tific work with more intense feeling than he would afterward have oth-ers believe."[13]

This, of course, is what the antivivisectionists had always main-tained about Bernard when they depicted him as a monster of cruelty, a man who chose to hide his delight in pain behind a mask of glacial calm. For his part, Bernard always insisted on the primacy of the phys-iologist in the quest for truth. Astronomers observed, the physiologist experimented, and those experiments would one day lead to perfection. When he described the physiologist in the *Introduction* he was speaking of himself: "The physiologist is no ordinary man: he is a scientist, possessed and absorbed by the scientific idea that he pursues. He does not hear the cries of animals, he does not see their flowing blood, he sees nothing but his idea, and is aware of nothing but an organism that conceals from him the problem he is seeking to resolve" (p. 132). It was a passage made famous by antivivisectionists, who saw in it the arrogant usurpation of moral authority by a group which, in popular opinion, had only recently been classed with butchers and bodysnatchers. Bernard argued for the morality of his ideas in words that were to provide a credo for his colleagues:

> In science, ideas are what give facts their value and meaning. It is the same in morals, it is everywhere the same. Facts materially alike may have opposite scientific meanings, according to the ideas with which they are connected. A cowardly assassin, a hero and a warrior each plunges a dagger into the breast of his fellow. What differentiates them, unless it be the ideas which guide their hands? A surgeon, a physiologist and Nero give themselves up alike to mutilation of living beings. What differentiates them also, if not ideas? (*Introduction*, p. 132)

And when the Queen asked Lord Lister to speak out against vivisection, Lister replied that "an act is cruel or otherwise, not according to the pain which it involves, but according to the mind and object of the actor."[14]

It was an awkward position to hold if one accepted that certain rules of behavior must be recognized and obeyed by all in society. Here were men standing apart and claiming the right to interpret their own actions as they saw fit, no matter how monstrous those same actions might seem to others. "Ouida," Louise de la Ramé, saw the physiologist as a man who "wraps up his own pursuit of idolatry in the specious pretext of a a pretentious solicitude for the welfare of mankind."[15] Stephen Coleridge was concerned with the whole question of rights and wondered what would happen to the general concept of law if some members of society could freely practice what was forbidden others. This was the question put by Frances Cobbe:

> Let us suppose, to aid our imagination, that something analogous to vivisection were going on in some other department of modern activity. There are legends that *dilettante* sovereigns in the Cinque-

cento age, when Art was supreme as Science is now, were so anxious to aid the great painters at their work that they beheaded
men to serve for models for John the Baptist, and crucified boys
to enable them to verify the details of Calvary. Were a similar ex-
pedient suggested in our day in the schools of the Royal Academy,
can we conceive the tempest of public indignation which would
gather round the head of the enthusiastic Art Director who
deemed the "end" of producing a noble and religious *picture* so
sacred that all "means" were lawful to attain it? Or suppose that,
for the sanitary interests of the community, it were proposed to
stamp out small-pox by administering poison to every person
seized with the disease. It is imaginable that such a scheme would
obtain a hearing?[16]

Shaw used the same arguments with considerably more wit, but
there was something more than a question of morality and law at
issue. Bernard and his followers were proclaiming a new faith with
all the ardor and intolerance of the newly converted. Society could
never hope to be saved from anarchy and benighted ignorance by an
Arnoldian profession of poetry or any number of mystical creeds, but
only by science. It was obvious that everywhere people could see and
enjoy the bountiful gifts of science: sailing ships giving way to steam,
horse carriages replaced by trains and motor cars, electric light in
shop windows and down city streets. And standing in the forefront of
the scientists, pointing the way to Utopia, was the physiologist, a priest
made righteous by his cause and sanctified by the blessings he would
shower down on humanity. Far from being a man who took pleasure
in the spectacle of pain, he endured it courageously so that others
might gain an earthly kingdom more glorious than any heaven promised by religion. Had Bernard not been a poet, a failed dramatist whose
verse plays speak for his vaulting ambition if not his talent, then he
might have expressed himself differently. However, Bernard's mind
always moved from the actual to the ideal by means of Biblical and
processional metaphors that give his prose a sacerdotal quality. It is
enough for him say that the frog is the "Job of physiology" to see a multitude of the creatures mutilated and maimed, and also to infer from
the passage that the frog was chosen by God to suffer and not by any
cruel whim of the vivisector. Yet by implication this new god of science
now had a distinctly human face. In the course of the struggle to subdue and control nature, the physiologist was endowed with the at-

tributes and language of divinity and given the keys to the earthly paradise.

Bernard believed that human perfection was possible, and that his passionate concentration would be rewarded with absolute truth. He could write in the *Cahier Rouge*, his laboratory notebook and diary:

> The struggle of men who keep thinking about the same thing. It is not in writing easily or in acting easily. It is to have an awareness of what is good—I have it. It always comes to this. This is the essential thing.
>
> When one returns to a subject later, one is always more satisfied. It is not any better for all that. Perfection is possible. The epoch will bear my mark.[17]

Vivisection was the one certain means by which the perfection of knowledge could be attained, because Bernard believed in accord with Descartes that men and animals were machines. Unlike Descartes he denied the human machine a soul and saw men and animals controlled not by God, but by their internal environment, the *milieu intérieur*, and when physiologists "go down into the inner environment of a living machine they find an absolute determinism that must become the real foundation for the science of living bodies" (*Introduction*, p. 108). Once the physiologist had mastered the organic nature of the animal's internal environment, he would then be able to understand and control the infinitely more complex working of man. Bernard would make the clocks self-conscious and pronounce the clockmaker obsolete.

It was a vision he expressed at the beginning of the *Introduction* in a series of extraordinarily sonorous images. The blood and anguish of so many tortured animals was the necessary sacrifice which the new priesthood must make to enable humanity to gain the kingdom of earthly delight, and his description of that goal spoke directly to the aspirations of the age. He begins by relegating the apostates and unbelievers to a limbo of disregard, then calls the reader to his side as he points to the road ahead:

> One must be brought up in laboratories and live in them, to appreciate the full importance of all the details of method in investigation, which are so often neglected or despised by spurious men of science who call themselves generalizers. Yet we will only attain really fruitful and illuminating generalizations about vital

phenomena by experimentation and, in hospitals, theatres or laboratories stir the foetid or throbbing ground of life. Somewhere it
has been said that true science is like a flowering and delectable
plateau which can only be attained by climbing craggy slopes and
tearing one's legs against branches and brambles. If I were to look
for a simile that would express my feelings about the science of
life, I should say that it was a superb hall, glittering with light, to
which the only entrance is through a long and horrible kitchen.
(P. 41)[18]

The antivivisectionists made this the most famous passage from
all of Bernard's writing, quoted and requoted as an example of the
shambles of science.[19] But it is far more than this, for Bernard was the
prophet of a religion that captured the imagination of a multitude of
people, and when the antivivisectionists denounced him as a devil,
they were only confirming his power. In this passage Bernard moves
first through a traditional landscape of religious belief: the narrow
path, the rocky steeps along which the pilgrim makes his difficult and
painful progress until in a high place he attains a flowering garden of
pleasure and contentment. Christian theology begins in a garden, and
tradition would have it that heaven too is a place of life-giving water
and a tree of life bearing twelve kinds of fruit and leaves for the healing
of nations (Revelation 22). Those who overcome sin will dwell in this
place forever, needing neither sun nor moon, but glorying in the light
of God.

Bernard deliberately sets this vision aside, just as he relegates
Darwin to the past, and proceeds to define a new and captivating
dream: a bourgeois heaven of social and material splendor, not a garden or a return to the natural world, but a salon lavishly furnished and
brilliantly lit. In Revelation 22 we are told that "night shall be no more;
they need no lamp or sun, for the Lord God will be their light, and they
shall reign for ever and ever." In Bernard's salon, the illumination will
be everlasting, but it will not require God for its source; man alone
will provide the energy. Bernard's lamps will shine forever in a *salon*—
nothing so ordinary as a *salle* or a *chambre*, but a place where art and
science meet in gracious accord, where conversation dazzles with wit
and education. It was an image that evoked a vision of culture, refinement, and exclusion. First there must be the ordeal of painful and
ghastly labor in a stinking kitchen, then the purgatory of experience
would end for the faithful worker as he put aside his implements of

toil and climbed the stairs to his reward in a world of luxury and leisure. Social aspiration, culture, and wealth were combined in one potent image.

In his own life, Bernard had followed a remarkable progress from the shabby squalor of his laboratory to the Académie française. He was born at St. Julien in 1813 to a small *vigneron* who was hard-pressed to find the money to educate the boy. After a traditional schooling, Bernard arrived in Paris in 1834 longing for a career as a poet and dramatist, but financial need made him enroll as a student at the Medical School. Here, he became an assistant to Magendie and learned physiology from the foremost vivisector of the day. The poet was never far from the scientist as Bernard began to formulate the theories behind his experiments, always aware that they should be presented with artistry and coherence. The *Cahier Rouge* shows him working deliberately to this end. In November 1850, he recorded an experiment which demonstrated the principle of endosmosis: "I injected potassium prussiate in the peritoneum of a rabbit; after a very short time, about ten minutes, I made the rabbit micturate and found that its urine contained prussiate. This was a phenomenon of endosmosis because I carried out the same experiment two days after death, and I saw that at the end of a very short time also, the prussiate of potassium had passed into the urine. This was most evidently by endosmosis pure and simple." Bernard then moves directly to a consideration of the philosophic implications of this experiment and concludes with a plan for a series of lectures on aesthetic principles:

> The mind moves along the same path in the production of the human mind. Everywhere, in music, painting, oratory of all kinds, sciences and arts, there is a similar principle for presenting the objects. It is this aspect that constitutes the *artist*.
> 1. There is an ensemble, a general harmony, a goal toward which all aspects converge.
> 2. Each of the aspects could thus also, strictly speaking, constitute a similar small, equally harmonious entity.

A lecture series on artistic feeling. It exists everywhere, even in the sciences. The art of the sciences, considered in their exposition.[20]

Bernard was as much concerned with the literary expression of science as he was with its factual content. A urinating rabbit was not merely an illustration of a scientific principle; it was one small part in the total unity of universal truth, a truth which would manifest itself as art. In this way, the *milieu intérieur* of the animal was a microcosm reflecting the macrocosmic nature of man, and the mastery of the less complex machine would eventually lead to control over the whole of nature. Religion is an exercise in language as well as belief, and Bernard continually transformed his experiments into dramas of life and death in which the sacrifice of an animal was like the offering of Abel's firstlings to God. When Abel offered up living flesh as the symbolic surrogate of his own body, he found favor with God, and throughout the *Introduction* this concept is implicit in Bernard's emphasis that the animal is the primitive and undeveloped form of man. He vigorously opposed experimentation on humans, even on condemned criminals, insisting on the sanctity of human life. Nonetheless, animals were the key to the mystery of man, and it is little wonder that a number of physiologists felt that if they ignored Bernard's prohibition and used patients for research, then humanity would be able to reach the brilliant salon more rapidly.

Even his enemies appreciated the tragedy of Bernard's life, a man who was vilified and deserted by his wife and daughters, but few expressed the nature of that tragedy with such insight as the poet John Davidson. In *The Testament of a Vivisector* (1901) he adopted the persona of Bernard, the vivisector who vivisects himself: "'Have I no pain?'—I live alone: my wife / Forsook me, and my daughters."[21] Remorselessly, the vivisector records his triumph and its agony in images which speak directly to the issues of women and animals:

> Submissively, like a somnambulist I found
> Who solves his problem in a dream,
> The atonement of it, and became its lord—
> Lord of the riddle of the Universe,
> Aware at full of Matter's stolid will
> In me accomplishing its useless aim.
> The whip's-man felt no keener ecstasy
> When a fair harlot at the cart's-tail shrieked,
> And rags of flesh with blood-soaked tawdry lace
> Girdled her shuddering loins. (P. 20)

Bernard's own language made the translation from animals to women inevitable. He described nature as a woman who must be forced to unveil herself when she is attacked by the experimenter, who must be put to the question and subdued (*Introduction*, p. 48). For Anna Kingsford, Frances Cobbe, and Ouida, Bernard was the arch-fiend, a Marquis de Sade in the garb of a scientist, for despite his ad-monitions against human vivisection, Bernard quoted at length from Galen and Magendie to prove that the experimental use of humans was frequently necessary. So, he noted approvingly that a "helmintolo-gist had a condemned woman without her knowledge swallow larvae of intestinal worms, so as to see whether the worms developed in her intestines after death" (*Introduction*, pp. 130–31).[22] Only John David-son saw Bernard discovering to his terror that matter's only medium of consciousness is pain, and the only release from pain is in death (*Testament*, p. 24).

The fear that animal experimentation would lead to the use of hu-man subjects remained, and Ouida wrote: "If the arguments of the priesthood be only followed out to their due and logical sequence, tens of thousands of men would be stretched on the torture-table be-side the dog and the horse, and should be sacrificed without hesita-tion in the pursuit of knowledge. Indeed, it would be more practical to sacrifice the idiot, the cripple, the mute, the sufferer from cutaneous or cerebral affections than to execute the healthy, sound, and useful animal."[23]

With considerable irony it was often the antivivisectionist who made the experiments of the physiologists better known to the public and who provided the vivisector with a special language. For example, it became customary after 1900 to speak of the vivisected animal as being "sacrificed" in consequence of an experiment, by contrast with the earlier "put down" or "killed." The first use of this euphemism was not in a physiologist's report but in a letter written by Dr. George Hoggan, an English physician who worked for a little over four months in Claude Bernard's laboratory. In his letter to the *Morning Post*, Feb-ruary 1, 1875, Hoggan wrote: "As nothing will be likely to succeed so well as example in drawing forth information on these points, I ven-ture to record a little of my own experience in the matter, part of which was gained as an assistant in the laboratory of one of the great-est living experimental physiologists. In that laboratory we sacrificed daily from one to three dogs, besides rabbits and other animals, and, after four months' experience, I am of opinion that not one of those experiments on animals was justified or necessary."

Increasingly, Bernard's exposition of physiology and medicine was furnished with a vocabulary that reflected the sacerdotal cast of his own mind. And it soon became apparent to the antivivisectionists that they were opposing something far more powerful than a scientific theory: they were combating a secular faith which was as appealing in its certainties as Marxist doctrine. Marx interpreted the role of man in society from a basis of historical determinism permitting of prediction, Bernard's experiments maintained the existence of absolute laws in nature which regulated men and animals alike: "Man's intellectual conquest consists in lessening and driving back indeterminism in proportion as he gains ground for determinism by the help of experimental method. This alone should satisfy his ambition, for by this alone he is extending, and can further extend, his power over nature" (*Introduction*, p. 93). Bernard called his disciples to do battle against ignorance, sentimentality, and conservatism, speaking always of the need for sacrifice and the necessity for death to make life possible: "To learn how man and animals live, we cannot avoid seeing great numbers of them die, because the mechanisms of life can be unveiled and proved only by knowledge of the mechanisms of death" (p. 108).

Certainly, it was a creed well suited to an age of mundane religion, with Spiritualism as one of the most popular and least spiritual faiths of all: the dead could be reached through any sympathetic medium, or communicated with by means of planchette and ouija board, just as messages were being tapped out along the telegraph wires. Reincarnation satisfactorily explained the obvious inequalities of human life, since the divine order, or karma, worked as efficiently as the bookkeeping section in a well-run business. Overdraw in this life, bankrupt in the next; provident, compassionate, and kind on this round of existence, healthy, happy, and rich in the next cycle. Spiritualism and its kindred beliefs had followers from the aristocracy to the working class. William Guthrie Spence, shearer and miner, founder of the Australian Workers' Union, travelled the bush with a planchette and prided himself on being able to read people's auras; Sir Arthur Conan Doyle was president of the Spiritualist Alliance and photographed ectoplasm and fairies. Parish churches may have been empty, but a well-known medium or mystic could always draw an audience. Nonetheless, only one group in society was described as a new priesthood, and this was the medical profession.

If doctors were feared in the later years of the nineteenth century, they were also venerated. "The repute which eminent medical men enjoyed is suggested by the fact that between 1850 and 1883 thirty-six were knighted and sixteen received baronetcies; Lister was made a baron."[24] Surgeons could no longer be associated with barbers in the public mind when so many of them were to be seen moving in the highest ranks of society. Viscount Haldane's brother was the physiologist John Haldane, and both were nephews of Sir James Burdon Sanderson, whose *Handbook for the Physiological Laboratory* was derived from Claude Bernard's *Introduction to the Study of Experimental Medicine*. Moreover, if Tom Nero had been unequivocally English, a working class Everyman, Bernard and Klein made it possible to see the vivisector as foreign, a demonic figure who had nothing in common with practical English medicine.

The altar was translated into the operating table, where the surgeon presided over the transformation of death to life. Demonstrations in the room invariably called an operating theatre were stirring dramatic presentations: "The physiological theatre offers plays that are as exciting, thrilling, and entertaining as any others; there is quite enough of murderous attempts and of struggle for life."[25] Louise Lind-af-Hageby was not the only observer who had witnessed the inherent drama in vivisection and surgery and seen the excitement of the audience. For her, and for many others, the lusts of bloodsport were now being sanctioned by scientific faith in the same way as burning a witch in a public square was a spectacle of torture and also a challenge to the powers of the devil.

An experiment became the expression of truth, and by its reenactment, indeterminism would be driven back and humanity brought closer to the glittering salon, just as the Mass bore endless witness to Christ's sacrifice. Those who denied the validity of animal experimentation were the opponents of progress, or, as Paramore says with weary contempt in Shaw's *The Philanderer* (1905): "Ignorance, superstition, sentimentality: they are all one. A guinea pig's convenience is set above the health and lives of the entire human race." Like the priest offering up the sacrifice of Christ's body and blood for the salvation of mankind, the vivisector killed his victims for the sake of humanity. Gradually the role of the calm, disinterested scientist envisaged by Bernard was changing to that of the tragic destroyer: "The pathologist sees beyond the pain which he inflicts to the pain which he prevents. The death of a few lower animals may be, and has in the past been the means of preventing pain and disease both to the animals themselves and to human beings also, who may be counted by thousands or even millions."[26]

Cast in this priestly role, doctors became spokesmen for moral and social issues.[27] The temperance societies preached the evils of strong drink, issued pamphlets, and occasionally produced homiletic plays, but the physiologist Charles Richet, a student of Claude Bernard and one of Anna Kingsford's teachers, knew a better way to illustrate the effects of alcohol:

> However little I may be a partisan of painful experimental demonstrations, I make one exception for an experiment which I consider it essential to present, in all its horror, before the young men who attend my lectures. I refer to absinthe. If two or three drops of essence of absinthe are injected into the veins of a dog, he is at once seized by a violent attack of epilepsy with hallucinations, convulsions, and foaming at the mouth. It is truly a terrible sight, one which fills with disgust and horror all who have witnessed this experiment. But it is precisely for the sake of arousing this disgust, this horror, that I perform the experiment. The unfortunate dog will, during ten minutes, have had an attack of intoxication and absinthean epilepsy; but at the end of an hour he will have recovered completely. At the same time, the two hundred students who have witnessed this hideous spectacle will retain, profoundly engraved on their minds, the memory of that epileptic fury, a memory which will remain with them to the end of their days. They will then be able, by their propaganda against absinthe, to exercize around them a salutary influence, to prevent perhaps ten, fifteen, one hundred human personalities from destroying themselves by the use of this abominable poison. After all, it is better to give a dog ten minutes of absinthism than to allow twenty human families to be plunged, by absinthism, into degradation and misery.[28]

Richet's demonstration embodied the physiological belief in the power of experiment. The physician would have found his absinthe victims in the vestibule of any charity ward in Paris, but Bernard had taught that the physician's mode of observation was fallible and generally controvertible. At worst, the physician was Molière's Sganarelle, at best a muddled and well-meaning theorizer. As Bernard stated: "Pile up facts or observations as we may, we shall be none the wiser" (*Introduction*, p. 48). Physiologists regarded themselves as the forerunners of medical science, and in their company and of their kind were the surgeons.

One of the most remarkable changes in public esteem of the century had involved the surgeon. The doctor, who had once been the agent of pain and suffering, was now hailed as the man who could effect miracles. This change had not come about as the result of his own efforts, certainly not because of Bernard's scathing comments about physicians, but in consequence of one of the greatest of all discoveries—anaesthesia. In labored but heartfelt verse S. Weir Mitchell lauded its use, and in the last line he managed to capture exactly what it meant to people who knew that any surgical operation meant certain agony and possible death:

> Whatever triumphs still shall hold the mind,
> Whatever gift shall yet enrich mankind,
> Ah! here no hour shall strike through all the years,
> No hours so sweet, as when hope, doubt, and fears,
> 'Mid deepening stillness, watched one eager brain,
> With God-like will, decree the Death of Pain.[29]

Few patients who had recovered from an operation performed without anaesthetic wrote of their sensations during the procedure. For most it was agony so excruciating that memory mercifully refused to record the ordeal, but occasionally an account was made and invariably the language falls into a Biblical cadence. For example, Sir James Simpson quoted the recollection of a medical colleague who had undergone an amputation without the aid of chloroform or ether. What he described is the dark night of the soul, the desolation of Job and the end of all things in Revelation: "Of the agony it occasioned I will say nothing. Suffering so great as I underwent cannot be expressed in words, and thus fortunately cannot be recalled. The particular pangs are now forgotten; but the blank whirlwind of emotion, the horror of great darkness, and the sense of desertion by God and man, bordering close upon despair, which swept through my mind and overwhelmed my heart, I can never forget, however gladly I would do so."[30]

Anaesthesia brought about the "death of pain," and doctors who were chary of mentioning miracles frequently quoted Shelley when describing its effects. With "God-like will," they could induce a sleep like death from which the patient would rise restored to health:

> How wonderful is Death,
> Death and his brother Sleep!
> One pale as yonder waning moon,
> With lips of lurid blue;
> The other rosy as the morn
> When, throned on ocean's wave,
> It blushes o'er the world.[31]

Twilight sleep was being used to save women from the agony of childbirth, and despite a measure of resistance to it from those who saw it as unnatural and a defiance of God's injunction, it was in wide use among the upper classes by 1900. Certainly, Queen Victoria's acceptance of twilight sleep gave it the sanction of royal approval. Not only did its advocates claim that it produced healthier babies, it was even going to restore the economy of the nation. William Greenwood exhorted his readers to consider what the refusal to accept anaesthesia in childbirth would mean to the country: "diminishing birthrate alongside an increasing infant mortality! Put it into cold commercial language—diminishing production, increasing expenditure. This means national bankruptcy."[32] But twilight sleep would encourage women to have more children, and in consequence the country would flourish.

Anaesthesia made the surgeon seem a god, and even the working class, wary of charity wards and doctors who used patients for research, had to admit that they had been freed from one of life's greatest terrors. If surgery was called for, it no longer meant unendurable torture. When fifty-four patients in London hospitals who had undergone surgery under anaesthetic in 1848 related their feelings to Sir James Simpson, only the images of fairy tale and magic could describe their emotions: "They were unanimous in their expressions of delight and gratitude at having been relieved from their diseases without suffering. . . . The old story of the magician in the Arabian Tales seemed more than realized before us, the ether being like the tub of water, one moment's dip of the head into which produced a life-long vision in the dreamer's mind."[33]

All the various parts of a new myth were now assembled: Claude Bernard had provided the creed, and anaesthesia, the authority. Admittedly, the surgeon was still feared, for he carried with him the traditions of the past, when he worked with the resurrection men; and the hooligan medical students reminded people of the days when apprentice surgeons were deliberately "hardened by education and custom as not to be affected by the sufferings of those submitted to their knives."[34] Nonetheless, the surgeon now controlled the relief of pain, and with anaesthesia, a multitude of surgical procedures were made possible which would formerly have meant death. The medical profession was invested with the trappings of religion, and the surgeon, as high priest, conducted the ceremonies in the new temples of laboratory and operating theatre.

Sacrifice has always been at the heart of religion, and it was in a spirit of sacrifice that animals were vivisected. Nothing outraged a physiologist more than the accusation that he was a sadist who enjoyed an animal's suffering, and he would promptly invoke Claude Bernard's description of the vivisector as a man engaged in the dispassionate experiments of science, enduring the spectacle of pain for the benefit of humanity, a man "sublime and terrible in martyrdom," to use Davidson's phrase. The antivivisectionists pointed to the human predilection for blood sports and wondered if the vivisector was indeed unlike his fellow men. Shaw spoke of "the psychology of credulity and cruelty," and told the surgeons that "you will soon prove that you are justified not only in vivisecting dogs and guinea-pigs, but in dissecting every human being you can get into your power."[35] He mocked medical pretensions, but he was always aware of the power of this new priesthood, and in an exchange with H. G. Wells over the issue of animal experimentation he freely admitted: "When a vivisector says in effect, 'I have a dread secret to wrest from Nature: so you must license me to sacrifice a guinea-pig', the Sambo in us assents; and the more hideously the guinea-pig is sacrificed the more we feel the importance of the secret. The vivisector can sell us anything as a cure next day."[36] To Shaw's sorrow the Sambos were now in a clear majority, and there was widespread acceptance for the necessity of animal sacrifice, provided that the detailed procedure of the sacrifice was not made known to disturb the sensibilities of the general public.

Antivivisectionists jeered when the Research Defence Society opened a shop alongside the British Union for the Abolition of Vivisection in Oxford Street in 1912. But the window of the Research Defence Society contained the icon that was to become an article of faith in people's lives, and one that would challenge and supersede Hogarth's progression of cruelty: a picture of a smiling woman with a baby on her knee and underneath it a question: "Which will you save—your child or a guinea-pig?"[37]

The only path to the glittering salon lay through a ghastly kitchen, and in that dark and terrible place there must of necessity be sacrifice and death. Here was a vision to win the heart of the most humane individual, who knew that heaven is never gained without bitter travail. Women and workers, many reluctantly, joined Claude Bernard's church and learned there to worship the new gods of science.[38]

10

The Sacrifice

When the 1876 Vivisection Act was being debated, Robert Lowe wrote that "the Bill was not introduced with any large or humane view, but merely for the purpose under the cloak of humanity of taking care of that rather restricted and exclusive class of the animal kingdom known under the name of pets."[1] Lowe's observation was remarkably shrewd and perceptive. Throughout the nineteenth century, animals, like people, were ranked by station and esteem, with dogs, cats, and horses in the first rank, frequently given individual names, and regarded as projections of their owners, even to definition by sexual affinity, with dogs seen as masculine and cats invariably feminine: pets were "a privileged species," to use Keith Thomas' phrase.[2] One reason that Henry Salt's work *Animals' Rights Considered in Relation to Social Progress* (1892) had a very limited appeal was because he roundly condemned the keeping of pets. In Salt's uncompromising view, the cherishing of pets was as much evidence of a love of animals as slavery bore witness to humanitarianism: "It seems to be forgotten, in a vast majority of cases, that a domestic animal does not exist for the mere idle amusement, any more than for the mere commercial profit, of its human owner; and that for a living being to be turned into a useless puppet is only one degree better than to be doomed to the servitude of a drudge. The injustice done to the pampered lap-dog is as conspicuous, in its way, as that done to the over-worked horse."[3] This was an attitude wholly at variance with contemporary opinion, which soared beyond most known forms of animism to a plane of belief where the domestic pet, and the dog in particular, was cherished in preference

170

to people and endowed with supernal qualities of character and clair-voyance. There is an old joke of the two young mothers in a railway carriage presiding over a noisy brood; one says to the other that she far prefers dogs to children, and one of the children whispers to his brother that he wouldn't mind having dogs for parents. Certainly, few incidents roused the public to greater fury than Dr. George Hoggan's account of the dogs in Claude Bernard's laboratory:

> During three campaigns I have witnessed many harsh sights, but I think the saddest sight I ever witnessed was when the dogs were brought up from the cellar to the laboratory for sacrifice. Instead of appearing pleased with the change from darkness to light, they seemed seized with horror as soon as they smelt the air of the place, divining apparently their approaching fate. They would make friendly advances to each of the three or four persons pres-ent, and, as far as eyes, ears, and tail could make a mute appeal for mercy eloquent, they tried in vain.
>
> Even when roughly grasped and thrown on the torture trough, a low complaining whine at such treatment would be all the pro-test made, and they would continue to lick the hand that bound them till their mouths were fixed in the gag, and they could only flap their tails in the trough as the last means of exciting com-passion. Often when convulsed by the pain of their torture this would be renewed, and they would be soothed by receiving a few gentle pats. It was all the aid or comfort I could give them, and I gave it often. They seemed to take it as an earnest of fellow feel-ing that would cause their torture to come to an end—an end brought only by death.[4]

Dogs were not simply people; they were more faithful, loving, and sympathetic than human beings. They were the children who never grew up to criticize or abandon their parents, the servants who were always obedient and grateful for a pat or a plate of scraps, the compan-ions whose greatest joy was to share your company. At the end of her days Ouida wrote, "I am weary of everything except my dogs."[5] And Galsworthy believed he shared the opinion of most people when he said, "If I were condemned to spend twenty-four hours alone with a single creature, I would choose to spend them with my dog."[6] Indeed, when physiologists felt called upon to justify their use of dogs, they frequently made use of these sentiments and described the dog as the willing sacrifice, eager to give its life for the benefit of its master: "The loyalty, devotion and self-sacrifice of the dog have often been emphasized; these noble qualities have their loftiest and most perfect expression when life is surrendered for the sake of the object worshipped."[7]

Nothing admits of more contradictory impulses than the ways in which we regard animals. They can be gods or toys, the embodiment of our most depraved passions or our better selves. For Galsworthy, the dog was "the nearest thing to man on the face of the earth, the one link that we have spiritually with the animal creation; the one dumb creature into whose eyes we can look and tell pretty well for certain what emotion, even what thought, is at work within; the one dumb creature which—not as a rare exception, but almost always—steadily feels the sentiments of love and trust."[8] At the same time, Galsworthy could use the image of the dog to speak for the unemployed, the lost dogs who had neither home nor master, and as that beast-dog and wife-beater, the brute incarnate who came out of the darkness in the shape of half-human flesh, to cry: "All my life I have been given that which will keep me alive, that, and no more. What I have got I have got; no one shall wrench it from my teeth! I live as the dogs; as the dogs shall my actions be! I am the brute beast; have I the time, the chance, the money to learn gentleness and decency? Let me be! Touch not my gnawed bones!"[9] A curious distinction can be discerned here between animal and beast: beastliness was to become a defining characteristic of the worst in human nature, whereas the animal spoke for all that was natural and expressive. When George Sturt wanted to characterize the heroic quality of man, he described it as the power of the animal in the human spirit, referring throughout his journals to the integrity and independence of animals.[10]

These contradictory images could be held at the same time about any particular animal, but the dog had always been the most mutable, capable of rousing fear as the mad dog—the carrier of rabies—or seen as noble and understanding as Ouida's *Dog of Flanders* (1872). By the end of the century the beast in the dog was like a small errant ghost emerging only occasionally to disturb the living embodiment of love and trust. The progress can be seen in Landseer, whose paintings of animals moved from the starkly realistic to those popular studies of dogs as human types. *Dignity and Impudence* must surely be one of the best known of all Landseer's works and the origin of all those paintings of dogs at the card-table or carousing across a bar counter. The antivivisectionists always recognized the dog as the animal most likely to elicit compassion and stressed the torture of dogs in their pamphlets and posters. Had it been a cat or a monkey operated upon contrary to regulation at London University in 1902, it is very doubtful whether there would have been such a passionate outcry. The statue of a dog patiently waiting for his master recalled Landseer's *The Old Shepherd's Chief Mourner* and all those other dogs in story and picture whose devotion extended beyond the grave.

Within this ambivalent maze of emotional convictions it was quite possible to identify with one group of animals while relegating others to the slaughterhouse. For example, the Duke of Portland was a noted sportsman and foxhunter; he was also chairman of the Battersea Dogs' Home, and when it was suggested by Mr. Starling in evidence before the Second Royal Commission of 1913 that unwanted dogs should be used for vivisection, the Duke considered "Mr. Starling's suggestion not only horrible but absurd; and one which should be resisted as entirely unacceptable to the Home."[11] In his notebooks, Richard Jefferies slyly noted: "It is wellknown that foxes like to be hunted by squires and farmers, but cannot bear to be chased by Cockney sportsmen."[12] Even Frances Cobbe, more in defense of her aristocratic patrons than foxes, declared, "It is almost ludicrous to compare a fox-hunt, for example, with its free chances of escape and its almost instant termination in the annihilation of the poor fox when captured, with the slow, long-drawn agonies of an affectionate, trustful dog, fastened down limb by limb and mangled on its torture trough."[13] Such incongruities were duly noted by the vivisectionists (as they had been in their day by William Windham), who discovered in themselves a fathomless well of pity for foxes. Cruelty was argued by degrees and qualified by class, and always those animals most resembling people benefited from the comparison.

Old patterns of behavior could be buried but never quite obliterated, and frequently they can be found contending for authority in an individual. For many, Dickens provided a most gratifying synthesis of the contrary impulses of savagery and compassion by an odd reversal of customary attitudes towards animals. At first sight Dickens can be seen as one of the most eloquent spokesmen for antivivisection: in 1866 he called upon the RSPCA to look after the "Royal Inhumane Society," in his article "Inhumane Humanity."[14] Later in a zoo he dwelt with fascinated horror upon the spectacle of snakes devouring a live mouse, or called for the reform of the Smithfield Markets, where scenes recalling the old days of bullbaiting could still be found.[15] However, a

number of critics, including John Carey, have questioned whether it
was really the abolition of cruelty which obsessed Dickens or the ex-
ploration of its most violent social manifestations.[16]

Bloodsports flourish in Dickens' novels, but in his mythic and
metaphoric universe these sports are conducted less as overt spec-
tacles than by people disguised as animals. It is as though Dickens has
the power to lead us back to a time when cats, dogs, and birds were
ritually tortured and put to death.[17] The world of Dickens' fiction is a
place of primitive magic and terror which speaks for the consciousness we find in some working-class memoirs of the period. An old
man in 1909 looked back to his childhood in the East End of London,
where he was born in 1823. Quite simply he wrote:

> My working life began with tragic suddenness. . . . I had the mis-
> fortune to upset the water-butt in our yard, and my father said,
> "You can go to work after that." We were living in the St. Pancras
> district, and I was presented to a shoemaker in Wells Street. The
> conditions were that I was to work for nothing and also "find my-
> self." I worked from 8.30 in the morning to eight at night, and all
> the time my master was threatening me. He terrified me by saying
> that if he had been a monkey he would have jumped down my
> throat.[18]

Here was the world of Dickens' childhood with his old nurse, Mary
Weller, regaling him with stories of gigantic black cats and ferocious
rats, but in the novels those fears are disguised by fictional projections
into a realm of ritual sacrifice where the most primitive rites of exorcism and sacrifice are conducted. In *Oliver Twist* (1837) Bill Sike's surrogate is his dog, Bull's Eye, which meets the same end as his master,
after Bill has futilely sought to destroy it as evidence of his guilt. In
Dombey and Son (1848) Carker is both human and animal, possessing
"two rows of glistening teeth whose regularity and whiteness were
quite distressing, and a smile so wide that there was something in it
like the snarl of a cat." The cat was a favorite subject for public and
private execution, as we have seen, ritually burned in ovens and bonfires to drive out evil spirits and ward off the devil. Feline and insinuating, Carker is Dombey's familiar, the destroyer of his business and his
home, and he meets his end in the fire of the locomotive that "spun
him round and round and struck him limb from limb, and licked his
stream of life up with its fiery heat." Dickens' metaphorical locomotive

owes very little to a steam engine, and a great deal more to the furnace, the fire, and the ancient rites of witchcraft. Similarly, Eugene Wrayburn of *Our Mutual Friend* (1865) denies all affinity with animals and scoffs at Boffin's injunction to look to the bees as an example of industry and thrift: "I object on principle, as a two-footed creature, to being constantly referred to insects and four-footed creatures. I object to being required to model my proceedings according to the proceedings of the bee or the dog, or the spider, or the camel." However, Eugene Wrayburn is thrown into the river like a dog with broken legs—and only then does he come to a recognition of his own humanity.

A popular sport of the early years of the century was the drowning of pairs of incongruous animals tied together, a duck and a cat frenziedly trying to escape each other and drowning in the process. In *Our Mutual Friend* it is Rogue Riderhood and Bradley Headstone who are condemned to die together like two ill-assorted animals. Headstone is the "passion-wasted nightbird; with respectable feathers, the worst nightbird of all." And when Rogue Riderhood bargains with Eugene and Felix, his hands turn and twist an "old sodden fur cap, formless and mangey, that looked like a furry animal, dog or cat, puppy or kitten, drowned and decaying." Headstone and Riderhood are found locked to each other in the ooze of the Lock Gates, bird and beast joined together.

This transposition of form and identity, the interchanging role of animate and inanimate, are some of the most obvious elements of Dickens' creative vision. What is less apparent is Dickens' outspoken opposition to animal suffering and the contradictory impulse whereby the torturing and killing of animals is tacitly admitted and defined. The cat burned alive in an oven was always a surrogate for a human victim; Carker consumed by the fire of the locomotive permitted the reader vicariously to enjoy a forbidden sport and to relive an ancient ritual of sacrifice.

The power of fiction enabled people to indulge in the forbidden sports, and one small aspect of Dickens' extraordinary control over the emotions and imagination of his readers lay in this ability to revive the forbidden rites in new disguises. It is not really animals which are tortured and killed in Dickens' novels, but men and women who die in animal shape. In effect, Dickens described what Anna Kingsford had seen in her visionary dream, where every vivisected animal embodied a human form, but then he reversed the image to restore the most ancient ritual of all—human sacrifice.

The antivivisectionists continued to insist that the experimental use of animals was a bloodsport no different from the cockfight or the bullbait and that far from being the calm and dispassionate man of science, the physiologist was a sadist who deserved to be shunned by all decent people. As Shaw said in response to H. G. Wells, "'The vivisector is distinguished from the ordinary run of limited scoundrels by being an infinite scoundrel. The proper place in organized human society for a scoundrel who seeks knowledge or anything else without conscience is the lethal chamber." [19] George Bigelow had noted: "Watch the students at a vivisection. It is the blood and suffering, not the science, that rivets their breathless attention." [20]

The response of the medical profession to these accusations was the blunt rejoinder that witnessing an experiment of vivisection in no way affected the character of the spectators or the operator. [21] But it was prudently decided to limit the audiences on these occasions, and secrecy was henceforth to become the hallmark of physiological research. Nonetheless, if the reality of animal sacrifice was no longer to be witnessed in a public spectacle, it found full expression in fiction.

As pets replaced livestock in the experience of townsfolk, there was an increased sensitivity to animal suffering. Tenants of council cottages in Battersea were not permitted to keep pigeons, goats, pigs, or any other farm animal, and slaughtering was not permitted on a butcher's premises after 1910. Many old residents of Battersea remembered the cattle being driven along Pig Hill and the horses straining up icy Battersea Rise, but these sights were vanishing as motor cars took the place of horses and meat was delivered to the butcher's shop as skinned carcasses. At the turn of the century the slaughterhouse had been a place of terror and excitement for children, in whom a new sense of compassion competed with the old lust to capture and kill. When Charlie Chaplin looked back to his own childhood, he saw the premise of all his later films in an incident which held within it the same conjunction of pity and cruelty, the comic and the tragic, that had helped to shape Dickens' creative vision. In both artists their fictional mode involved the transformation and exorcism of the savagely primitive by means of laughter.

At the end of our street was a slaughterhouse, and sheep would pass our house on the way to be butchered. I remember one escaped and ran down the street, to the amusement of onlookers.

Some tried to grab it and others tripped over themselves. I had giggled with delight at its lambent capering and panic, it seemed so comic. But when it was caught and carried back into the slaughter-house, the reality of the tragedy came over me and I ran indoors, screaming and weeping to Mother, "They're going to kill it! They're going to kill it!"[22]

What had been a routine occasion in the life of a country child was now a horrifying nightmare for a city child accustomed to seeing objects on his plate called sausages and cutlets that bore no resemblance by name or shape to a living animal. By the early years of the twentieth century few people had to bother themselves with that particular nightmare. The slaughterhouse, like the physiological laboratory, was closed to the public. Children and their parents were no longer called upon to witness scenes of animal suffering, and what was out of sight was effectively out of mind. Antivivisectionists had to devise ingenious schemes to infiltrate physiology laboratories to find out what was being perpetrated there; indeed, most of their information was to be derived from the published reports of the vivisectionists.

It has been said that a visit to an abattoir would make a vegetarian of the most convinced carnivore among us; however, the number of people who had actually seen animals killed for food was becoming fewer every year, and those who wanted to know the process whereby the crown of lamb had arrived on the dining room table were fewer still. When Molly Hughes was attending an education conference in America in the 1890s, two of her colleagues decided to investigate the Chicago stockyards:

We had been warned not on any account to visit the stock-yard, because the killing of the pigs was an insufferable sight. Of course we had heard that the organization was so complete that the pig walked in at one end and came out at the other in the form of sausages. Two of our party felt that such marvellous management must be well worth seeing, and really *ought* to be investigated, if Chicago was to be thoroughly visited. So they went to the office and explained to the man in charge that they wanted to see something of the processes, but to avoid the actual scene of the killing. "Sure," said he, scenting no doubt that he had some elegant hyper-sensitive English ladies to deal with, and immediately he ushered them straight into the slaughter-house where some thousand pigs were being dispatched. They rushed away and were really ill for a few hours. I had a sneaking sympathy with that man.[23]

Molly Hughes could remember looking out of her bedroom window in London to the opposite side of the street where the neighborhood butcher killed sheep, and she had spent a good part of her childhood on a farm in Cornwall. For her, killing was a necessary part of eating, but to eat meat while refusing to recognize it as the occasion of some animal's death was hypocrisy at its worst.

Contrary to what antivivisectionists said, the physiologists were not unaffected by the new sensitivity towards animal suffering. Some hardened themselves in the same way that surgeons had become inured to the spectacle of pain before the days of anaesthesia; others worked by the priestly code of Claude Bernard and spoke in sacerdotal euphemisms of sacrificing animals for the sake of human progress; others still contrived to invest the whole process of animal experimentation with language and attitudes that recalled the early days of the century, when bloodsports were translated into comic metalepsis for the fainthearted. Comedy has often been an evasive strategy, the means of creating distance between subject and viewer, thus rendering it possible to endure the intolerable. Murder, as Thackeray wrote, "is a great inspirer of jokes."[24] Obscenity was always the stock in trade of medical students and a customary way of relieving tension in the operating theatre. So, when some physiologists and surgeons recorded their memoirs, it was as though Pierce Egan or Jonathan Badcock were the inspiration for their prose. It was in this particular mode that Franklin Martin recalled his early years of experimentation with dogs and the necessary pain of the surgery inflicted upon them:

My eager assistant was keen for the job, for then as now the word "Research," regardless of its usefulness or futility, was a term to conjure with. . . . Our "Master of Hounds," Adam, the janitor of the laboratory, soon became an enthusiastic cooperator. It was up to him to provide the dogs, to act as operating-room assistant, to care for the convalescent patients in our little animal hospital, and to keep them alive, and frequently to act as chief mourner and grave digger at the occasional obsequies. . . . No. 13 was a large Shepherd dog named Bruce, who, presumably had come from a higher social sphere than our other animals. We suspected that he had been purloined by the "The Master of the Hounds" from some place east of State Street.[25]

The inflation of tone, the sentimental asides, and the comic euphemisms in the context of sport are reminiscent of Badcock and Egan, serving to conceal the unsavory reality of dog-stealing and a long series of experiments involving the transplant of ureters into the animals' intestines. Dogs were continually being stolen for use in experimental medicine, and at one time the antivivisectionists considered keeping a watch on University College in London to prevent stolen dogs being smuggled into the laboratory.[26] Franklin Martin's defense against the reality of suffering was the language of sport, and he praised his "Master of Hounds" for the ability to lure suitable dogs away from the very feet of their owners.

When the brown-doggers of 1907 rioted down the Strand with a stuffed replica of the brown dog, they sang their own version of "The Little Brown Jug":

As we go walking after dark,
We turn our steps to Latchmere Park,
And there we see, to our surprise,
A little brown dog that stands and lies.

    Ha, ha, ha! Hee, hee, hee!
    Little brown dog how we hate thee.
    Ha, ha, ha! Hee, hee, hee!
    Little brown dog how we hate thee.

If we had a dog which told such fibs
We'd ply a whip about his ribs;
To tan him well we would not fail,
For carrying such a monstrous tale.

    Ha, ha, ha! Hee, hee, hee! etc.[27]

The parody and the puns were traditional, but the antivivisectionists were outraged by this revival of sporting and comic forms. They countered with some lachrymose and colloquial verses of their own which sought to revive the old fears of bloodsports waking the beast in man:

Them 'thusiastic student chaps
　'Ad best let dead dogs be,
Or they may wake a Frankenstein,
　Wot ain't quite good to see.[28]

With the spectacle of animal suffering no longer a commonplace for people, the natural world was being subtly rearranged in their experience. Pets were now a subspecies of humanity, the beloved children and preferred companions, and this anthropomorphism even affected the minds and attitudes of the scientists themselves. The contradictions are apparent between the dog as laboratory subject and the dog as family pet, the animals to be sacrificed in the laboratory by the physiologist and those which he cherished in the home. The same contradictions are apparent in a number of popular works of natural history. Coupin and Lea's *The Romance of Animal Arts and Crafts* (1907) endured for many years as a school text and carried the stern admonition that "we must be careful not to attribute human motives and reason where they have no existence." Then in the same passage the work is described as "an interesting account of the spinning, sewing, manufacture of paper and pottery, aeronautics, raft-building, road-making, and various other industries of wild life."[29] Naturally, the animals commended were those which best imitated the works of men.

Admittedly, there is no settled view of animals in this period or any other, as Keith Thomas has shown, for even within one social or religious group there can be a number of different attitudes towards animals. Theosophists and Spiritualists argued heatedly whether animals had individual or world souls; if the latter, then the death of a single dog would no more affect the universal Dog Soul than the plucking of an apple from the tree.[30] When Father Bernard Vaughan, speaking at Liverpool, castigated those who had raised an idol to a dog in the Latchmere Recreation Ground and went on to denounce the new paganism of "cat and dog worship," he was deluged with telegrams of protest and letters insisting that dogs had souls.[31]

What can be argued is that from the middle of the nineteenth century, animals were sacrificed to fiction before they were sacrificed to science. In the fiction of this period we find animals assuming mythic roles that rival and eclipse the reality of animals in the known world. Peter Rabbit and Toad of Toad Hall took their places alongside Mr. Micawber in a universe of the imagination where animals were not simply people; they were more human than people—as a great many pet lovers were maintaining. Moreover, although these creations had a long ancestry going back to Aesop and La Fontaine, they were infinitely more complex than the masquerade animals of the old cautionary fables. Another crucial difference was the context of the tales, for although animal stories were derived from the first myths of humankind, the nineteenth century was the beginning of a time when society no longer had any direct perception of natural life other than by means of pets and zoos. Eighteenth-century children recited rhymes about Mother Goose and then could see geese and ducks in any farmyard: the distinction between the reality and the imaginary was always apparent. But for the city child of the latter years of the nineteenth century, the goose was Christmas dinner and a colored picture of a fat old lady wearing feathers and a black bonnet.

It was never easy for a child to become accustomed to animals being killed: Flora Thompson wept bitterly when the family pig was slaughtered, and it needed some coaxing from her mother before she overcame her repugnance and ate it. There were always ambivalences and evasions reminiscent of the comic distancing of the sporting writers when the killing of an animal was discussed in the presence of young people. Thackeray's "jingling antithesis" is apparent in Anna Fay's recollection of life at Oakly Park near Shrewsbury in 1851:

> The season for shooting birds is over, but Uncle Richard enjoys very much ferreting rabbits; you would enjoy this very much.
> A ferret is a little gray or white animal which they use instead of a dog. They sew up the poor thing's mouth; otherwise it would eat the rabbit and attend more to its own appetite than to the pleasure of the sportsman. The keeper puts a string around its neck, places it at a hole, and soon you hear a rumbling in the earth and in a trice the rabbit pops out the other entrance to its house. The sportsman stands ready with his gun, and poor Bunny no sooner escapes from one enemy than he falls victim of another still more relentless. His hapless body is thrown into the bag, is carried to the larder with his unfortunate companions, and hung up by the legs, till the cook thinks that it is time he should be either smothered with onions or made a pie of, in which latter form I frequently discuss his merits at breakfast or luncheon.[32]

In the course of a single paragraph the rabbit is humanized and the pain of its animal death deflected by its rendering as fiction, and eventually a pie. Anna Fay uses comedy to obscure her guilty suspicion that she is a discriminating cannibal, then speaks of the rabbit only as pie, an object demonstrably free of all feeling. Paradoxically, fiction can produce a sympathetic awareness of reality or separate us from it, and the resulting fiction can be quite contrary to that intended by the writer. Ostensibly *Black Beauty* was written to awaken sympathy for the plight of horses forced to endure the bearing rein, but it could also be argued that horses that spoke to each other and recorded their autobiographies made an actual horse seem a very inferior and deficient kind of animal. It then became possible to make the fictional animal the privileged species and the real animal an anomalous species without rights or status.

In the past there had always been a shadowy notion that if animals had duties they also had rights, however limited. Animals were never placed on trial in England, although there were instances in America and Europe of dogs and other domestic animals being tried and sentenced to death for savaging their masters. However, the idea of rights was evident when John Brown recorded the fate of the sagacious William, the dog who had been rescued from a ritual drowning by a group of village boys. William became a thief, and one day John Brown's grandmother gave the milk-boy twopence to hang the dog for purloining a leg of mutton.[33] William paid the penalty for his crime with a punishment meted out to human criminals in the early years of the century and one that indicated the dog's responsibility for his act. In a society where dogs had become pets, however, such an action would have been deemed barbaric. Children were being exhorted to be kind to animals by means of tracts and homilies—but the most effective means of inculcating this behavior was with fictional animals: animals like Black Beauty and Diamond who pleaded their own cause with the younger reader.

The fiction written for children in the nineteenth century was always "a very lightly sugared pill of instruction, or a highly dramatised warning," to use J. S. Bratton's description.[34] Mrs. Trimmer and Hannah More regularly enjoined kindness to animals as one of the approved virtues of the good child, but in all their works the animals remained animal. There was a marked change when Charlotte Tucker published the *Rambles of a Rat* (1857). Here, an engaging rat of Norman ancestry is made the narrator of the story, and his adventures and those of his sprightly friends provide a story which still manages to convey the customary messages of obedience, honesty, and cheerful acceptance of class. The difference between Charlotte Tucker (who wrote under the pseudonym of "ALOE"—"a Lady of England") and previous writers of animal stories is that her rats carry the full burden of narration. They are not objects to illuminate the main human subject; rather, they are the means whereby the human characters are observed and assessed. Charlotte Tucker's rats are inordinately clever chaps with great stores of information, but as far removed from real rats as the moon is from green cheese. Nonetheless, whether these stories are told by an animal like Anna Sewell's Black Beauty or Charlotte Tucker's Ratto, the imprint is human, and inevitably the animals are all translated into pets, or little people.

Animal stories proliferated as the actual world of animals receded to reveal a landscape of fictional creatures who existed only to provide a moral message for children. Beatrix Potter's Peter Rabbit wore clothes like any small boy and had to be taught not to lose them and never to stray into Farmer Macgregor's cabbage patch. And it was Peter Rabbit who became the reality for children and a great many adults, leaving ordinary rabbits to be killed, cooked, and eaten with impunity. When *Black Beauty* was published in the United States, it carried the commendations of veterinarians and horse lovers, who all stated that nobody had presented the mind and feelings of horses as effectively as Anna Sewell. Within the maze of these frequently contradictory distinctions, it was always possible to relegate the mute animal of everyday life to the rank of a subspecies. Whatever horses in general gained from the sympathy accorded Black Beauty was lost when they failed to measure up to the anthropomorphic equines of fiction. Unfortunately for horses, *Black Beauty* was not being read as fiction, but as a realist tract, and surely, the ultimate *tour de force* of the creative artist is when reality itself is changed in accord with a fictional imperative.

Fiction has the power to alter the perception people have of the real world: a poem will strike us with a shock of recognition as though we have just written it ourselves; a novel or drama will make us weep and laugh as we identify with the characters. G. K. Chesterton was aware of this when he observed that Dickens was not simply an event in English literature; Dickens was an event in English history.[35] And just as a Dickensian quality can be seen affecting the way people celebrated Christmas, the fictional depiction of animals altered the contemporary perception of the natural world. Anna Sewell believed she had faithfully recreated the mind of a horse, and her achievement was generally praised on her own terms. Charlotte Tucker's Ratto was regarded as a contribution to natural history, and it was approvingly noted that at no time did her rats discuss religion or mention God, confining themselves to mundane questions of history, geology, and engineering.[36] Autobiographies of animals soon became one of the most popular forms of children's fiction, and the same praise which had been given Anna Sewell for her delineation of equine psychology was accorded a writer like Gordon Stables, whose *Sable and White* (1894) was subtitled *The Autobiography of a Show Dog*.

A strong opponent of vivisection, Stables tried to visualize the suffering from an animal's point of view:

> Some instinct seemed to tell us both that a fearful crime was about to be perpetrated on our helpless bodies; that, in fact, we were to undergo the torture that I had often heard poor Professor Huxley speak about, the torture of vivisection; that, in a word, we would be tied to a bench or stool and cut to pieces alive, and all for the supposed benefit of that proud biped, the microbe man. . . .
>
> Here we could see in the ghostly moonlight, not only rabbits and birds alive and half dissected, fastened down to the tables and stools just as the operator had left them, but many dogs as well. One was face downwards on a species of saddle like a grating, and even as we looked at him he lifted up his head, and once more the thrilling and terrible medley of mingled barking, howling, and moaning resounded through the rooms. Another poor sufferer was in a standing position, between horizontal and upright bars, to the upper ones of which he was slung. Still another wretched dog had both its jaws tied to bars that kept the mouth open wide, and from the throat protruded strange-looking pipes and instruments.[37]

Joe manages to escape from the vivisector and continues his adventures until he finds a comfortable home in the country, where he settles down as the family pet. The difficulty for writers with a message like Stables' was that the episode of the vivisector's laboratory was seen as part of the whole fictional account and was moved insensibly away from realism and into that part of the imagination where fiction holds sway.

Stables wrote with considerable vigor, but the same could not be said of his imitators. Marshall Saunders' *Beautiful Joe* (1901) was another canine autobiography, and Saunders' belief that she had been gifted with the ability to transcribe the language of dogs and a great

many other animals was confirmed in Hezekiah Butterworth's introduction: "The wonderfully successful book entitled 'Black Beauty',
came like a living voice out of the animal kingdom. But it spoke for the
horse, and made other books necessary, it led the way."[38] Marshall
Saunders was happy to oblige, and *Beautiful Joe* was followed by
Beautiful Joe's Paradise (1903), which illustrated her belief in the im-
mortality of animals. She went on to write autobiographical accounts
of fox terriers, canaries and other finches, monkeys, and kittens; and
all were praised for their faithful delineation of animal consciousness
and behavior. In every case, of course, what can be learned from these
books is a code of behavior applicable to children: animals are used to
demonstrate social rules for English children in much the same way
that the Little Black Sambo storybooks taught the European child how
to behave. These are conduct books written at the expense of the animals they purport to describe.

Increasingly a large part of the fictional world was being taken over
by animals, with Kipling moving easily between the arbitrary assaults
of the boarding school in *Stalky and Co.* (1897) and the authoritarian
rules of *The Jungle Book* (1893). Stalky, the future hero of Empire,
gleefully shoots stray cats and rabbits, leading his chosen followers
against neighboring dormitories; and when he is not meting out punishment to others, he cheerfully accepts a flogging from the Head. The
Law of the Jungle is the code of the boarding school, with the animals
sorted out into comparable roles of masters and student. Mowgli, the
man cub, is cuffed into an education by Baloo the bear and tutored
less painfully by Bagheera the black panther. But always man holds
sway over the animal kingdom by divine right, and nothing can withstand Mowgli's clear-eyed stare. Even though Mowgli lives with the
creatures of the Jungle, and frequently owes his life to them, he is set
apart by a special power of natural authority. The Law is still Mac-
Donald's universal law of obedience, and one that must be learned by
all who wish to live in Kipling's society of eternal adolescence. At the
conclusion of "Her Majesty's Servants" in *The Jungle Book*, an old
Asian chief marvels at a ceremonial military advance with camels,
horses, and elephants marching in unison with men:

"But are the beasts as wise as the men?" said the chief.
"They obey, as the men do. Mule, horse, elephant, or bullock,
he obeys his driver, and the driver his sergeant, and the sergeant
his lieutenant, and the lieutenant his captain, and the captain his

major, and the major his colonel, and the colonel his brigadier commanding three regiments, and the brigadier his general, who obeys the Viceroy, who is the servant of the Empress. Thus it is done.[39]

Kipling's animals were as real to his readers as his human characters: Bagheera, Baloo, Shere Khan, and Ikki embodied the inhabitants of the jungle, assuming that strange half-human shape that seemed to allay so many deep-rooted fears of the natural world. It was comfortable to believe that all living things obeyed the same law, which was "like the Giant Creeper, because it dropped across every one's back and no one could escape."[40] Then to be told that none but man had the right to execute the Law was an implicit confirmation of Claude Bernard's assumption of man's duty to shape nature according to his will. Indirectly, the animal stories that purported to teach compassion and respect for animals did more to confirm man's authority over animals than the tales of adventure written by travel writers like Frederick Courteney Selous with their bloody accounts of buffalo shooting and hippo hunts in crocodile-infested rivers.[41] At least in works like these, animals were seen as dangerous adversaries and were accorded the dignity befitting a worthy enemy, but the writers of animal fiction trivialized and demeaned the natural world by humanizing it.

If Kipling's enormously popular *Jungle Books* made the animals of the jungle seem like members of a rough-and-tumble boarding school, Kenneth Grahame took the animals of the English countryside and turned them into a social object-lesson in *Wind in the Willows* (1908). The work was an instantaneous success with an almost mythic power over the consciousness of its readers: the River-Bankers, Rat, Mole, Badger, Otter, and Toad stood for the old gentry which felt itself threatened by the gathering strength of the trades unionists and Socialists. Over the River lived the stoats and weasels, scruffy, impudent, and anarchic, waiting to lay waste to the property of any gentleman like Mr. Toad who refused to accept the social responsibilities entailed by ownership of Toad Hall. Grahame had narrowly avoided being shot in 1903 by an insane Socialist, George Robinson, when he was Secretary of the Bank of England, and *Wind in the Willows* is a passionate evocation for the old order of deference and class.[42] Ratty, Mole, Otter, and Badger are model country gentlemen, living quietly and never giving offense—but there is inevitable riot and revolution when Toad tries to break the old social order by recklessly rushing into the machine age in his motorcar. No sooner is he arrested than the Wild Wooders scramble to take possession of his property, where they live in a squalor of unmade beds and dirty dishes.

The social message of *Wind in the Willows* did not go unremarked, but what gave the work such enduring appeal was the imaginative power invested in its animal characters. They were animal in a sense, shaking paws whenever they met, but they wore clothes, rode horses and drove motor cars, and always knew that they belonged to a lesser world than that inhabited by humans. The relationship between animal and human shifts and turns upon itself throughout the work: at one moment Toad is at the wheel of his automobile, barreling down the highway at reckless speed and being arrested by a policeman; another moment he disguises himself as a washerwoman and is chatting to a barge-woman until she recognizes him as an animal daring to masquerade as a human:

> The woman moved nearer to him and peered under his bonnet keenly and closely. "Why, so you are!" she cried. "Well, I never! A horrid, nasty, crawly Toad! And in my nice clean barge, too! Now that is a thing that I will *not* have!"
> She relinquished the tiller for a moment. One big mottled arm shot out and caught Toad by a fore-leg, while the other gripped him fast by a hind-leg. Then the world turned suddenly upside down, the barge seemed to flit lightly across the sky, the wind whistled in his ears, and Toad found himself flying through the air, revolving rapidly as he went. (Chap. 10)

Grahame continually turns his readers upside down in this fashion, reminding them that the world is made for humanity and that animals belong to an imaginary realm which may infiltrate the human world but can never hope to control it. One cold night, when they have left Mr. Badger's house, Rat and Mole pause in a village to look through the cottage windows: "The two spectators, so far from home themselves, had something of wistfulness in their eyes as they watched a cat being stroked, a sleepy child picked up and huddled off to bed, or a tired man stretch and knock out his pipe on the end of a smouldering log" (Chap. 5). They know that they can never enter those houses and never hope to belong to the real world. Again and again in the work Grahame pauses to emphasize the nature of his animals as imaginative fictions, then sends them off on fresh adventures where they emulate the ways of human society.

It is precisely these contradictions that came to characterize the way people regarded animals and permitted the natural world to be mutilated and destroyed. If Mr. Toad was accepted as the quintessential frog, then there was no reason to suffer any qualms as an actual frog was vivisected in a biology class, while Rat sculling down the River was surely no relation to a race of laboratory rats. As Cecil Hart of Battersea unconsciously knew, it is deceptively simple to translate reality into the more comfortable modes of fiction.

The antivivisection movement failed, and the statue of the brown dog was broken up and the fragments buried. The experimental use of animals "enjoyed a spectacular growth," to quote Richard French, and although people like Charlotte Despard and Louise Lind-af-Hageby continued to work to alleviate the suffering of animals, they could not withstand the new priesthood and the gods of science. Yet, even some of the most ardent antagonists of the brown dog and all it stood for were troubled by some of the later developments in medicine. William Howard Lister, the politically astute young medical student, had organized the brown-doggers and led the students across the river to Battersea, then went from one meeting to another to shout down the antivivisectionists as misguided and sentimental. When the war broke out, he immediately enlisted and saw service on several fronts until he was killed at Asiago in 1918. In one of his letters home he wrote with considerable disgust of "a physiologist who wanted to come up with me so as to get at Boches who had just been killed, cut out bits of their central nervous system, with a view to the effects of a prolonged bombardment on the nervous system."[43]

The cause of animals was not helped when they were seen as surrogates for women, or workers, or when they were translated into fictions, no matter how appealing. If we look at animals and see only the reflection of ourselves, we deny them the reality of their own existence. Then it becomes possible to forget their plight, and a man like Cecil Hart can pause and remember the role of the dog in the Brown Dog Riots as nothing more than an "advertizing story."

Notes

Index

Notes

Chapter 1: The Brown Dog Riots of 1907

1. *Reflections on Battersea*, collected by the Vocational Committee of the Rotary Club of Battersea (Battersea: Rotary Club of Battersea, 1980), p. 9.
2. Gillian Tindall, *The Fields Beneath* (London: Granada, 1977), pp. 22–28.
3. Charles Booth, *Life and Labour of the People in London*, 3d ser., 5 (London: Macmillan, 1902): 150.
4. Sherwood Ramsbury, *Historic Battersea* (pamphlet, Battersea, n.d.), p. 2.
5. Mrs. W. Chapman, in *Reflections on Battersea*, p. 19.
6. Janet Roebuck, *Urban Development in Nineteenth-Century London: Lambeth, Battersea, and Wandsworth, 1838–1888* (London: Phillimore, 1979), pp. 121–22.
7. Andro Linklater, *An Unhusbanded Life: Charlotte Despard* (London: Hutchinson, 1980), p. 68.
8. *Reflections on Battersea*, p. 33.
9. Booth, *Life and Labour of the People in London*, 9 (1903): 312.
10. *Daily Mail*, 23 May 1902 and 9 Dec. 1902.
11. *Second Royal Commission on Vivisection*, Parl. Papers 1907, Cd. Q. 11624.
12. *Tribune*, 3 October 1906. The Progressive campaign for the 1906 election was managed by the Trades and Labour Council, which represented nearly forty political and labor organizations in the borough. Forty Progressive candidates were nominated, comprising eight laborers, three compositors, two bricklayers, three carpenters, two plasterers, three painters, two general foremen, one electrician, one school attendance officer, one insurance agent, three schoolmasters, an organizer of Polytechnic lectures, one barrister, and three "independent gentlemen."
13. *South-Western Star*, 23 Sept. 1902.

14. *Battersea Council Records*, Minutes of Proceedings, 13 May 1903, 2:60.
15. *Law Reports, Public General Statutes*, 39 & 40 Vict. c. 77. The provisions and limitations of the act are outlined in Richard D. French's study, *Antivivisection and Medical Science in Victorian Society* (Princeton: Princeton University Press, 1975).
16. Stephen Coleridge succeeded in forcing Lord Cromer, president of the Research Defence Society, to resign from the Council of the RSPCA in 1911. Cromer argued that his membership in a society dedicated to animal research did not affect his work for the RSPCA, but after Coleridge had addressed the members, he was forced out of office by a vote of 55 to 48. Coleridge then demanded the resignation of Stewart Stockman, who actually held a number of licences for animal experimentation. *Lancet*, 27 May 1911.
17. Lizzy Lind Af Hageby and Leisa K. Schartau [*sic*], *The Shambles of Science: Extracts from the Diary of Two Students of Physiology* (London: Ernest Bell, 1903).
18. *Daily News*, 19 Nov. 1903.
19. Ibid., 20 Dec. 1903.
20. *Lancet*, 1830, p. 751.
21. W. H. Lister, then a medical student, was one of two representatives examined by the Commission on University Education in London in 1909. When questioned about the value of representation on the senate, Lister replied: "'What was at the back of our minds was not so much the fact that representation would be of value, but that the actual election would be the great point if you granted us this. That the election taking place once in two years or something of that sort would be a most tremendous help in bringing to the students of London the realisation that they are units of one whole University, especially if carried out on party grounds. . .' 'Political party grounds?' asked one of the commissioners. 'Yes,' was the reply." Quoted in Eric Ashby and Mary Anderson, *The Rise of the Student Estate in Britain* (Cambridge: Harvard University Press, 1970), p. 54.
22. *Battersea Council Records*, 11 July 1906, 7:109.
23. Ibid. At Coleridge's advice the Church Antivivisection Society remained the nominal owner of the statue and indemnified the council to the extent of £300 in any possible action for libel. *Lloyd's*, 16 Sept. 1906. A description of the fountain and the popular songs which it inspired are found in a pamphlet by Edward K. Ford, *The Brown Dog and His Memorial* (London: Miss Lind-Af-Hageby's Anti-Vivisection Council, 1908).
24. *South London Mail*, 16 Nov. 1906.
25. *Lloyd's*, 16 September 1906.
26. *South-Western Star*, 17 September 1906.
27. Ibid., 22 Aug. 1907.
28. *Tribune*, 4 May 1907.
29. Linklater, *An Unhusbanded Life*, p. 112.
30. Walter Seton, *William Howard Lister* (London: Medici Society, 1919), p. 20.

31. The fine was noted with considerable approval by the Battersea Council, 17 Nov. 1907.
32. *Daily Express*, 6 Dec. 1907.
33. Ford, *The Brown Dog and His Memorial*, p. 9.
34. *Daily Chronicle*, 15 Nov. 1907.
35. *Battersea Council Records*, 22 Jan. 1908.
36. Ibid.
37. *Tribune*, 17 Dec. 1907.
38. *Daily Chronicle*, 7 Feb. 1908.
39. *Daily Graphic*, 15 Jan. 1908.
40. Stephen Paget became the first secretary of the AAMR in 1882. In 1908 he became secretary of the Research Defence Society. At the annual general meeting of the British Union for Abolition of Vivisection, Robert Hadwen described the RDS as "a nine days' wonder [which] will shortly fizzle out like predecessors of a similar type." *Abolitionist*, 20 May 1908.
41. Ken Young, *Local Politics and the Rise of Party* (Leicester: Leicester University Press, 1975), p. 93.
42. Flyer, 1908, Battersea Municipal Library. Antivivisection hospitals were without exception controlled by boards of lay people. The Battersea General was the last of its kind in England; two years before, St. Francis Hospital in New Kent Road had been an antivivisection institution, but a group of local doctors campaigned against the board and gained a majority.
43. *Hospital*, 31 July 1909.
44. E. G. Morris remembered the street carnivals for the "Old Anti" with floats, horses, and decorated carts, walkers, and bands. *Reflections on Battersea*, pp. 19–20.
45. *Daily Telegraph*, 29 Dec. 1909.
46. *Tribune*, 29 January 1907. It was noted that Battersea was more affected than any other division by the "latch-key" decision and that the Moderates were organizing most effectively.
47. *Municipal Gazette and London Argus*, 13 December 1907.
48. *Daily Mail*, 7 Dec. 1909.
49. *Morning Leader*, 22 Feb. 1910.
50. Letter from Marjorie F. M. Martin, daughter of borough surveyor, Battersea, in *British Medical Journal*, 15 September 1956.
51. *Daily Graphic*, 21 Mar. 1910.
52. *Daily Express*, 8 Jan. 1908.
53. Raymond Postgate, *The Life of George Lansbury* (London: Longman Green, 1951), p. 128.
54. French, *Antivivisection and Medical Science*, p. 239.
55. Ibid., p. 240.
56. Edward Maitland, *Life of Anna Kingsford* (London: Macmillan, 1913), 1:309.
57. James Turner, *Reckoning with the Beast* (Baltimore: Johns Hopkins University Press, 1980). Turner argues that the self-interest of the middle class re-

quired them to divest the guilt they felt about the working poor upon animals. Brian Harrison challenges this view in his review of Turner's work in the *Times Literary Supplement*, 29 January 1982.

58. *Abolitionist*, 1 Aug. 1912.

59. Patrick White, *The Vivisector* (London: Allen Lane, 1973), p. 135.

60. *Abolitionist*, 1 Aug. 1912.

Chapter 2: What about the Workers!

1. Walter Thornbury and Edward Walford, *Old and New London* (London: Cassell, Petter and Galpin, 1904), 2:308 and 6:477.

2. Broomfield House was demolished in 1904.

3. *Speeches of William Windham* (London: Longman, Hurst, Rees, Orme and Brown, 1812), 3:353.

4. Ibid., p. 346.

5. *Diary of the Right Hon. William Windham*, ed. Mrs. Henry Baring (London: Longmans Green, 1866), p. 437.

6. E. P. Thompson, *The Making of the English Working Class* (London: Gollancz, 1963), p. 59.

7. Anthony Trollope, *An Autobiography* (1883), chap. 1.

8. Flora Thompson, *Lark Rise to Candleford* (London: Allen Lane, 1979), p. 182.

9. Edgar Johnson considers Salem House to be Wellington House Academy in Hampstead Road: "Mr. Jones, the headmaster, was a sadist, forever smiting the palms of offenders with 'a bloated mahogany ruler,' 'or viciously drawing a pair of pantaloons tight with one of his large hands, and caning the wearer with the other.'" *Charles Dickens: His Tragedy and Triumph* (New York: Simon and Schuster, 1952), 1:49.

10. Quoted in Sydney H. Coleman, *Humane Society Leaders in America* (New York: Humane Association, 1924), p. 74. An account of the relationship between the RSPCA and the SPCC is given in George Behlmer's *Child Abuse and Moral Reform in England, 1870–1908* (Palo Alto: Stanford University Press, 1982), pp. 68ff.; the history of the early founding of the ASPCC may be found in Coleman, *Humane Society Leaders*.

11. Thompson, *Lark Rise to Candleford*, pp. 174–75.

12. Ivy Pinchbeck and Margaret Hewitt, *Children in English Society* (London: Routledge and Kegan Paul, 1969–73), 1:247.

13. Mrs. B. G. Golding, in *Reflections on Battersea* (Battersea: Rotary Club of Battersea, 1980), p. 18.

14. Mrs. J. Scholefield, ibid., p. 10.

15. Philip P. Hallie, *The Paradox of Cruelty* (Middletown, Conn.: Wesleyan University Press, 1969), chap. 3.

16. Ernest George Morris, in *Reflections on Battersea*, p. 33.
17. Elizabeth Gaskell, *The Life of Charlotte Brontë* (London: Smith, Elder, 1857), vol. 1, chap. 2.
18. Leon Radzinowicz, *A History of English Law* (London: Stevens and Sons, 1948), 3:204.
19. Elizabeth Gaskell, *Wives and Daughters* (1866), chap. 1.
20. Gaskell, *Life of Charlotte Brontë*, vol. 1, chap. 2.
21. Frances Power Cobbe, "The Indigent Class: Their Schools and Dwellings," *Fraser's Magazine*, vol. 73, (1866).
22. RSPCA, *Annual Report*, 1865, p. 132.
23. Brian Harrison, "Religion and Recreation," *Past and Present*, no. 38 (1967): 118.
24. Gordon Boswell, *The Book of Boswell: Autobiography of a Gypsy* (London: Gollancz, 1970).
25. W. M. Thackeray, "Going to See a Man Hanged," *Fraser's Magazine*, August 1840.
26. G. Kitson Clark, *The Making of Victorian England* (Harvard: Harvard University Press, 1962), p. 126.
27. T. F. T. Dyer, *British Popular Customs* (London: George Bell and Sons, 1891), p. 440.
28. S. Reynolds Hole, *More Memories* (New York: Macmillan, 1894), p. 186.
29. Wilkie Collins, *My Miscellanies*, vol. 20 of *The Works of Wilkie Collins* (New York: Collier, 1900), pp. 29–31.
30. Samuel Hynes, *The Edwardian Turn of Mind* (Princeton: Princeton University Press, 1968), p. 76.
31. Brian Harrison, "Animals and the State," in *Peaceable Kingdom* (Oxford: Clarendon, 1982), p. 116.
32. *Animals*, no. 1 (September 1899).
33. Brian Harrison, "Animals and the State in Nineteenth-Century England," *English Historical Review* 88 (1973): 805.
34. Florda Thompson has related how the children of her village were passionate egg stealers, despoiling the nests of wild birds, but after the Band of Mercy had come to the area, birds were spared. See also John Ranlett, "Checking Nature's Desecration: Late-Victorian Environmental Organization," *Victorian Studies* 26 (1983): 206.
35. *Reflections on Battersea*, pp. 9–10.
36. Ibid., p. 19.
37. B. L. Coombes, *These Poor Hands* (London: Gollancz, 1939), p. 76.
38. Robert Tressell, *The Ragged Trousered Philanthropists*, with an Introduction by Allan Sillitoe (London: Granada, 1981).
39. Quoted in Paul Thompson, *The Edwardians* (London: Paladin, 1979), p. 296.
40. *Tribune*, 1 March 1907.
41. *Daily Graphic*, 6 January 1910.

Chapter 3: Ignorant Prejudices

1. W. Wynne Nevison, *Life's Fitful Fever* (London: Macmillan, 1920), p. 74.
2. Quoted in Paul Thompson, *The Edwardians* (London: Paladin, 1979), p. 246.
3. Iain McLean, *Keir Hardie* (New York: St. Martin's Press, 1975), p. 123.
   Keir Hardie's secretary, Mary Travers-Symon, was a suffragette and took part in several demonstrations. There is no question that Hardie's support for Mrs. Pankhurst isolated him within the Independent Labour Party. Labour politicians customarily agreed to support women's franchise but did very little to make it a reality.
4. George Lansbury, *Looking Backwards and Forwards* (London: Blackie & Sons, 1935), pp. 97–98.
5. Henry Pelling, *A History of British Trade Unionism* (London: Macmillan 1966), p. 81.
6. J. Ramsay MacDonald, *Women in the Printing Trades* (London: Grant Richards, 1904), pp. 65–66.
7. *The Worker* (Brisbane), 1 March 1890.
8. Edith Abbott, *Women in Industry* (New York: D. Appleton, 1924), p. 319.
9. There is an excellent study of the link between feminism and Owenite socialism in Barbara Taylor's *Eve and the New Jerusalem* (London: Virago, 1982).
10. Charles V. Drysdale, *Why Men Should Work for Women's Suffrage: The Wages and Employment Question* (pamphlets, Birmingham, 1911?), pp. 10–11.
11. Ibid., p. 25.
12. Suzann Buckley states that if they were married, working-class women were generally satisfied with their roles. "The Family and the Role of Women," in *The Edwardian Age*, ed. Alan O'Day (London: Macmillan, 1979), p. 138.
13. Miss Mason of Tyneham Close, in *Reflections on Battersea*, p. 18.
14. Vera Brittain, *Lady into Woman: A History of Women from Victoria to Elizabeth II* (New York: Macmillan, 1953). In his study of women in the printing trades Ramsay MacDonald wrote that "the progressive young woman eager to show that she is man's equal and can do man's work, seems to be a product of the middle classes." *Women in the Printing Trades*, p. 65.
15. Kenneth D. Brown, *Labour and Unemployment, 1900–1914* (London: Roaman and Littlefield, 1971), p. 14.
16. Peter Lynebaugh, "The Tyburn Riot against the Surgeons," in *Albion's Fatal Tree*, ed. Douglas Hay et al. (New York: Pantheon, 1975), p. 71.
17. William Gaunt, *The World of William Hogarth* (London: Jonathan Cape, 1978), p. 93.
18. Hogarth's art was increasingly popular in the latter years of the nineteenth century, and his works were reprinted in the three volumes entitled *Hogarth's Works* by John Ireland and John Nichols (London: Chatto and Windus, 1875). Austin Dobson published a study of Hogarth in 1879.
19. James Mill, *Analysis of the Phenomena of the Human Mind*, ed. with addi-

tional notes by John Stuart Mill (London: Longmans, Green, Reader, and Dyer, 1869), 1:320.

20. Ibid.

21. Charles Mitchell, "Pictorial Satire," *Times Literary Supplement*, 20 Nov. 1948. The *Four Stages of Cruelty* and the prints' reception are discussed by Ronald Paulson in *The Art of Hogarth* (London: Phidon, 1975), p. 61, and in *Hogarth: His Life, Art, and Times* (New Haven: Yale University Press, 1971), 2:108.

22. Edwin Chadwick, "A Supplementary Report on the Results of a Special Inquiry into the Practice of Interment in Towns . . . ," *Quarterly Review*, no. 146 (March 1844).

23. Arthur Morrison, *Tales of Mean Streets* (London: Macmillan, 1895), p. 163.

24. Henry Lonsdale, *A Sketch of the Life and Writings of Robert Knox* (London: Macmillan, 1870), p. 50.

25. Ireland and Nicholls, *Hogarth's Works*, 2:62.

26. *Annals of Labour: Autobiographies of British Working-Class People, 1820–1920*, ed. John Burnett (Bloomington: Indiana University press, 1974), p. 289.

27. R. L. Stevenson, "The Body-Snatcher," in *Tales and Fantasies* (London: Chatto and Windus, 1911), p. 105.

28. E. G. Morris, in *Reflections on Battersea*, p. 20.

29. *Standard*, 24 November 1883.

30. Aesculapius Scalpel [Edward Berdoe], *Dying Scientifically: A Key to St. Bernard's* (London: Swan Sonnenschein, and Lowrey, 1888), p. 7–12.

31. Edward K. Ford, *The Brown Dog and His Memorial* (London: Anti-Vivisection Council, 1908), p. 5.

32. Richard B. Fisher, *Joseph Lister* (London: Macdonald and Jane's, 1977), p. 218.

33. T. F. Thiselton Dyer, *British Popular Customs, Present and Past* (London: George Bell and Sons, 1891), pp. 387–88.

34. John Brown, *Rab and His Friends and Other Papers and Essays* (London: J. M. Dent, 1906), p. 64.

35. John K. Walton, "Mad Dogs and Englishmen: The Conflict over Rabies in Late Victorian England," *Journal of Social History* 13, no. 3 (1979). The Anti-Muzzling Association and the Canine Defence Association were both active in the campaign against enforced muzzling of dogs in summer to protect people from rabies.

36. *Tribune* 5 October 1907.

37. Ibid.

Chapter 4: Black Beauty and Other Horses

1. Miss L. Evans, in *Reflections on Battersea* (Battersea: Rotary Club of Battersea, 1980), p. 29.

2. William Howitt, *The Northern Heights of London* (London: Longmans, Green, 1869), p. 76.

3. The publication figures for *Black Beauty* are given by Susan Chitty in *The Woman Who Wrote "Black Beauty"* (London: Hodder and Stoughton, 1971), pp. 223–28.

4. Mary Sewell, "The Butterfly," in *The Children of Summerbrook: Scenes of Village Life* (London: Jarrold and Sons, 1859), p. 28.

5. *Speeches in Parliament of the Right Honourable William Windham, Acct. of Life by Thomas Amyot* (London: Longman, Hurst, Rees, Orme and Brown, 1812), 1:193.

6. *The Girl's Own Paper*, 4 Apr. 1885.

7. Windham, *Speeches in Parliament*, 3:345.

8. Mary Allen, *Animals in American Literature* (Champaign: University of Illinois Press, 1983), p. 13.

9. Geoffrey Gorer, *Exploring English Character* (London: Cresset, 1955), pp. 15–18.

10. Edward O. Wilson, *On Human Nature* (Cambridge: Harvard University Press, 1978), pp. 105–6.

11. Gorer, *Exploring English Character*, p. 262.

12. Ibid., p. 180.

13. Ibid.

Chapter 5: Horrible and Indecent Exposure

1. Quoted in Kenneth Hudson's *Men and Women: Feminism and Anti-Feminism Today* (London: Hutchinson, 1968), p. 23.

2. Élie de Cyon, "The Anti-Vivisection Agitation," *Contemporary Review* 43 (1883): 506.

3. "The Old Maid," in *Woman: An Historical, Gynaecological, and Anthropological Compendium* (London: William Heinemann, 1935), 3:245–51, sees every aged, unmarried woman lavishing affection on a cat or a dog.

4. Richard D. French, *Antivivisection and Medical Science in Victorian Society* (Princeton: Princeton University Press, 1975), pp. 239–40. Also noted in Judith Hampson's dissertation, "Animal Experimentation, 1876–1976: Historical and Contemporary Perspectives" (University of Leicester, 1978).

5. James Turner, *Reckoning with the Beast* (Baltimore: Johns Hopkins University Press, 1980). Note particularly Brian Harrison's review of Turner in the *Times Literary Supplement*, 29 January 1982.

6. Medical students were frequently castigated as "medical hooligans," and the *Star* of London, 11 December 1907, carried a leader under this title concluding: "What excites the curiosity of the public most keenly is this problem. At what stage in his evolution does the medical hooligan become the humane scientist?"

7. Elizabeth Blackwell, *Pioneer Work in Opening the Medical Profession to Women* (London: Longmans Green, 1895), p. 72. James Webster had been medical dean at Geneva (1844–1847), director of the Philadelphia School of Anatomy, and editor of the *Medical Record*.

8. In *Female Complaints* (New York: W. W. Norton, 1979), p. 81, Sarah Stage observes that "Blackwell, who abhorred vivisection, fought sexual surgery on the grounds that doctors who experimented on live animals were simply extending their experimentation to female patients."

9. Edward Maitland, *Anna Kingsford: Her Life, Letters, Diary, and Work* (London: George Redway, 1896), 1:82. This account was first published under Edward Maitland's name in a letter to the *Examiner*, 17 June 1876.

10. *Memoirs and Letters of Sir James Paget*, ed. Stephen Paget (London: Longmans Green, 1901), pp. 50–51.

11. This quotation is from J. J. Garth Wilkinson's pamphlet *The Forcible Introspection of the Women for the Army and Navy by the Oligarchy Considered Physically* (London, 1870). Garth Wilkinson was an early supporter of Frances Cobbe and her Victoria Street Society. Details of working-class responses to the Contagious Diseases Acts are to be found in Ruth Walkowitz, *Prostitution and Victorian Society* (New York: Cambridge University Press, 1980), pp. 108ff.

12. Edward Maitland, *Life of Anna Kingsford* (London: Macmillan, 1913), 1:82.

13. Quoted in Richard A. Cordell, *Somerset Maugham* (Bloomington: Indiana University Press, 1961), pp. 33–34.

14. See Samuel Jean Pozzi, *A Treatise on Gynaecology* (London: New Sydenham Press, 1892), p. 174; also Henry Maudsley, *Body and Mind* (London: Macmillan, 1870), p. 37.

15. Blackwell, *Pioneer Work*, p. 164.

16. *Lancet*, 3 August 1895.

17. *British Medical Journal*, 15 March 1884.

18. Quoted in Aesculapius Scalpel [Edward Berdoe], *Dying Scientifically: A Key to St. Bernard's* (London: Swan, Sonnenschein, and Lowrey, 1888), p. 170.

19. *Lancet*, 21 October 1876.

20. This procedure was characterized by Elizabeth Blackwell as "the castration of women" in *Essays in Medical Sociology* (London: Longmans Green, 1909), 2:119–20.

21. Maxence Van der meersch, *Bodies and Souls*, trans. Eithne Williams (London: Pilot Press, 1948), p. 37. See also Vander meersch, *Pourquoi j'ai ecrit "Corps et âmes"* (Paris: A. Michel, 1956).

22. Sir Comyns Berkeley and Victor Bonney, *A Textbook of Gynaecological Surgery* (London: Cassell, 1935), p. 54.

23. Blackwell, *Essays in Medical Sociology*, 2:82.

24. Edward Berdoe, *The Futility of Experiments with Drugs or Animals* (London: Swan, Sonnenschein, and Lowrey, 1889), p. 31.

25. Blackwell, "Erroneous Method in Medical Education," *Essays in Medical Sociology*, 2:117.

26. Ibid., p. 43.

27. Frances Cobbe, "Schadenfreude," *Contemporary Review* 81 (1902): 662. "The conclusion which I, for my part, have reached after a quarter of a century of such painful study, is that we have done vivisectors more than justice heretofore when we have credited them with either a burning zeal for therapeutic discoveries or for the advance of Science; and have merely blamed them for *disregarding* the claims of humanity in view of such high aims. I am persuaded that what (no doubt by a slip of undesigned candour) is described in the recent *Life of Claude Bernard* by an eminent English physiologist as the "JOYS of the Laboratory,' are very real 'joys' to the vivisector; that is, *Schadenfreude,*—Pleasure in the Pain he witnesses and creates."

28. Ibid.

29. Sir Rickman John Godlee, *Lord Lister* (Oxford: Clarendon, 1924), p. 380.

30. Evidence given before the Royal Commission on Vivisection, 1906, quoted in *British Medical Journal*, 17 September 1906.

31. Maitland, *Life of Anna Kingsford*, 1:338.

32. Quoted in *The Poems and Plays of Robert Browning* (New York: Random House, 1934), p. 1065. In the poem the dog Tray dives into the water and rescues a drowning child. The response of the vivisector is: "John, go and catch—or, if needs be, / Purchase—that animal for me! / By vivisection, at expense / Of half-an-hour and eighteenpence, / How brain secretes dog's soul, we'll see!"

33. Maitland, *Life of Anna Kingsford*, 2:268.

34. *Reflections on Battersea*, p. 15.

35. George W. E. Russell, *Collections and Recollections* (London: Harper, 1898), pp. 76–77.

Chapter 6: Riding Masters and Young Mares

1. Ruth Padel, "Saddled with Ginger: Women, Men, and Horses," *Encounter*, November 1980.

2. Susan Chitty, *The Woman Who Wrote "Black Beauty"* (London: Hodder and Stoughton, 1971), p. 197.

3. Christopher Johnston of Baltimore devised an operating chair with stirrups in 1860. James V. Ricci, *The Development of Gynaecological Surgery and Instruments* (Philadelphia: Blakiston, 1949), pp. 492–93.

4. Jenni Calder, *Women and Marriage in Victorian Fiction* (London: Thames and Hudson, 1976), p. 65.

5. The first reference to *The Way of a Man with a Maid* is in a work entitled *Parisian Frolics*, with a subheading: "tr. from the French by the author of The way of a Man with a Maid" (London: For Private Circulation Only, 1896).

Patrick Kearney in *The Private Case: Erotica Collection in the British Museum Library* (London: Jay Landesman, 1981), attributes the authorship of both works to John S. Farmer, a well-known writer of pornographic fiction.

6. "Man ennobles nature, woman, animal, by imposing suffering on 'her' and the male author naturally endorses the inevitablity of such a pattern, since he is, ultimately, the creator and destroyer." Padel, "Saddled with Ginger," p. 53.

7. Thomas Hardy was a convinced antivivisectionist and protector of animals who annoyed his neighbors by his opposition to foxhunting and shooting. In 1909 he wrote to a friend in New York: "The discovery of the law of evolution, which revealed that all organic creatures are of one family, shifted the centre of altruism from humanity to the whole conscious world collectively. Therefore, the practice of vivisection, which might have been defended while the belief ruled that men and animals are essentially different, has been left by that discovery without any logical argument in its favour. And if the practice, to the extent merely of inflicting slight discomfort now and then, be defended (as I sometimes hold it may) on grounds of it being good policy for animals as well as men, it is nevertheless in strictness a wrong, and stands precisely in the same category as would stand its practice on men themselves." Florence Emily Hardy, *The Later Years of Thomas Hardy (1892–1928)* (New York: Macmillan, 1930), pp. 138–39.

8. L. Lind-af-Hageby and L. K. Schartau, *The Shambles of Science* (London, 1913 ed.), pp. 77–78.

Chapter 7: A Woman Is Being Beaten

1. Steven Marcus, *The Other Victorians: A Study of Sexuality and Pornography in Mid-Nineteenth-Century England* (New York: Basic Books, 1966), pp. 264 and 286.

2. Gillian Beer, *Darwin's Plots* (London: Routledge and Kegan Paul, 1983), p. 5.

3. Jeffrey M. Masson, "Freud and the Seduction Theory," *Atlantic Monthly*, February 1984, pp. 33–68.

4. Frank Cioffi, "The Cradle of Neurosis," *Times Literary Supplement*, 6 July 1984.

5. Jeffrey M. Masson, *The Assault on Truth: Freud's Suppression of the Seduction Theory* (New York: Farrar, Strauss and Giroux, 1984), p. 85.

6. Marie Jahoda, *Freud and the Dilemmas of Psychology* (New York: Basic Books, 1977), pp. 86–87.

7. "The girl's recognition of the fact of her being without a penis does not by any means imply that she submits to the fact easily. On the contrary, she continues to hold on for a long time to the wish to get something like it herself and she believes in that possibility for improbably long years; and analysis can show that, at a period when knowledge of reality has long since

rejected the fulfilment of the wish as unattainable, it persists in the unconscious and retains a considerable cathexis of energy. The wish to get the longed-for penis eventually in spite of everything may contribute to the motives that drive a mature woman to analysis, and what she may reasonably expect from analysis—a capacity, for instance, to carry on an intellectual profession—may often be recognized as a sublimated modification of this repressed wish." Sigmund Freud, "Femininity," in *The Standard Edition of the Complete Psychological Works of Sigmund Freud*, trans. James Strachey, 12 (London: Hogarth Press, 1960): 125.

8. Freud, "Anxiety and Instinctual Life," ibid., p. 104.

9. Ernest Jones, *The Life and Work of Sigmund Freud* (New York: Basic Books, 1961), 1 :43.

10. "The expenditure of force on the part of the physician was evidently the measure of a *resistance* on the part of the patient. It was only necessary to translate into words what I myself had observed, and I was in possession of the theory of repression." Freud, *Autobiography*, trans. James Strachey (New York: W. W. Norton, 1935), p. 53.

11. Marcus, *The Other Victorians*, p. 260.

12. Freud, "A Child Is Being Beaten," *Complete Psychological Works*, 17 :191.

13. Charles Reginald Dawes, "A Study of Erotic Literature in England Considered with Especial Reference to Social Life" (1943), British Library Mss. 364.d.15.

14. *My Secret Life* (published anonymously ca. 1891), 5 :46. "Walter" occasionally buys a young man among his more usual female purchases; for example, he seduces an out-of-work house decorator who could have stepped from the pages of *The Ragged Trousered Philanthropists*, after first examining his hands to make sure that the lad is not a common laborer (8 :215).

15. Frances Cobbe, "Schadenfreude," *Contemporary Review* 81 (1902): 658.

16. Frances Cobbe, "Wife-Torture in England," *Contemporary Review* 32 (1878).

17. Nancy Tomes, "A 'Torrent of Abuse': Crimes of Violence Between Working-Class Men and Women in London, 1840–1875," *Journal of Social History* 11, 3 (Spring 1978), pp. 328–45. George K. Behlmer notes in *Child Abuse and Moral Reform in England, 1870–1908* (Palo Alto: Stanford University Press, 1982) that "all crimes of violence against the person dropped sharply in late Victorian England" (p. 15).

18. Beatrice Faust, *Women, Sex, and Pornography* (New York: Macmillan, 1980), p. 19.

19. Peter Gay, *The Bourgeois Experience* (New York: Oxford University Press, 1984), p. 370.

20. "Characteristic of 'obscene' works is the fact that in these seduction scenes the 'victim' is more often than not, a *willing collaborator*. In other words, the women who figure prominently in 'obscene' books are generally as anxious to be seduced as men are to seduce them." Eberhard Kronhausen and

Phyllis Kronhausen, *Pornography and the Law* (New York: Basic Books, 1964), p. 237.

21. James V. Ricci, *The Development of Gynaecological Surgery and Instruments* (Philadelphia: Blakiston, 1949), pp. 323–492.

22. Croonian Lectures, 1891, reproduced in flyer of the Animal Defence and Anti-Vivisection Society, 170 Piccadilly W. (1912?).

23. Lizzy Lind Af Hageby and Leisa K. Schartau, *The Shambles of Science* (London: Ernest Bell, 1903), pp. 19–20.

24. Ibid., p. 29.

25. Frances Cobbe, *The Nine Circles* (London: Swan, Sonnenschein, 1893), p. 4. When this work was first published in 1892, it met with a fiery response from Sir Victor Horsley, whose long letter in the *Times*, 25 October 1892, listed numerous instances of error in Cobbe's account. The work was subsequently reprinted with corrections and a preface by Dr. Edward Berdoe, who observed that if Frances Cobbe had failed to note that in some cases the animals had been chloroformed, Sir Victor had overlooked the fact that animals were frequently left in considerable pain after an experiment, with death sometimes occurring after days and weeks. The account of this controversy is generally given in Sir Victor Horsley's favor, but this is not quite fair to Frances Cobbe, and particularly not to Edward Berdoe.

26. Lind-af-Hageby and Schartau, *The Shambles of Science*, p. 29.

27. Gay, *The Bourgeois Experience*, p. 497.

28. Shaw, Preface to *The Doctor's Dilemma* (1906).

29. Edward J. Bristow, *Vice and Vigilance: Purity Movements in Britain since 1700* (Dublin: Gill and Macmillan, 1977), pp. 43–44.

30. Wilhelm Reich, *The Sexual Revolution* (New York: Orgone Institute Press, 1945), p. 159.

Chapter 8: The Truths of Fiction

1. R. D. French, *Antivivisection and Medical Science in Victorian Society* (Princeton: Princeton University Press, 1975), p. 104.

2. Sir Edward Sharpey-Schafer, *History of the Physiological Society during Its First Fifty Years, 1876–1926* (London: Cambridge University Press, 1927), p. 32.

3. "Report of the Royal Commission, Q.3537ff.

4. Leonard Huxley, *The Life and Letters of Thomas Henry Huxley* (New York: Appleton), 1 (1900): 473.

5. George MacDonald, *Paul Faber, Surgeon* (London: Chatto and Windus, 1878).

6. Wilkie Collins, *Heart and Science* (New York: J. W. Lovell, 1883).

7. Dickens to Collins, 12 July 1854, quoted in Edgar Johnson, *Charles Dickens: His Tragedy and Triumph* (New York: Simon and Schuster, 1952), 2:799.

8. Dugald B. MacEachen, "Wilkie Collins' *Heart and Science* and the Vivisection Controversy," *Victorian Newsletter*, no. 19 (Spring 1976); Kenneth Robinson, *Wilkie Collins* (New York: Macmillan, 1952); William H. Marshall, *Wilkie Collins* (New York: Twayne, 1970); and most recently, Sue Lonoff, *Wilkie Collins and His Victorian Readers* (New York: AMS Press, 1982), in which Lonoff speaks of the novel's "deserved obscurity" (p. 78).

9. Robinson, *Wilkie Collins*, p. 302.

10. Marshall, *Wilkie Collins*, pp. 104–5.

11. Patrick Brantlinger, "What is 'Sensational' about the 'Sensation Novel,'" *Nineteenth-Century Fiction*, June 1982, p. 27.

12. Daniel Farson, *Jack the Ripper* (London: Michael Joseph, 1972), p. 11.

13. Michael Durey, *The Return of the Plague* (London: Gill and Macmillan, 1979), p. 171.

14. Edward Berdoe, *Dying Scientifically: A Key to St. Bernard's* (London: Swan, Sonnenschein, and Lowrey, 1888), p. 7.

15. James Turner, *Reckoning with the Beast* (Baltimore: Johns Hopkins University Press, 1980), p. 119.

16. Edward Berdoe, *St. Bernard's: The Romance of a Medical Student* (London: Swan, Sonnenschein, 1887).

17. Marie Daal, *Anna, the Professor's Daughter*, trans. from the Dutch by Colonel Charles Mueller (London: Swan, Sonnenschein, 1885).

18. Biographical details of Sarah Grand are given by Elaine Showalter in the preface to *The Beth Book* (London: Virago, 1980).

19. *Life and Letters of Thomas Henry Huxley*, 2:374–82.

20. Lovat Dickson, *H. G. Wells: His Turbulent Life and Times* (New York: Athenaeum, 1969), pp. 66–69.

Chapter 9: The New Priesthood

1. R. D. French, *Antivivisection and Medical Science in Victorian Society* (Princeton: Princeton University Press, 1975), pp. 288–96.

2. E. Westacott, *A Century of Vivisection and Anti-Vivisection* (Philadelphia: C. W. Daniel, 1949), pp. 170–73.

3. *The George Eliot Letters*, ed. Gordon S. Haight (New Haven: Yale University Press, 1954), 6:364. The incident occurred on 23 April 1877. Lewes had given evidence to the Committee of Inquiry in 1875.

4. Paget begins his essay with an attack upon the antivivisectionists and continues in this polemical vein.

5. Claude Bernard, *Introduction à l'étude de la médecine éxpérimentale* (Paris, J. B. Baillière et fils, 1865). References throughout the text are to the readily available translation by Henry Copley Greene in the Collier Books Library of Science edition of 1961. However, a more scholarly edition of Bernard's work is Paul Cranefield's *Claude Bernard's Revised Edition of his*

"Introduction à l'étude de la médecine expérimentale" (New York: Science History Publications, 1976).

6. G. H. Lewes, *The Physical Basis of Mind* (London: Trüber, 1877), pp. 225–35.

7. Edmond de Goncourt and Jules de Goncourt, *Journal: Memoires de la vie littéraire* (Monaco: Academie Goncourt, 1956), 8:192–93.

8. Thoughout *The History of the Physiological Society during Its First Fifty Years, 1876–1926* (London: Cambridge University Press, 1927), Sir Edward Sharpey-Schafer pays tribute to the work and genius of Claude Bernard, described by John Burdon Sanderson as "the most inspiring teacher, the most profound thinker, and the most remarkable experimentalist he had ever known" (pp. 22–23). See also Sir Michael Foster, *Claude Bernard* (New York: Longmans, Green, 1899).

9. In *Le Roman Expérimentale*, Zola stated that the naturalistic novel was written in accord with Bernard's precepts. *The Experimental Novel and Other Essays* (New York: Cassell, 1894), pp. 1–40. However, Henry Céard's assertion that Zola did not actually study Bernard until 1879 has been accepted as authoritative. Nonetheless, it is clear that Zola was influenced by Bernard and that before he had studied Bernard's writings, he was acquainted with the received views of Bernard's theories. See Reino Virtanen, *Claude Bernard and His Place in the History of Ideas* (Lincoln: University of Nebraska Press, 1960), p. 121.

10. Gillian Beer discusses Claude Bernard's influence on narrative in *Darwin's Plots* (London: Routledge and Kegan Paul, 1984), pp. 274–75.

11. John Scott Burdon-Sanderson, *Handbook for the Physiological Laboratory*, compiled by E. Klein, J. Burdon-Sanderson, Michael Foster, and T. Lauder Brunton, 2 vols. (London: J. & A. Churchill, 1873).

12. Frederick Lawrence Holmes, *Claude Bernard and Animal Chemistry* (Cambridge: Harvard University Press, 1974), pp. 375–76.

13. Ibid., p. 376.

14. Sir Rickman John Godlee, *Lord Lister* (Oxford: Clarendon, 1924), p. 380.

15. Ouida, "The New Priesthood," *The New Review* 8 (1892): 151.

16. Frances Cobbe, "The Moral Aspects of Vivisection," in *The Modern Rack* (London: Swan, Sonnenschein, 1889), pp. 4–5.

17. *Claude Bernard and Experimental Medicine*, ed. Francisco Grande and Maurice B. Visscher (Cambridge, Mass.: Schenckman, 1967), p. 37.

18. In Bernard's own words, "un salon superbe tout resplandissant de lumière, dans lequel on ne peut parvenir qu'en passant par une longue et affreuse cuisine." Henry Copley Greene's translation of *salon* as *hall* does not quite convey the sense of *salon* in French, which denotes more a drawing room in high society.

19. John Vyvyan, *In Pity and in Anger* (London: Faber and Faber, 1969), p. 37.

20. *The Cahier Rouge of Claude Bernard*, in Grande and Visscher, *Claude Bernard and Experimental Medicine*, p. 6.

21. John Davidson, *The Testament of a Vivisector* (London: Grant Richards, 1901), p. 24.
22. Bernard qualified his restriction against human vivisection in the following passage: "Among the experiments that may be tried on man, those that can only harm are forbidden, those that are innocent are permissible, and those that may do good are obligatory" (p. 131).
23. Ouida, "The New Priesthood," p.152.
24. Richard D. Altick, *Victorian Studies in Scarlet* (New York: Norton, 1970), p. 146.
25. Lizzy Lind Af Hageby and Leisa K. Schartau, *The Shambles of Science* (London: Ernest Bell, 1903), p. 88.
26. W. D. Halliburton's preface to *The Pros and Cons of Vivisection*, by Charles Richet (London: Duckworth & Co., 1908), p. xii.
27. Particularly John Haldane, T. Lauder Brunton, and Stephen Paget, who wrote widely on matters of public health and social hygiene.
28. Richet, *The Pros and Cons of Vivisection*, pp. 15–16.
29. S. Weir Mitchell, "The Birth and Death of Pain," quoted in *The Semi-Centennial of Anaesthesia, 1846–1896* (Boston: privately printed for the Massachusetts General Hospital, 1897), p. 81.
30. J. Y. Simpson, *Anaesthesia; or, The Employment of Chloroform and Ether in Surgery, Midwifery, etc.* (Philadelphia: Lindsay & Blakiston, 1849), p. 27.
31. Shelley, *Queen Mab*, quoted in David Cheever's address in *The Semi-Centennial of Anaesthesia*, p. 45.
32. William Osborne-Greenwood, *A Study in Twilight Sleep* (London: 1916), p. 7.
33. Simpson, *Anaesthesia*, p. 27.
34. Ibid., p. 36.
35. *Shaw on Vivisection*, comp. and ed. G. H. Bowker, for the National Anti-Vivisection Society (London: G. Allen & Unwin, 1949), p. 23.
36. Shaw's reply to Wells was published in the *Sunday Express*, 24 July 1927.
37. *Abolitionist*, 1 Aug. 1912, p. 2.
38. Paraphrasing the last line of "The Female Animal: Medical and Biological Views of Woman and Her Role in Nineteenth-Century America," by Carroll Smith-Rosenberg and Charles Rosenberg, *Journal of American History* 60 (1973): 356.

Chapter 10: The Sacrifice

1. Robert Lowe, "The Vivisection Act," *Contemporary Review* 38 (1879): 719.
2. Keith Thomas, *Man and the Natural World* (New York: Pantheon, 1983), pp. 100–120.
3. H. S. Salt, *Animals' Rights* (New York: Macmillan, 1894), pp. 33–34. Henry Salt's supporters in the Humanitarian Society included Edward Carpenter and Annie Besant, who preached vegetarianism to G. B. Shaw. See also James

Turner, *Reckoning with the Beast* (Baltimore: Johns Hopkins University Press, 1980), p. 136.

4. *Morning Post*, 1 Feb. 1875.

5. Eileen Begland, *Ouida, the Passionate Victorian* (New York: Duell, Sloan and Pearce, 1951), p. 211.

6. John Galsworthy, "Vivisection of Dogs," in *A Sheaf* (New York: Macmillan, 1916), p. 85.

7. Walter B. Cannon, "The Dog's Gift to the Relief of Human Suffering," (New York: American Association for Medical Progress, 1926), p. 2.

8. Galsworthy, "Vivisection of Dogs," pp. 81–82.

9. Galsworthy, "The Lost Dog" and "Demos," in *A Commentary* (London: Macmillan, 1908), pp. 19–31.

10. *The Journals of George Sturt* (Cambridge: Cambridge University Press, 1967), 2:15.

11. Quoted with commentary in E. Westacott, *A Century of Vivisection and Anti-Vivisection* (Philadelphia: C. W. Daniel, 1949), p. 302.

12. Samuel J. Looker and Crichton Porteous, *Richard Jefferies: Man of the Fields* (London: John Baker, 1964), pp. 187–88.

13. Frances Cobbe, *The Modern Rack* (London: Swan, Sonnenschein, 1889), p. 10.

14. Charles Dickens, "Inhumane Humanity," *All the Year Round* 15 (1866): 238–40.

15. Dickens, "The Heart of Mid-London," *Household Words*, 4 May 1850.

16. John Carey, *The Violent Effigy: A Study of Dickens's Imagination* (Oxford: Oxford University Press, 1973).

17. Coral Lansbury, "Sporting Humor in Victorian Literature," in *Mosaic* (Winnipeg: University of Manitoba Press, 1976), pp. 66–67.

18. *Evening News*, 11 May 1909.

19. *Shaw on Vivisection*, comp. and ed. G. H. Bowker for the National Anti-vivisection Society (London: G. Allen & Unwin, 1949), p. 33.

20. Lizzy Lind Af Hageby and Leisa K. Schartau, *The Shambles of Science* (London: Ernest Bell, 1903), p. 27.

21. Ibid., p. 29.

22. Chaplin quoted in David Aberbach, "Chaplin: Of Crime and Genius," *Encounter*, May 1983, p. 89.

23. Molly Hughes, *A London Home in the 1890's* (Oxford: Oxford University Press, 1980), p. 47.

24. W. M. Thackeray, "Going to See a Man Hanged," *Fraser's Magazine*, August 1840. See also Lansbury, "Sporting Humor in Victorian Literature."

25. Franklin H. Martin, *Fifty Years in Medicine and Surgery* (Chicago: Surgical Publishing Co., 1934), pp. 253–55.

26. "Animal Defence and Anti-Vivisection Society Reports," Resume of Report, 1928, p. 13.

27. Edward K. Ford, *The Brown Dog and His Memorial* (London: Anti-Vivisection Council, 1908), p. 3.

28. "There's Life in the Brown Dog Yet," *John Bull*, 18 Jan. 1908.

29. H. Coupin and John Lea, *The Romance of Animal Arts and Crafts* (London: Seeley, 1907), introduction.

30. The argument was settled firmly in favor of individual souls in the first issue of *Animals*, Feb. 1889, but a great many spiritualists, including Sir Arthur Conan Doyle, maintained a belief in a "World Soul."

31. *Tribune*, 30 Mar. 1907.

32. Anna Maria Fay, *Victorian Days in England: Letters of an American Girl, 1851–1852* (Boston and New York: Houghton Mifflin, 1923), pp. 123–24.

33. John Brown, *Rab and His Friends and Other Papers and Essays* (London: J. M. Dent, 1906), p. 69.

34. J. S. Bratton, *The Impact of Victorian Children's Fiction* (London: Croom Helm, 1981), p. 47.

35. G. K. Chesterton, *Charles Dickens* (London: Methuen, 1906), p. 11.

36. Bratton, *Impact of Victorian Children's Fiction*, pp. 76–77.

37. Gordon Stables, M.D., *Sable and White: The Autobiography of a Show Dog* (London: Jarrold and Sons, 1894), pp. 265–66.

38. Hezekiah Butterworth, Introduction to *Beautiful Joe: The Autobiography of a Dog*, by Marshall Saunders (London: Jarrold and Sons, 1901). Butterworth was president of the Boston Humane Society.

39. Rudyard Kipling, "Her Majesty's Servants," *The Jungle Book* (New York: Doubleday, 1924), p. 302.

40. Kipling, "How Fear Came," *The Second Jungle Book* (New York: Doubleday, 1925), pp. 1–2.

41. Frederick Courteney Selous, *Travel and Adventure in South-East Africa* (London: R. Ward, 1893), p. 300.

42. Peter Green, *Kenneth Grahame* (London: John Murray, 1959), pp. 103–7.

43. Walter Seton, *William Howard Lister* (private circulation, London, 1919), p. 86.

Index

TEXT DESIGN BY MIKE BURTON
COMPOSED BY G&S TYPESETTERS, AUSTIN, TEXAS
MANUFACTURED BY EDWARDS BROTHERS, INC., ANN ARBOR, MICHIGAN
TEXT AND DISPLAY LINES ARE SET IN ZAPF BOOK LIGHT

Library of Congress Cataloging in Publication Data
Lansbury, Coral.
~~The~~ old brown dog. *etc*
Includes index.
1. Vivisection—England—History.   2. Animals,
treatment of—England—History.   3. Social movements—
England—History—20th century.   ~~I. Title.~~
HV4943.G7E535   1985   942.082'3   85-40369
ISBN 0-299-10250-5